MAI
AND

MALAY POISONS
AND CHARM CURES

BY
JOHN D. GIMLETTE
M.R.C.S., L.R.C.P.

KUALA LUMPUR
OXFORD UNIVERSITY PRESS
LONDON NEW YORK MELBOURNE

Oxford University Press
Oxford London Glasgow
New York Toronto Melbourne Auckland
Kuala Lumpur Singapore Hong Kong Tokyo
Delhi Bombay Calcutta Madras Karachi
Nairobi Dar es Salaam Cape Town
and associate companies in
Beirut Berlin Ibadan Mexico City

⬤*Oxford University Press 1971*
First published in 1915
Reprinted in 'Oxford in Asia paperbacks' 1971
Third impression 1981

ISBN 0 19 638150 9

Printed in Malaysia by Ampang Press Sdn. Bhd., Ampang Jaya, Selangor
Published by Oxford University Press, 3, Jalan 13/3,
Petaling Jaya, Selangor, Malaysia

PREFACE TO THE THIRD EDITION

THANKS to the continued encouragement and financial aid of the Government of the Federated Malay States, it has become possible to publish this the third edition of " Malay Poisons and Charm Cures," the second edition having been some time out of print. If excuse be needed it is surely found by the requirements of the Institute for Medical Research, F.M.S., by newly joined cadets of the Malayan Civil Service, and by several Courts of Law in the Far East. Hence the attempt to bring the book up to date, retaining, however, the original style. Many additions and corrections have been made. The index has been revised and enlarged.

A collection of most of the poisons referred to in the book has been accepted by Dr. Andrew Balfour, C.B., Head of the new London School of Hygiene and Tropical Medicine. The specimens, about sixty in number, arranged by General Sir Wilfred Beveridge, K.B.E., the organiser of the new museum, should be of educational value. With the sanction and good-will of H.H. the Sultan of Kelantan, K.C.M.G., and his Adviser who forwarded them, they form probably an unique collection of their kind. Dr. A. T. Stanton, formerly Director, Government Laboratories, F.M.S., now Chief Medical Adviser to the Secretary of State, Colonial Office, London, has referred the need for further investigation of Malayan poisons to the new Colonial Medical Research Committee.

I am again indebted to many friends for assistance, especially to C. Otto Blagden, D.Litt., Reader in

Malay and Dean of the School of Oriental Studies,
London University, who has rescued me from many
mistakes in Malay, and who has most kindly translated
cognate matter from a report on poisons occurring in
the Dutch East Indies. This monograph *Indische
Vergiftrapporten*, by the late Dr. M. Greshoff, was sent
to me from the Royal Colonial Institute of Holland,
through the kindness of Miss T. van Bethem Jutting,
of the Zoological Institute, Amsterdam. Mr. H. N.
Ridley, C.M.G., has most kindly revised the botany,
and with Mr. I. H. Burkill, has given me valuable
notes. I must thank Mr. N. E. Penzer for reference
to his " Romance of Betel-Chewing "; Dr. R. O.
Winstedt, M.C.S., C.M.G., for his help, and Mr. William
Churchill for much kindly assistance. I gratefully
acknowledge the wise counsel of my old friend H. E.
Durham, and the influence of Sir Hugh Clifford, M.C.S.,
G.C.M.G., G.B.E., now Governor, S.S., and High
Commissioner, F.M.S., on my early training under him
when he was British Resident of Pahang.

J. D. G.

Upper Weston,
Bath.

PREFACE TO THE SECOND EDITION

ABSENCE on leave, granted on the grounds of public policy during the period of the Great War, interrupted any further active work on " Malay Poisons and Charm Cures " for five years. The original book, now long out of print, was found useful for medico-legal reference in the Lower Courts of Law, and has been revised. By additions and readjustments the production of a larger and more complete edition has resulted, but as the exigencies of the Service have not allowed me to return to the Federated Malay States, from where I was seconded for duty in Kelantan in 1909, my notes are almost entirely confined to this State, and a better title might have been " Kelantan Poisons and Charm Cures."

The pioneer work contained in the first edition was generously recognised by the Government of the Federated Malay States, and I am indebted to Dr. R. O. Winstedt, D.Litt.(Oxon.), now Principal, Raffles' College, Singapore, for a bonus awarded in 1915 by the Committee for Malay Studies, which defrayed the initial cost of publication. A similar grant has been promised for the publication of this edition. On my return to Kelantan in 1919 the late Sultan Sir Mahomed IV., K.C.M.G., with kindly friendship deputed Dato' Mĕgat Lela 'diraja, Secretary to the Kelantan Ecclesiastical Council (*Majlis Ugama Islam*), as well as two of the "medicine-men" to the Royal Household, to help in preparing a second edition of " Malay Poisons and Charm Cures."

Dato' Mĕgat Lela 'diraja, a Malay of good birth, has a competent knowledge of the English language, and has been helpful more especially in translating some of the passages relative to the Black Art. The two " medicine-men " proved to be illiterate, self-made Kelantan men who had no knowledge of English. To'

Bomor Haji Awang the senior has been very reticent in disclosing the secrets of his profession, but his colleague To' Bomor Ĕnche' Harun bin Sĕman has been most generous. Although much information has been obtained first-hand, I have borrowed largely from the works of others ; to them I can only express my obligations by recording, as far as possible, their names in the text and in the lists of references. Want of a reference library and the absence of a chemical laboratory in a native State such as Kelantan have been serious handicaps. The revision was completed on my retirement from the Colonial Medical Service. I hope that others still on the active list may be incited to continue and complete further investigations.

Many Malay friends have made this field of research a pleasant tilling ; towards them I shall always cherish feelings of affection and gratitude. I am again indebted to my friends Mr. W. W Skeat, Mr. I. H. Burkill, and Dr. H. E. Durham, Sc.D.(Cantab.), F.R.C.S. (Eng.), M.B., B.C., *Pawang juga*, for much help. I must thank Major J. C. Moulton, O.B.E., B.Sc.(Oxon.), Director of Raffles' Museum and Library, Singapore, for much kindness, also Mr. A. F. Worthington, British Adviser, Kelantan ; but I am more especially indebted to Mr. H. W. Thomson, British Resident, Pahang, for his kindness in reading and correcting the manuscript, to Dr. Winstedt in helping so much with the magic, and to Dr. Durham in so generously contributing to the section on Tuba. Sir William H. Willcox, K.C.I.E., C.B., C.M.G., M.D., F.R.C.P., has assisted with analyses and given kindly encouragment. Mr. C. Otto Blagden, Reader in Malay and Dean of the School of Oriental Studies, London Institution, has also given some much appreciated help.

Bath, 1923.   J. D. G.

PREFACE TO THE FIRST EDITION

EIGHTEEN years' service in the Government of the Federated Malay States, ten of which have been spent in Kelantan, has afforded me time and opportunity to prepare these notes. They are made from consultation with friendly Kelantan " medicine-men " (*bomor* or *pawang*) and converse with other Malay " witch-doctors " (*bomor* or *pawang*), as well as from actual acquaintance with the individual drugs mentioned. The original notes formed a paper on " Some Malay Poisons," which is published by the Government of the Federated Malay States. They are expanded and supplemented by reference to the published works of Mr. H. N. Ridley, C.M.G., F.R.S., M.A., formerly Director of the Botanic Gardens, Singapore ; to Henry's " Plant Alkaloids," published in 1913 ; Brown's " Punjab Poisons," 1888 ; Skeat's " Malay Magic," 1900, and other general sources, including some Dutch authors, chiefly Greshoff and Boorsma. Much scientific work was done in the Malay Archipelago by the late Professor Greshoff, and the poisonous plants described by him and by Boorsma are generally found also in the Peninsula.

We know very little about Malay poisons, and our knowledge, indeed, of Malay drugs seems to be confined to Ridley's " Materia Medica," published in the Agricultural Bulletins of the Straits Settlements for 1906, and afterwards translated into Dutch by Professor Greshoff, of Haarlem (" De Indische Mercuur," 1907). I am greatly indebted to Mr. I. H. Burkill, M.A., F.L.S., the present Director of the Botanic Gardens,

Singapore, for a very great deal of help, especially in naming most of the plants. The flora of Kelantan is but little known, and many of the botanical specimens sent to him for identification have found a resting-place in the Herbarium at Singapore, while others have been sent to Kew Gardens.

I must thank Dr. R. Hanitsch, Ph.D., Director of Raffles' Museum, Singapore, for identifying a few specimens from the animal kingdom, and as Hon. Secretary of the Straits Branch of the Royal Asiatic Society, for giving me permission to incorporate my notes on " Some Superstitious Beliefs Occurring in the Theory and Practice of Malay Medicine " (Journ. No. 65, 1913) in the present work.

The British Adviser to the Government of Kelantan, my brother officers in this State, and Dr. H. E. Durham, Sc.D., M.B., F.R.C.S., have given me much kindly encouragement and criticism. Mr. R. De Munick, Assistant, Sĕmambu Estate, Kuantan, Pahang, has supplied me with a good deal of interesting information and some botanical specimens which were very valuable as cross-references. I am also indebted to Mr. W. W. Skeat for a good deal of help.

The " witch-craft " of the " medicine-man " is always of general interest, but the investigation of Malay medicines, poisons, and their antidotes is of special scientific interest. It presents a large field for medical research, the ground of which is hardly broken in the following pages.

J. D. G.

Kota Bharu,
Kelantan, 1915.

CONTENTS

FOREWORD

An especial and absorbing interest is attached to a description of medicine as practised in a country into which modern medicine has not yet penetrated, for one is carried back to the times far distant when in one's own country the practitioners of medicine were striving to see light amidst the medley of faith cures, charms, and herbal and animal remedies which had formed the Materia Medica of their forefathers.

Dr. John D. Gimlette has given a fascinating scientific account of medicine as practised by the " medicineman " in the Federated Malay States, and no one is so well qualified to undertake such a task, for since 1896 he has devoted his life to the study and advancement of medicine in this remote part of the world.

Dr. Gimlette has done more than this, because, as is well known, he has gained the confidence and affectionate regard of the natives of the Malay Peninsula for his self-sacrificing and devoted help to them in times of illness and distress. The reader of this work should know that the author in the course of his practice in Malaya nearly lost his life and permanently impaired his health from an infection received while performing a difficult surgical operation to save the life of a native of the country.

The work which, during a period of long and painful illness, Dr. Gimlette has so bravely completed forms a very valuable addition to our knowledge of Medicine and Toxicology.

The Government of the Federated Malay States is to be congratulated on its wise policy in giving support to the publication of this work, which is a piece of research leading the way to discoveries of importance in modern medicine.

Mr. A. W. Churchill is well known as a publisher of standard medicine and scientific works, and in this

capacity has done much for the advancement of
scientific knowledge. By his far-sighted policy in
publishing a work which must of necessity have a
somewhat limited sale he has shown that true interest
in the advancement of medical knowledge for which
he is so much appreciated.

From a careful study of this work I am quite certain that many of the animal and vegetable poisons
described by Dr. Gimlette have potent active principles
which would find a useful place amongst modern
therapeutic remedies. For example, no less than
eighteen of the animal poisons and twenty-three of
the vegetable poisons mentioned have undetermined
active principles.

What a field of research is open to the physiologist
and pharmacologist !

To quote one instance—Dr. Gimlette in 1919 sent me
a number of Ibul nuts from Kelantan, and these on
extraction were found to contain an active principle
having a very pronounced effect on the heart, pro-
longing diastole and strengthening systole, the details
of which research are being published by Dr. V. G.
Walsh and Mr. J. Webster. There is no doubt that
similar investigations of other reputed poisons would
lead to like productive results.

As an old friend and admirer of the author, I con-
gratulate him on his self-denying labours, which have
added to the knowledge of Medicine and Toxicology
and point the way to fertile fields of medical research.
I thank him also for the privilege of writing this
short " Foreword " to his admirable and interesting
work.

W. H. WILLCOX,
K.C.I.E., C.B., C.M.G., M.D., F.R.C.P.,
Medical Adviser to the Home Office.

MALAY POISONS AND CHARM CURES

PART I

CHAPTER I

METHODS OF POISONING AND MALAY CHARMS IN GENERAL

MALAYS, like other Eastern people, are skilled in the art of poisoning, which is " of all the forms of death by which human nature may be overcome the most detestable, because it can of all others be the least prevented, either by manhood or foresight." Murder is commonly accomplished by Malays in a fit of passion or blind jealousy by stabbing with the national weapon, the kris (kĕris : a dagger, the kris or creese), with a spear, or by slashing with the narrow-bladed Malay chopper, as well as by the more deliberate use of fire-arms. Malays are not a timid people, and, although in India secret poisoning became one of the most prominent, if not the most prevalent, of court atrocities under Mussulman rule, the Muhammadan Malay, as a general rule, attempts vengeance by means of poison when he is bearing a grudge and brooding, and when violent or other measures appear to him to be too dangerous or too uncertain. Very often, when jealousy or malice inspires him, the intention is rather to cause annoyance or injury less serious than death. With such object in view, poison is frequently put into wells and water jars. Malay women are generally held to be the accredited agents, at any rate, in many cases of poisoning, because naturally the cooking is left almost entirely to them.

Malaya is richly supplied with medicinal plants and herbs ; they form the stock-in-trade of the *bomor* or " medicine-man," many of their properties, either deadly (*rachun*) or intoxicant (*mabok*), are known, as well as their medicinal value, to Malays of most classes. This is especially true of the uncultured folk who live in rural districts, but their knowledge is often restricted to the locality, thus explaining the fact of so many various country poisons being used by Malays for felonious purposes. Familiarity with these drugs and with potent imported poisons, such as cyanide of potassium, white arsenic, strong acids and opium, gives considerable scope for the selection of poisons. It is not surprising that the common datura or thorn-apple, with its power of gradually reducing the astutest intellect into a state of drivelling fatuity, and arsenic, which destroys more speedily with symptoms which the most learned native doctors can hardly distinguish from Asiatic cholera, have been used, as in India, as the closing act of a great political contest, as a means of removing a stubborn minister or an intriguing kinsman (Ref. 8).

Some of the poisons used in Kelantan are common to India ; for example, Plumbago rosea (*chĕraka merah*), Excœcaria agallocha (*bĕbuta*), Datura fastuosa (*kĕchubong hitam*), opium (*chandu*), arsenic (*warangan* or *tuba tikus*), the horse-radish tree (*mĕrunggai*), and glass in powder (*sĕrbok kacha*) combined with bamboo and other fine vegetable hairs. Malays do not hesitate to use well-known poisonous drugs as medicines, especially, perhaps, Datura fastuosa, Alocasia denudata (*kĕladi chandek*), Goniothalamus tapis (*kĕnĕrak*), Gly-

cosmis citrifolia (*nĕrapih*), opium and white arsenic.
Indeed, as regards poisons derived from the vegetable
kingdom, all those mentioned in subsequent chapters,
except *bĕbuta, pokok batu pĕlir kambing, langkap, ibul,
pokok ipoh, tuba, rĕngas, binjai* and *rengut*, are used
either externally or internally as Malay medicines.
Malay thieves frequently use poisonous plants to
cause no more than stupefaction (*mabok*) of their victims
as a preliminary to the main venture. Robbers employ
sand, powdered glass, quicklime and other powders to
disconcert their pursuers. Rogues claim to be able to
cause loss of voice lasting for seven or eight days by
the administration of certain poisons by the mouth.
Two or three clinical cases have occurred in Kelantan
in which it was alleged that witnesses in court could
not give evidence for this reason. Aphonia was complete but temporary, but the poison could not be produced. To' Bomor Ĕnche' Awang, a Kota Bharu
" medicine-man," or *bomor*, said that a powder made
with lime used in betel-chewing, and scrapings from
the smooth, dry, shiny inner bark of a forest vine (*rotan
sĕga;* Calamus, sp. Palmæ), the familiar " cane " of
boyhood, was used for this purpose. This was prepared
by the " medicine-man " (To' Bomor Ĕnche' Awang),
and given by arrangement, in a draught of water, to a
strong Chinese ward attendant in the State hospital at
Kota Bharu, Kelantan, but it had no ill effect on him.
The amount of powdered rattan bark was probably
too small in quantity, owing to nervousness on the
part of the *bomor* who prepared it. He was a vaccinator
on the hospital staff.

Suicide by poisoning, or indeed by any other method,
is almost unknown among Malays, except, perhaps,
when the wild beast part of a distracted man comes
uppermost and brooding sullenness changes to frantic
frenzy. A Malay may then start to " run amuck "

with a stabbing or cutting weapon in his hand, perhaps with the idea of suicide, killing indiscriminately, and expecting to be slain, perchance, at the end of his reckless " running amuck " (*měngamok*). Poison mixed with honey is sometimes smeared on the under surface of a knife. The poisoner, sharing a meal with his enemy, divides a water-melon in half with the poisoned blade, but is careful to eat only the upper and harmless portion as his share of the fruit. This method of poisoning is said to be common in Trengganu ; potassium cyanide is employed. In Kelantan a long-bladed kitchen knife, the *pisau ajam*, is used and the ordinary water-melon, *labu China*, chosen. This ingenious form of poisoning by smearing a powerful drug on the blade of a knife is a very old one. Sir Thomas Browne remarks : " The poyson of Parysatis reported from Ctesias by Plutarch in the life of Artaxerxes whereby anointing a knife on the one side, and therewith dividing a bird : with the one half she poisoned Statira, and safely fed herself on the other, was certainly a very subtile one, and such as our ignorance is well content it knows not."—(Browne, Thomas, Knight, 1672, " Enquiries into Vulgar and Common Errors." Sixth and last edition. Book VII., p. 431. London.) We know from Plutarch's " Life of Artaxerxes " that " Statira dying with dreadful agonies and convulsions, was herself sensible of what had happened to her," and from this may infer that the Persian queen was poisoned with arsenic smeared on the blade of a carving knife.

The Kris.—On the west coast of the Malay Peninsula it has been denied very generally that the blade of the kris is ever deliberately poisoned, but in Kelantan I have been told by the late Dato' Lela 'diraja and the Ěngku Said Husain of Kota Bharu that arsenic is sometimes smeared on the blades of Malay weapons with criminal intent. Reference to this practice is made in a quaint little book entitled " Six Months Among the Malays," published in London in 1855. The author, Dr. Yvan, who was physician to a scientific mission sent by France to China, writes as follows : " I changed the subject by inquiring whether it were true that the Malays poisoned their arrows and other weapons. ' As true,' he replied, ' as that I am the son of my father.' On my inquiring further into the subject he said he would return on the morrow and show me something relative to it ; so on the following day Abdala arrived carrying a number of small paper parcels, which he spread out on the table and allowed me to examine. There were several fragments of a whitish substance which I immediately recognised from its form to be a species of lime ; another ingredient reduced to a white powder, some coco-nut oil, a citron, and an extract of some kind of a dark colour and virous smell. Abdala took up a long, thin kriss, touched the side of it with the lime, then spread it over with the white powder and squeezed a little of the citron juice upon it ; this being done, he exposed it to the heat of the sun and when the blade was quite dry he took up the black extract and put a small quantity of it upon the part which had previously been covered with lime, touching it lastly with the coco-nut oil. He then proceeded to prepare the other side of the kriss in the same manner, and, to convince me that he perfectly understood the whole affair, he wounded a fowl which died a short time afterwards. The white substance was, I found, a mixture of arsenic, and the extracted matter was from the bark of the menispermum coculus ; the poisonous properties of the kriss were, probably, owing principally to the latter ingredient " (Ref. 9). The writer was shrewd in his inference if it is correct. Menispermum cocculus is Anamirta cocculus, Linn.—

Menispermaceæ, the fruit of which (Cocculus indicus, fish-berry or Levant nuts) was once used by poachers in " foxing " fish, and by bad characters in " hocussing" people. It contains the poisonous principle picrotoxin, a crystalline non-alkaloidal body, easily absorbed through the skin, discovered in the seeds by Boulay in 1812. Picrotoxin is a powerful convulsive poison. The lethal dose is ½ grain (0·03 gramme), and two powdered seeds (2·4 gramme) have caused death. Though Anamirta cocculus extends southwards from South India to New Guinea, in the Malay Peninsula, Anamirta Loureiri takes its place.

Sometimes the blade of the kris is dipped in human urine with the idea of rendering penetration of the steel more easy when attacking a so-called invulnerable man. Even to-day Malays still think that certain persons can acquire impenetrability of the skin to shot and steel by means of some very powerful charms. In 1895 a notorious Malay rebel—the Orang Kaya Pahlawan of Pahang—was a case in point. This Malay was endowed with much cunning, great physical strength, courage, and a power of imagination so developed that he could persuade people to believe in the quaint infallibility of his ideas. Except for a silver bullet he was safe. The idea of invulnerability of the flesh was also attached to To' Janggut, a ringleader in the Kelantan rising of 1915, but he was shot dead by the Sikh troops of the Malay States Guides. Charms intended to procure invulnerability nearly always take the form of a belt. A girdle-charm of this kind was found on a Kelantan robber who was speared to death, in 1917, in a seaside village of northern Kelantan ; this particular belt was tied with the knot in front.

Certain Malay weapons are endowed with magic properties, especially the kris and some of the short Malay daggers called *tumbok lada*. In 1917, His Highness the

late Sultan allowed a very beautiful and valuable
straight, long-bladed kris to be taken from his palace
to the hut of an elderly woman living near the Residency
in Kota Bharu. She had been bitten at dusk on the
foot by a poisonous snake, and expired at daybreak.
Several Malay " medicine-men " were in attendance ;
she died, however, before the arrival of a very famous
bomor who had been sent for from afar and into whose
hands it was intended to place the Sultan's magical
kris. As a charm cure the point of the naked blade is
applied by the *bomor* to the punctures of snake-bite.
No special formula is chanted. Death from snake-bite
is rare in the Malay Peuinsula, although more than
thirty poisonous snakes have been described ; the
royal kris had been borrowed in the hope of restoring
the woman to health.

His Highness the present Sultan showed me his
father's famous kris in 1921. It is called *kĕris bari*,
from the name of the steel, *bĕsi bari*, from which the
blade is made ; the blade is undamascened and rough
like the surface of fine emery paper, it is also black ;
but this is only due to the fact that, like the blades of
all Malay weapons, it has been treated with white
arsenic and the juice of the lime fruit to prevent it
from rusting. His Highness also showed me another
very beautiful gold-mounted kris, which he said was
of even higher quality than the *kĕris bari*. It was a
short, straight kris, also undamascened, called *kĕris
melela*, the usual name for an undamascened blade.
The Sultan told me that in the event of a hair being
swallowed and sticking in the throat, the resulting
irritation will quickly disappear when a little oil in
which the point of this kris has been dipped is administered by the mouth. A Malay dagger (*tumbok
lada*) with a blade forged from *bĕsi bari* is one of the
treasured possessions of the To' Bomor Ênche' Harun

of Kota Bharu. This old "medicine-man" told me that in days gone by his enchanted dagger would float in water, but owing to repairs to the hilt its magic had been lost. The magic kris is generally of Javanese manufacture ; a rare variety is reputed to have a blade of steel made by finger pressure alone. One of these weapons (*kĕris pichit*) is said to be in the possession of the Raja d' Hilir of Perak. Generally speaking, the value of the weapon does not depend on its costly ornamentation, but upon the accuracy of proportion in its blade ; while a kris that has frequently shed blood is greatly increased in superstitious value. Different forms of damascening produce different effects—" with one kind the owner of such a kris cannot be overcome ; others are generally auspicious ; another gives luck to its wearer when trading or voyaging " (Ref. 6). Arrows and darts poisoned by means of the deadly upas sap are now no longer used for homicide, being confined to the killing of game by the jungle folk living in caves and trees, on the hills or plains, *i.e.*, by the Sakai and other jungle tribes of the Malay Peninsula.

Betel-Chewing.—The method of conveying poison in a betel " chew " is a very old one. Francois Bernier (1656–1668) mentions the case of a young Indian nobleman who was poisoned in this way. "As a mark of distinguished favour the King presented the *betel* in the presence of the whole court to the unsuspecting youth, which he was obliged immediately to masticate, aggreeably to the custom of the country. . . . Such, however, was the activity of the poison that he died before he could reach home " (see Vincent Smith's edition, 1914, pp. 13–14, Oxford). The conservative Malay is said to employ this method by smearing poison on the gambier which is enclosed in the betel packet (see pp. 134, 231).

Bile.—The bile of reptiles, birds and mammals is a

favourite ingredient of many Malay poisons. Probably its use by Malays as a practical poison is not very efficacious, and it may be used only in " make-believe," as an excipient, or to give a finish to a known deadly combination. Bile is much prized as a medicine ; for instance, that of the bear, porcupine, snake and crow, especially that of the racquet-tailed drongo or king-crow (Dissemurus platurus), is used by the *bomor* either as a practical or fanciful drug. The dried gall-bladder of the bear is used as a medicine in Borneo ; but the Malay *bomor* only administers the bile of the honey-bear (Helarctos malayanus) internally as a " pick-me-up " in cases of accidental falls from a tree or height ; it is more commonly applied by him to the navel of children suffering from emaciation caused by intestinal worms. The bile of the large porcupine (Hystrix longicauda) is used in cases of suppressed yaws (*bunga puru ta' jadi*) ; that of the king-crow or monkey's slave is used as a fanciful and very disgusting kind of aphrodisiac.

Blood.—Human blood is sometimes used in the making of love charms and gambling charms. The blood must be derived from the corpse of a man who has suffered death from violence, and, for the future success of the charm, it is essential to obtain his for-giveness before his death. This superstition is quite common in Kelantan ; Nik Ismail, one of the Kelantan Malays on the hospital staff at Kota Bharu, told me that when cases of murder are in the wards, charm-mongers frequently approach him begging for a little post-mortem blood. The following incident came under my personal observation in 1920. Shortly after the execution of a Malay (Awang Dogol bin Dĕris) by hanging for murder, a fellow prisoner of the deceased man was caught trying to collect blood (in sufficient quantity to soak a few bits of thread) from the forearm of the dead criminal. The culprit was a Kelantan *bomor* who had been sentenced to two years' rigorous imprisonment for cheating ; he said he had obtained the thread from the native gaoler for the purpose of making a charm. His object was the making of a love charm, but the charm could also have been used in playing the Chinese gambling game of Poh (*main po*). It was to have been prepared by saturating seven pieces of thread in the blood of the dead man and that of a pink water-buffalo, adding the eyes of a tiger and those of a black cat, and burning the whole to ashes. As with other Malay philtres of a harmless, fanciful, or disgusting kind, this one was supposed to have the power of creating love by smearing it either on the skin of the owner, or on the apparel, after mixing the ashes with coco-nut oil.

To appreciate its use as a gambling charm it is necessary to describe shortly the game of Hai Weh, or Poh. This game is played with a die placed in a square brass box fitting it accurately, which in turn slides into a brass cover. The lower end of the box is bevelled, and, the die having been inserted, the box is spun on a board or mat marked with a diagonal cross. The faces of the die are coloured red and white, and the stakes having been placed on the mat, those opposite the red portion of the die when it ceases spinning are the winners (Ref. 3). The blood charm is supposed to enable the owner to see what is inside the brass box by smearing the ashes mixed with coco-nut oil over the eyebrows. In India " a native pharmacopœia prescribes bruised dhatura, mixed with a person's blood, and smeared between the eyes, as a potent love charm, which causes any one who sees a woman thus decorated to become her slave " (Ref. 2). Poisonous drugs are not added to, or employed in, the manufacture of Malay love philtres for sinister purposes. Great

attention is paid to the proper combination of drugs
for curative purposes, and so also with poisonous
preparations. Some of the Malay poisons, especially
those which act through the skin and mucous membranes, are devised with an almost incredible refinement
of cruelty.

"**Time-Poisons.**"—It has often been said, but
without authority, that an accomplished Malay criminal
can give a single dose of poison and time the death of
his victim within three months, six months, or even
three years, according to the dose and the particular
combination he uses. A system of slow poisoning is
supposed to have prevailed in the Middle Ages. Thus,
Linschoten, writing (1583) on the manner and customs
of Portuguese and half-caste women in India, remarks :
" There are many men poysoned by their wives, if
they once be mooved : for they know howe to make a
certaine poyson or venome, which shall kill the person
that drinketh it, at what time or houre it pleaseth
them : which poyson being prepared, they make it in
such sort, that it will lye sixe yeres in a mans body and
never doe him hurt, and then kil him, without missing
halfe an houres time." Pyrard de Laval reported (1619)
that the women of Goa acted in the same way : " elles
l'empoisonneront avec vue certaine drogue, qui le
pouurra faire encore durer six mois au bout il faut qu'il
meure " (Ref. 5). It has been suggested that datura
may have been the drug employed in this system.
Croton oil has also been suggested (see p. 163). Again,
the possibility of the existence of such a poison which
will kill at any distance of time when the hour
approaches for which it has been planned, is supported
by the tale of La Spara, who was hanged in Rome in
1648 with thirteen of her companions, while a number
of her clients were whipped, half naked, through the
streets. Hieronyma Spara, the reputed witch, supplied

young matrons who wished to resent the infidelities of
their husbands with an elixir which was a slow poison,
clear, tasteless and limpid, and of strength sufficient
to destroy life in the course of a day, week, month or
number of months, as the purchaser preferred. In this
case arsenic has been suggested as the most likely
poison (see p. 264). A similar organisation was led by
Tofania, an old woman of Naples, who was tried and
strangled in 1719, after she had caused, directly or
indirectly, the deaths of more than 600 persons with
her " Acqua Tofana " or the Manna of St. Nicola of
Bari (Ref. 1). This notion obtains in Java and exists
in Persia to this day. I tried to verify the Malay story
in an up-country district of southern Kelantan known
as the Ulu Kĕsial district. This part of the State had
long enjoyed an evil reputation for efficiency in poisoning until the District Officer, Mr. A. J. Sturrock,
treated it with a considerable amount of judicial attention in the year 1912. Many of my notes have come
from Ulu Kĕsial ; but of late years it has become
increasingly difficult to chat about poisons in this part
of Kelantan. Native experts there say that the idea
of a time-poison is unfounded (*bohong*), but that the
effect of a certain deadly poison, presently to be
described, is greatly accelerated or delayed if certain
fruit and vegetables, such as papaw, water-melon,
pumpkin and cucumber, happen to be eaten soon after
the ingestion of the poison, or not until some days
after its administration. This Ulu Kĕsial poison serves
as an example of the great attention to detail which
must be paid in the preparation of old-fashioned
Malay poisons. It is said to cause the spitting of blood
with fever.

The fruit of a poisonous palm (*ibul*) and of a poisonous
jungle climber (*rengut*) are taken as well as a pill-
millepede and the gall-bladder of the honey bear, that

of a common toad and that of a horned toad-frog ; each is carefully and separately dried and then toasted over a fire. They are then pulverised, and kept in separate packets until the time arrives to use them. If it is desired to administer this poison in water, an equal quantity of the six powders is taken, mixed together, and put into the water jar. If it is to be mixed with food, the galls of the frog and the toad must be fresh, and, when fresh, mixed with the four dry powders, and the resulting mass then heated over a fire until it becomes black and sticky like opium prepared for the pipe. It is now ready to be put into a curry or any kind of rice-broth. In three or four days the victim is said to cough blood. A fine black powder, prepared by an Ulu Kĕsial villager and said to contain all the ingredients, was sent to me in 1920 to experiment with. It was given to a dog, but the result of the experiment was not known owing to the pariah slipping its chain and escaping shortly after it had swallowed the poison. This particular combination is said to be so deadly that it must not be prepared inside a house or in a market town, but in the solitude of thick jungle. An evil-doer (Mat Hasan), I am told, neglected this precaution when making it, and so caused his own death. He was getting it ready in his house, had reduced the millepede to fine powder and the galls of the bear and the toad, when a puff of wind blew the dry powders into his mouth and nostrils and he died in three days. The villagers said he had died of fever, but those who " knew " declared Mat Hasan had accidentally poisoned himself.

Some apparently quite harmless things are avoided (*pantang*) when combined, because they are said to be poisonous (*mabok*) in combination : for example, mangosteen fruit with sugar, for fear the sap of the rind will mix with the sugar ; water-melon with honey,

for the same reason ; the heart (*umbut*) of the coco-nut
tree with shell-fish ; the heart of the *nibong* palm
with oysters. Fish and other food must be fried
only with vegetable oil, *i.e.*, coco-nut oil ; a stew
made of the flesh of the mouse-deer and pineapple
is said to cause death. It is said that the durian
fruit must not be eaten with brandy, so also even in
England that eating a banana with a glass of Curacoa
at dessert is " very unwise." On the other hand,
tradition says it is unwise to eat the pear without
wine (" Pear, Wine and Parson "—Cotgrave's French
Dictionary, 1650) :—

> Après la poire,
> Le vin ou le prêtre.

And again in the " Art of preserving Health " by
doctors of famous schools of Salermo (Italy) early
twelfth century (Ref. 4) :—

> La poire crue est un poison . . .
> Elle charge trop l'estomac. Étant cuite,
> Elle y porte la guérison . . .
> Quand on a mangé de la poirre,
> Que le premier soin soit de boire.

(Translation of Brunzen de la Martinière, 1749.)

On the other hand, the fermented juice (perry) was
accredited with therapeutic properties (" La Maison
Rustique," Ch. Estienne and Liébault, 4t, livre iii.,
p. 405, 1589). In Kelantan no spells are muttered
during the process of mixing drugs with criminal
intent ; no special " precious rod " of gold or silver
is used as in ancient Egypt, but no doubt magic enters
during the preparation of the compositions.

Serious cases of poisoning are recognised as being
beyond the power of the *bomor*, but he has antidotes
for every poison, many of them being made up of
products from the animal and vegetable kingdoms.
One, for instance, which occurs in a manuscript book

on Malayan medicine, belonging to the Pharmaceutical
Society of London, is to take *těras* (the core or pith) of
api-api, a mangrove tree, and that of *pandan pudak*,
a screw-pine, and rub both together on a stone into a
thick mass. Administer this in the form of a draught,
morning and evening, and rub whatever remains in the
cup or vessel upon the chest. Emetics do not seem
to be specially employed as in Western practice, but
prescriptions for inducing vomiting may be found in
the manuscript books used by the *bomor*, and one
which occurs in the book on Malayan medicine quoted
above, is to add scrapings from the root of the herb
akar tutup bumi (Elephantopus scaber, Linn.—Com-
positæ) to the " betel-chew." This prescription shows
how greatly the Malay is impressed by the idea that
evil spirits cause illness. The plant, E. scaber, is also
called *tapak Sulaiman*, or *t. leman* (*tapak*, the palm, or
sole of the foot), because it has a rosette of leaves
which suggests the pentacle, *i.e.*, the seal of Solomon
used in controlling the jinns. When prescribed for the
purpose of sealing the jinns underground it is called
akar tutup bumi (*tutup*, shutting ; *bumi*, the earth).
As a medicine, Elephantopus scaber appears to be
simply mucilaginous. Another emetic, given in the
same book, is to take seven pieces of mouse dung with
a little white pepper. This is also administered in the
" betel-chew " : " place these in a *sireh pinang* (betel-
packet) and give him to chew in order that he may
vomit."

Fresh coco-nut water when obtainable is promptly
used as a household remedy in nearly all cases of Malay
poisoning. It is slightly acid, diuretic, and contains
much sugar with a small proportion of fat, and may be
of practical value. Should the supernatural aid of
magic be sought, the prospect of cure by charms rests
entirely on the power of the formula chanted by the

bomor and on the significance of his blowing (*tiup ;*
Kelantan, *siup*) upon the face or body of the patient
during the process of the cure. This practice is called
jampi-jampi ; the cure depends, in fact, on the patient
himself, on his faith in the talismans and amulets that
he happens to be wearing for good luck ; on his
conservative belief in old traditions, and on his depend-
ence on the will of the *bomor* who tries to cure him by
suggestion.

It is said in Kelantan, that a criminal with poison
concealed about his person can be recognised by the
absence of the top part of his shadow—*i.e.*, the shadow
of his head and neck is not projected. Many think
that poisoned food can be recognised by the shadow
of the right hand and fingers not being cast when
eating rice. Some say that a stirring rod of ivory will
become dusky if poison should have been put into
food, such as curries and other stir-abouts. In Perak
a spoon made of the beak of a hornbill is said to turn
black if it touches poison.

The *bomor*, like Mithridates the Great, king of
Pontus and Bithynia, can make an antidote for any
kind of poison ; his compounds differ from the royal
prescription, which consisted of " two dry walnuts, and
as many good figs, and twenty leaves of rue, bruised
and beaten together, with two or three corns of salt,
and twenty juniper berries, which taken every morning
fasting, preserveth from danger of poison and infection
that day it is taken " (Ref. 7). For instance, one is
prepared from the wing-bone of a goose, the horn of
the wild goat, the spine of the sea porcupine, the tusk
of a toothed whale, and various yet unidentified jungle
roots and barks. These are to be rubbed down in hot
water on a stone, and after careful straining the water
is to be given by the mouth. A formula must be
recited and a powerful rendering given at the same time

by the *bomor* who owns the charm. This prescription
was used by the late To' Bomor Ēnche' Abdullah, a
" medicine-man" to H.H. the late Sultan of Kelantan ;
the charm that he used is given on p. 53.

Burnt tiger's whiskers in coco-nut oil as an internal
remedy for chronic rheumatism ; the ashes of a cat's
whiskers in liquid opium as an antidote to poison ;
hairs from an elephant's tail as toothpicks in the
toothache of children, and medicines derived from the
sperm whale, and such a rare local animal as the
Malayan wild goat, strongly suggest the idea of " make
believe " or sympathetic magic on the part of the
bomor, much in the same way as " a saffron bag, worn
at the pit of the stomach," cures rheumatism, and the
digging foot of a mole serves to cure cramp in Devonshire.

REFERENCES

(1) " Chambers' Encyclopædia." 1927. New ed., " Secret Poison-
    ing," Vol. VIII., p. 251. London : Chambers.
(2) CROOKE, W. " Things Indian." 1906. " Poisoning." London :
    Murray.
(3) DENNYS, N. B. " A Descriptive Dictionary of British Malaya."
    1894. " Gambling." London.
(4) LEROY, ANDRÉ. " Dictionnaire de Pomologie." 1867–79.
    Vol. I., p. 65. Paris and Angers.
(5) LINSCHOTEN, JOHN HUYGHEN VAN. " The Voyage of Linschoten
    to the East Indies." From the old English translation of
    1598, edited by Burnell and Tiele. 1885. Vol. I., p. 211.
    London : Hakluyt Society. No. LXX.
(6) McNAIR, Major F. " Perak and the Malays." 1878. London :
    Tinsley.
(7) PARKINS, Dr. " The English Physician," p. 330. 1814. London :
    Crosby.
(8) SIMPSON, A. P. " Native Poisons of India." *Pharmaceut. Jour.
    and Trans.* (London). 1871. 3, II., p. 602.
(9) YVAN, Dr. " Six Months Among the Malays and a Year in
    China," p. 145. 1855. London : Blackwood.

CHAPTER II

THE WORK OF THE *BOMOR* IN RELATION TO CLINICAL MEDICINE

CLINICAL medicine was closely allied with the forbidden sciences in the popular creed of the Middle Ages, and Magic maintains its hold firmly to-day in the Far East. In Malaya its practice has come down to the Malays, not only from a very conservative belief in ancient folklore, subsequently ingrafted with Indian mythology and Arabian quasi-science, but it still definitely persists as a part of their primitive religion, which was pure nature worship and consequently spirit worship. The original beliefs of the Malay were animistic and saw souls in trees and rocks and every living thing, " sermons in stones, books in the running brooks." Then came the influence of Brahmanism with its magical precepts and hymn charms, which the Malay " medicine-man " kept secret. Finally Islam, coming from India 600 years ago, brought him the Sufi mysticism, which some suggest has been derived ultimately from Neo-Platonism.

The Bomor.—Malays of all classes still respect the " medicine-man " : it is still his business to give advice in matters of sorcery ; to propitiate devils, to chide or coax evil spirits as occasion seems to demand, and to prescribe *taboo* for everyday life. His vocation survives in the common practice of magic by incantation (*jampi-jampi*) and in the not uncommon performance, in Kelantan, of *Main Pětěri*, or the practice of the Black Art in raising spirits. He compromises himself to-day in practising a pagan faith, but his lapse from Islam

is sanctioned by the devout but not very orthodox
Malay as consistent with conflict between the ancient
Law of Custom, which Islam recognises everywhere
(*Hukum Adat*), and the strict Law of the Prophet
(*Hukum Shara*).   As a concession many old pagan
charms are prefaced with a prayer, " In the name
of Allah, the All-Compassionate and All-Merciful,"
and concluded with the pious termination, " There
is but one God, and Muhammad is His Apostle "
(Ref. 9).

The folklore of Malaya is so abundant and so varied
that the " medicine-man " must of necessity be an
expert specialist.   The sea, with all the lore of naviga-
tion and deep-sea fishing, is the department of a
specialist in magic called the *pawang-di-laut ;* the land,
on the other hand, is the domain of the *pawang-di-
darat :* one an expert in the folklore of hunting and
trapping, another in procuring camphor wood, others
in finding eagle-wood, in securing good luck for newly
opened tin or gold mines, in the many strange customs
surrounding the cultivation of rice, in propitiating the
spirits of a district, and so on.   They perform magical
rites in order to secure good catches of fish, to find
alluvial tin, to ensure good crops, etc.

In Kelantan, a *pawang* whose vocation is clinical
medicine is commonly known as a *bomor, i.e.*, a person
who practises the healing art by utilising the magic art.
There are physicians of this kind of either sex ; they
are generally crafty old Malays, but there is no reason
why a *bomor* should not be a Siamese, a Turk, or even
a Tamil.   The origin of the *bomor* is told in a quaint
Kelantan legend.   As narrated by To' Bomor Ênche'
Harun it is as follows : " In olden days a son was born
to Abdul Kutok and Siti Ajam in a country called San
in Arabia.   The father was the chief of all the Saints,
and the little boy was known as Akmal Hakim.   When

he was quite young the trees would speak to him and tell him if their roots and leaves were useful as medicines, even teaching him how to make combinations which would bring the dead to life. For such time as Akmal Hakim stayed in that country no deaths occurred in the land; but he began to get proud and God became angry with him. One day Akmal Hakim decided to cross a river and go to a distant country, taking all his books on medicine with him. God commanded the Archangel Gabriel to take the disguise of a boatman and upset the boat during the crossing. Gabriel did this and Akmal Hakim was drowned. When the boat upset all the books were lost in the water except fragments which floated away to various countries. From these torn sheets the finder learned to become a *bomor* or physician." This Kelantan legend is corroborated by a Selangor account (Ref. 18, p. 46). Akmal Hakim is probably identical with the celebrated Lukman (or Luqman) al-Hakim of Arabian fable. Very little is known about this mysterious person. Accounts differ as to his parentage and date. He is mentioned in the Koran, and is generally supposed to have been a philosopher (Ar. *hakim*), the supposed author of a collection of Arabian fables, and, like Æsop, a slave noted for his ugliness. He is referred to again in the sacrificial song of the To' Bomor Pĕtĕri (Chapter IV., p. 81), and his name occurs in other neutralising charms given by Skeat (Ref. 12).

Possibly Luqman al-Hakim was Hakam the son of Abu'l Hakam (Ref. 2, p. 16), a Christian, and one of the earliest known Arabian physicians (Ar. *hakim*). Both Abu'l Hakam and his son lived to be centenarians, but do not appear to have written anything. 'Isa, the son of Hakam, is supposed to have written a large treatise on the Art of Medicine, of which no fragment remains.

A prescription ascribed to Luqman al-Hakim contains Euphorbia hirta (E. pilulifera), a medicine used to-day in Western practice for the relief of asthma and bronchitis. Luqman al-Hakim's prescription was for a cough : Take about 4 gallons of the stems of *Sudu-sudu* (succulent Euphorbias, such as E. nerefolia and *ara tanah*, E. hirta—Euphorbiaceæ), chop into very small pieces and dry well. Boil about a gallon of unhusked rice, dry well and beat off the husk. Mix the stems with the clean rice, pound into a flour and preserve carefully. " When a patient has to be treated, provide him with no more than half an ounce " (translated from the manuscript quoted on p. 14).

Regarded as a physician, the *bomor* is held in honour for his sagacity and for the fortunate use of the curative or remedial plants and other drugs that he may employ. He is a self-made handy-man who lives by his wits, with or without the aid of magic. He wears no special dress ; his office is only inherited if the soul of a dead *bomor*, in the form of a tiger, passes into the body of his son ; as a rule he qualifies for his title (To' Bomor) by natural ability and skill. He is an independent practitioner individually resorted to, likely to be called in at birth and at death, for any accident or illness. He generally accepts small payments for his services and is secretive, so that it may happen that one *bomor* is quite ignorant of the magic employed by another. Only a few are experienced in the black art of spirit-raising ; but most of them are skilled in the lore of incantation. Very often the village *bomor* is merely a herbalist, and a lovable old fellow ; he is always well qualified in the use of local native drugs and the folklore connected with them. The late To' Bomor Ênche' Jalal, whose photograph is given as an illustration, was a practitioner of this type. His conception of therapeutics was based on the medical doctrines of mediæval times :—

> He knew the cause of everich maladye,
> Were it of hoot or cold, or moiste, or drye,
> And where engendered, and of what humour ;
> Prologue to the " Canterbury Tales."—Doctour.
> (W. W. Skeat. " The Works of Chaucer." 1900. Text, p. 13.)

The village *bomor* is a pillar of local society ; but the Malay " medicine-man " who specialises in poisoning is a dangerous citizen and not a person to offend. The spirit-raising *bomor* is best regarded as a priest-physician ; he is a master in the occult science which is only within the reach of the few ; he professes to rule demons by means of special incantations which they are unable to disobey, and in general is beneficial rather than noxious to his fellow-men. He is not, as a rule, a mere impostor as long as people believe in him. If his magic works, no matter how, why should he not use it ? When dealing in magic he endeavours, without asking the consent of the higher power, to move the occult powers to exert a healing influence by means of traditional rites, and may try to protect people against mysterious enemies.

I once found it advisable to seek advice from a Kelantan *bomor* about dispersing a swarm of wild honey-bees from a bookcase in my study. Provided they are allowed to remain undisturbed, bees swarming by chance in a house are considered harbingers of good fortune. To' Bomor Ĕnche' Harun came and conducted a ceremony in the study with great dignity and import-ance ; he prepared a feast of comestibles customarily offered to spirits by the *bomor* who practises sorcery (see Chapter IV), and intoned some formula that I did not understand. Eventually he concluded the exorcism in a practical way by removing the bees in the book-case to another house in the compound (Ref. 6).

The consideration of exorcism, anathema, incantations and charms used by the *bomor* is a vast subject. Briefly, Skeat divides the medical rites into " ceremonial inspection," *i.e.*, diagnosis, by divination and ominous signs, etc., and " therapeutical rites," such as propitiation of evil spirits, the destruction or neutralisation of evil principles, the casting out, or sucking out, of evil principles, and the recalling of a sick man's soul (" Malay Magic," Ref. 12, p. 408).

The *bomor*, again, is the Malay surgeon, as well as physician, and in Kelantan he is not unskilful in his treatment of simple fractures by means of circular splints made of slips of split bamboo fastened together (*bĕlat*, a kind of Gooch splint) and applied outside a vegetable poultice.   He is not always so successful in his minor surgery, which, according to the Muhammadan religion, is mostly confined to the operations of circumcision, ear-boring and tooth-filing.   I have seen a clinical accident in which a Kelantan *bomor* completely severed the male organ at the root during the circumcision of a young lad ; but most of the failures which drift into the Government hospitals are due to sepsis. Midwifery, and all the lore pertaining to it, is the province of a woman, the *bidan* or Malay widwife ; the *bomor* is called in only when the help of magic seems to be indicated in a difficult labour caused by *hantu* or evil spirits.   Charms known as *tawar sĕlusoh* are used in cases of transverse and other abnormal presentations.

Hantu.—It is necessary to dwell on the word *hantu* (ghosts, evil spirits and goblins) in order to explain the work of the *bomor* in relation to clinical medicine. Just as the hawthorn is under the protection of the fairies in Ireland, its small red fruit the pixies' pear of Dorset, and darnel is sown by the devil in Wiltshire at midnight, so in Malaya there are wild plants which are said to be planted and cultivated by *hantu* or spirits.

Pokok kapas hantu (Hibiscus abelmoschus, Linn.,
Malvaceæ), a shrub used in medicine, having musky
perfumed seeds, and *akar kĕmĕnnyan hantu*, a climbing
plant (Hedyotis capitellata, Wall., Rubiaceæ), also
called *akar lidah jin*, or Satan's tongue, are examples.
Also may be noted the river weed called *akar kĕmang
hantu* (Neptunia oleracea, Lour., Leguminosæ), the
root of which is used in Kelantan as an external remedy
for necrosis of the bones of the nose and hard palate
(*rĕstong*), one of the late manifestations of syphilis. In
this case the word *hantu* is used on account of the soft
white " floats " of very loose cortical tissue which give
the plant an uncanny appearance in the water.

Ridley refers to the use of the word *hantu* as corresponding to the word " false " as applied to plant
names. He gives several others in addition to those to
which reference has been made in his " List of Plant
Names." Among them are *bunga hantu*, the " ghost
flower " (Strophanthus jackianus, Wall., Apocynaceæ),
and *limau hantu*, the wild pomelo (Citrus decumana,
Linn., var. Rutaceæ) ; but the most interesting of them
all is *paku langsuir*, the bird's-nest fern of Selangor
(Thamnopteris nidus-avis, Linn., Filicies). The *langsuir*, a terrible female vampire afflicting pregnant
women, is supposed to make her home in this wild
jungle fern. Wilkinson, on the other hand, says that
hantu, when applied to plant names, has the meaning
of " wild " as against " cultivated " (by human agency),
the theory being that ghosts themselves plant these
wild plants. Certain jungle trees (*tualang* or *sialang*)
in which wild bees nest are supposed to afford abiding
places for spirits in the large hollow projections from
the trunk by which they are characterised. The owl,
a harbinger of calamity, is called the " ghost-bird " on
account of its ghostly flight in the darkness ; the
dismal fish-owl, with its repulsive laugh (*haw, haw, haw,*

ho), is nicknamed *To' kĕtampi*, or " old-man-winnow-the-rice-for-the-burial-feast," and Sir Frank Swettenham gives two more gruesome names—*tumbok larong,* " nail-the-coffin," and *charek kafan,* " rend-the-shroud." Probably these names are suggested by the unearthly cries of the ill-omened owl. The slow loris (*kongkang*) is supposed to be always unhappy because it sees ghosts with its large, staring eyes, and it often sits with its hands in front of its face as if it were shutting out some dreadful spectacle. Certain clouds, when of very quaint or changing form (*hantu dagok*), are believed to be the ghosts of murdered men. In Kedah an evil spirit called *Hantu Doman* is a survival of the Monkey-God, *Hanuman,* who occurs in the Hindu legend Ramayana. It is described as having the face of a horse and the body of a man. The word *hantu* is applied to the middle finger (*jari hantu*), perhaps supporting the old superstition of " making the horns " against the Evil Eye ; a sea-shell called *siput laut*, unidentified, is called *hantu,* and the word *siput,* if used in another sense, signifies the lines or markings on the hands used in palmistry (Ref. 16).

The very superstitious Malay takes it for granted that a certain class of these evil spirits, the *hantu pĕnyakit,* cause him illness. For example, among others are the *hantu kĕmbong,* that afflicts him with stomach-ache and distension of the abdomen ; the *hantu kĕtumbohan,* that brings on small-pox ; the *hantu chika,* that causes severe colic at night-time ; the *hantu mambang* of jaundice ; the *hantu buta* and *hantu pĕkak* of blindness and deafness. The *hantu uri,* an evil spirit of the after-birth connected with the caul, is held responsible for the gurgle (*agah*) of an infant during sleep. The Malay even thinks that evil spirits can control both the occurrence and the march of disease. To' Bomor Ênche' Harun, one of the " medicine-men " to the Kelantan royal household, gave me the following scrap of information. He took it from one of his old hand-copied, magico-medical books, and said it was genuine knowledge in magic : " A Haji on his return voyage from Mecca passed an island, where he caught sight of many *hantu* sitting on the ground. He landed and at first walked about keeping his own counsel. At last he met the king of the island, and addressed him not knowing at the time that it was the king. He asked the name of the place. The king of the phantoms said ' It is the island of Kiran ; you are addressing the king, who is *Raja Sinar Pati ;* my men are called *hantu sĕgĕdah.*' The Haji then inquired as to the nature of their work. *Raja Sinar Pati* replied ' I am the evil spirit of Cholera, and when I feel hungry I go to other countries and devour men.' "

The Malay word *jin* corresponds to the Arabic *djin, jinn* or *jin,* which stood for the fairies who, according to Arabian fable, were created from " smokeless fire " 2,000 years before Adam was made of earth (Ref. 1). They are generally, but not necessarily, supposed to be evil spirits and are said to be governed by *Nabi Sulaiman* (King Solomon). Sir Frank Swettenham states in his book " Malay Sketches " : " The following legend gives the Malay conception of the origin of all *jin, hantu, bajang,* and other spirits. The Creator determined to make Man, and for that purpose He took some clay from the earth and fashioned it into the figure of a man. Then He took the spirit of Life to endow this body with vitality and placed the spirit on the head of the figure. But the spirit was strong, and the body, being only clay, could not hold it and was reft in pieces and scattered into the air. These fragments of the first great Failure are the spirits of earth and sea and air. The Creator then formed another clay figure but into this one He wrought some iron, so that when it received the vital spark it withstood the strain and became Man " (Ref. 15). McNair gives a different idea which is also taken from Malay literature : " God, in order to render steadfast the foundations of the watery expanse, girt it round with an adamantine chain, viz., the stupendous mountains of Caucasus, the wondrous region of genii and aerial spirits " (Ref. 10). A more detailed view is that when the twins Cain (*Kabil*) and Abel (*Habil*) were in the womb of their mother Eve they bit their thumbs till the blood came, and when they were born the blood turned into spirits both good and bad. The blood which spurted to the clouds became the Black Spirits (*Jin Hitam*), and that which fell on the ground the White Spirits (*Jin Puteh*) (Ref. 12).

Some Malay teachers in Kota Bharu, Kelantan, say that there are two classes of spirits, the external jin and the internal jin. The *bomor* of this school says the external jin are created by God from the wind, and that they can be seen by people who have faith and who are learned in spirit lore. He says that spirits can be seen by a man in a trance or in unconscious moments. This kind of spirit-raising *bomor* claims also that he can reflect the external spirits, by means of special magic, on to the finger nails of innocent little boys, a statement which suggests in its application the idea of scrying or crystal gazing. He imagines, moreover, that spirits have the power of conversing among themselves at certain times :—

> In each low wind methinks a spirit calls,
> And more than echoes talk along the walls.
> (Pope. "Eloisa to Abelard." Elwin, Vol. ii., p. 254.)

The spirit language in Kelantan is confined to sixteen words which differ from the ordinary Malay terms : for example, *sarong* (a sheath or covering) corresponds to *sĕmar* among the jin ; *tĕlur* (egg) to *burok ; mari* (come) to *samal;* *sireh* (the betel vine) is *sĕlambak;* and *matahari* (the sun) is *sinar,* which elsewhere means a " ray of sunlight." Skeat gives a different and larger list of specimen words of the spirit language used by the *pawang* in other Malay States (Ref. 12).

Some notes written for me in 1913 by To' Bomor Engku Said Abdul-Rahman of Kota Bharu, after consultation with the wise men of the town, refer to the two classes of Malay jin, *i.e.,* those inhabiting the bodies of men and those living outside. The contributors concurred in the statement that there are many different kinds of jin, and that their influence is evil, but the external jin are not able to afflict us except in co-ordination with the jin who live in our internal organs (internal jin). In dealing with the origin of disease they say it is because the thought of mankind is fixed upon disease with increasing persistency that the disease grows, a statement which is in some way comparable to Christian Science. They say, further, that the mind is fixed on the disease owing to the strength of the imported spirit (external jin) acting with the jin that controls the will of man. According to To' Bomor Ênche' Sĕnik of Panambang, Kota Bharu, a yellow jin, the *jin kuning pancha indĕra,* is the internal spirit that is supposed to control the five senses of man (*indĕra,* Sanskrit *indriya,* " sense ").

The family of external jin is a very large one. Some of them, known collectively as *Ma' Kopek,* are denizens of the forests and hills, and of these *hantu rimba,* that is so alarming to the lonely traveller in big jungle, the *langsuir,* already mentioned, who is the terrible vampire in the guise of an owl that haunts the nursery and sucks the blood of infants and women in childbed out of revenge for her own origin in the lying-in room, and the *hantu raya* are well-known examples. These dwellers of forests and hills, of land and sea, *Panglima*

A KELANTAN VILLAGE BOMOR.
To' Bomor Ĕnche' Jalal—Ulu Kelantan.

Sulong, Awang Kĕbĕnaran and *Hantu Laut,* the " Ghost of the Sea," together with all the black jin, are known as " Earthly Beings " ; they are distinct from " Celestial Beings," who are the fairies (*jin, pĕri, dewa, mambang*), and include, with nixies and elves, all the inferior divinities of the clouds, such as *chĕndĕra* and *indĕra* (Sanskrit, *Indra*). Many of the black spirits are ghosts, for example, the *hantu pĕmburu* or *hantu raya,* the Malay Spectre Huntsman, an avatar of Siva the Storm-God, who haunts river, pool, mere and lake with his bird *berek-berek,* the square-tailed bee-eater, and his three blood-sucking hell-hounds. There is, among others, the *hantu bankit,* a graveyard goblin or " sheeted ghost," the departed spirit of a man in his grave-clothes so hampered by the winding-sheet that it can move only by rolling over the ground ; there is also *balong bidai,* an evil spirit supposed to live in rivers and to have the form of an open mat in which it envelops and drowns its victims. The Malay were-tiger that results from a man turning himself into a tiger by magic agencies is in a class by itself, and is probably an example of impulsive insanity (lycan-thropy). It is akin to the were-wolf and the were-leopard, and the hare of Queen's County, recorded by Yeats, that was eventually traced to the person of an old Irish witch (Ref. 19). The reader will find much additional information about Gods, Spirits and Ghosts in Winstedt's " Shaman, Saiva and Sufi " (Ref. 18).

Many Kelantan people think that disease is sent by God. According to the teaching of To' Bomor Ĕnche' Harun it came about in this way : " During the time of King Solomon, a son of the Prime Minister was walking in a garden, when, without warning, he fell down suddenly as if bereft of his senses. The sad news of this event soon reached his father the *Mĕntĕri Asaf,*

who, taking his son (father) [1] *Berkhia* with him, went
at once to *Nabi Allah Sulaiman* (Solomon) and said
' He is my son.'   When King Solomon saw what had
happened to *Berkhia* he was very much surprised, and
said it was owing to the Will of God that such an event
had occurred.   He remarked that he had heard from
Jibrael (the Archangel Gabriel) that this kind of illness
is the most important of all diseases ; it is called
Rihul'-ahmar (Ar.) or *Angin Merah* (Malay ' red
wind ').   The king asked permission from God to
cast this disease out of the body of the Prime Minister's
son, but the Archangel appeared and told Solomon to
give an account of it to God, and Solomon did as he
was bidden.   God called the Devil and commanded
him to go to King Solomon.   Satan went to the king,
but when the Ministers saw him coming, every one
except Solomon ran away because they were very much
frightened at his appearance which was like a red
blanket of fire.   The Devil approached the king, at the
same time giving salutation, and King Solomon asked
him his name and occupation.   The Devil made reply :
' I am *Rihul'-ahmar* or the *Jin Angin Merah ;* if I
enter the body of a human being by the right nostril,
he gets the disease called *gajah-gajah* (hemiplegia) and
falls down unconscious like a dead man.   If I enter by
the left nostril, he gets *busong ayer* (dropsy) and is
unable to eat or drink owing to pain.   If I get in by
the anal aperture, he suffers from piles.   If I get in by
the orifice of the urethra, he gets *uluran* (any testicular
swelling).   If I enter by the mouth, it becomes offensive, if by the eye, it becomes blind : if by the tongue
it stiffens and prevents speech, if by the leg it palsies,
if by the hand it loses power.   If I get in by the brain,
the man goes mad, and if I get in through his skin, he

---

[1] One notes that Kelantan folk-lore wrongly makes Asaf the father instead
of the son of Barakhya (" Encyclopœdia of Islam," No. VIII., p. 476, *sub*
Asaf).— R.O.W.

gets a hundred thousand diseases.' King Solomon then said to the Jin of the Red Wind : ' All that you have just told me depends upon the Will of God ; you are misfortune a cause of human suffering.' "

Solomon plays a great part in the history of Magic. Josephus states in his " Antiquities of the Jews," when referring to the cure of a lunatic by Eleazar : " He put a ring that had a root of one of those sorts mentioned by Solomon to the nostrils of the demoniac, after which he drew out the demon through his nostrils ; and when the man fell down immediately, he adjured him to return into him no more making mention of Solomon, and reciting the incantations which he composed " (Ref. 7).

Again, continues the To' Bomor Ĕnche' Harun, in the days of the Prophet, two of the Prophet's friends, Omar and Abu Bakar, suddenly became paralysed. Muhammad was very surprised to see this ; but presently Gabriel came with a prayer invocation and asked the Prophet to read it over his two sick friends (here follows a long passage from the Koran). Muhammad did as Gabriel directed, and both Omar and Abu Bakar soon recovered. The practice of reading this passage from the Koran, in cases of hemiplegia, is in vogue in Kelantan to-day. Chewing betel while reciting verses of the Koran and spitting afterwards on the head of the patient is at times considered very valuable.

In some respects the Ĕngku Said Abdul-Rahman and other Kelantan physicians still follow the medical philosophy of the Dark Ages and believe that disease brought by evil spirits springs from the four elements, earth, water, fire and wind (air). Various ailments emanate from earth, especially those characterised by cold and dryness, such as giddiness (Ar. *sautha*, lit. to blacken), which is significant of burnt-up blood

causing a state of dry chill. If a hot wind blows over
this state of dry chill, dimness of vision with a rush of
blood to the head (*pitam*) ensues, making the earth
seem as if it were being folded up to engulf us. This
kind of dizziness (gastric vertigo) is ascribed by the
bomor to two demons, the *Nenek Jin Hitam* and the
Sĕmar Hitam, both black jin belonging to the class of
" Earthly Beings," one the grandfather of a thousand
dangers, the other the black sheath enfolding the
earth ; a thousand dangers signifies a thousand kinds
of illness caused by piercing and stabbing winds.
Many diseases, characterised by heat and moisture,
come from Air ; in these cases the red demons, especially *Jin Angin Merah*, personified in *Rihul'-ahmar*, and
Jin Raja Burong, the spirit that is king of the birds,
are to blame. From Fire we get nausea or squeamish-
ness (*hati mĕdu*), as well as heartburn (*pudas hati*)
with fever, conditions of dry heat which turn into hot
fevers when affected by hot dry winds. The yellow
jin are blamed for these conditions—for example,
external spirits, such as *jin tĕlok baranta*, and *jin
layang-layang*, the " swallow-ghost," also *anak jin
burok api*, and *hantu mambang*, one of the male
" Celestial Beings " personified in the glow of the
sunlight. Reference has already been made to *jin
kuning pancha indĕra*, the yellow jin of the five senses.
Many diseases come from Water ; those with symptoms of damp chills and catarrhal vomiting (Ar.
balgham, lit., " to spit ") develop into ague when
meeting with white ghosts, such as the ghost, *Sultan
Mahmud Raja-di-Laut* (The Ruler of the Sea), and *Jin
Puteh nur-i-Muhammad*.

The *bomor* got Neo-Platonic ideas from the Persian
Sufism he learnt from Muhammadan India, and it
may be noted that one of the Neo-Platonic philosophers
who flourished under the patronage of Khusraw, the

great Persian king, was an Arab physician, Harith ibn
Kalada, who was contemporary with the Prophet
Muhammad (Ref. 2, p. 11). In the *Lancet* of May 22nd,
1915, a reviewer of the original edition of this book
wrote as follows : " It is curious to note the survival
of ancient Greek philosophy in the modern Malay
bomor, whose belief is given on p. 5 as follows :
' According to the Kelantan bomor, disease is sent by
God, and it springs from the elements fire, air, earth,
and water.' Compare with this Plato in the Timæus,
cap. 82 : ' Now everyone can see whence diseases
arise. There are four natures out of which the body
is compacted, earth and fire, and water and air, and
the unnatural excess and defect of these . . . produce
diseases and disorders.' In the Kelantan belief, the
elements have spirits (jinn) associated with them, and
every human being has in addition an internal jinn
peculiar to himself, without whose cöoperation the
external jinn of the element (earth, air, fire or water)
is powerless. Seeing that the Malays are Mohammedans
the elemental doctrine probably reached them by way
of Galen and the mediæval Arabic physicians."

A study of Browne's " Arabian Medicine," however,
shows clearly that this doctrine of the four natural
properties rather than elements formed the basis of
Arabian medicine and reached the Far East from
Arabia and Persia. Again, the care taken by the
bomor in treating everyday diseases with foods and
drugs of an appropriate kind may perhaps be based
on the conception of trying to " preserve the balance
of power " among the four natural properties which
are Heat and Cold and Dryness and Moisture, and the
four Humours.

Ĕngku Said Abdul-Rahman followed the teaching
of Galen in regarding earth as cold and dry ; the
bodily humour that corresponded was black bile

located in the spleen, according to the Arabs. He looked upon Air as hot and moist ; the corresponding humour is blood located in the liver. He conceived Fire as hot and dry ; the corresponding humour is yellow bile located in the gall-bladder, and regarded Water as cold and moist, corresponding to phlegm, which is not located by the Arabs. The reader is referred to Browne's " Arabian Medicine " for much further information (Ref. 2, Lecture IV). The excess of these humours was a cause of disease ; the ·" distemperance " could be either " simple " or " compound."

> For Hot, Cold, Moist, and Dry, four champions fierce,
> Strive here for mastery, and to battle bring
> Their embryon atoms :
>
> (Milton, " Paradise Lost," 11., 898.)

The doctrine of the four natural properties is followed to-day all over native Asia ; it is explained at length in Chapter I of the Taju's-Salatin, a Malay classic of the beginning of the seventeenth century. Part of this was quoted in Malay by Dr. Winstedt in his review of the second edition of " Malay Poisons and Charm Cures." The passage is given at the end of Appendix I. A translation kindly given to me by Dr. Blagden is as follows : " The essence of humanity is made up of four matters, differing from one another in their properties, and termed the four elements ; and each of the four is in conflict with one another, like earth, water, wind, and fire. These four matters are the essence of every individual man as long as his being subsists ; and the properties of these four matters, which are in the essence of every individual man, are always different from one another in all men, without regard to the man's will, so that during the whole term of his life he is not at rest. For God has put into the body of each individual man various matters of which one is in conflict with another in its properties and characteristics, phlegm, bile, dryness, humidity, heat, etc., which are in conflict with one another. If the properties of all these matters are normal in a human body, neither deficient nor in excess, the human body is in good health and at rest ; but if they are not normal, but are deficient or in excess, then sundry diseases arise in the human body by reason of this fact." The passage goes on to explain how various diseases, mentioned by name, develop when the " balance of power " is not maintained.

The excess of bodily humours has to be treated by the *bomor* with appropriate food and drugs ; the qualification of them into hot, cold, moist and dry, and the compounds, such as cold and warm, warm and humid, cold in the third degree, etc., is elaborate. A simple example of *makan-sireh* (betel-chewing, see p. 231) is here given : betel-leaf or *sireh* is warm in the first degree, cold and dry in the second, judging from the taste and scent ; *chunan* or lime made from shells for smearing over the leaf, is much warmer ; *pinang* or areca nut, folded in the leaf, is cold and temperate, and *gambir* or gambier, also folded in the leaf, is cold and dry. The taboo prescribed by a *bomor* in regard to diet in illness is always strict : two examples will suffice—beef, mutton, three kinds of pumpkins and mango fruit may not be eaten in conditions of any kind of fever, nor in gonorrhœa, eye diseases and painful joint affections ; eggs and milk may be taken. Eggs of all kinds, coarse brown sugar (jaggery), and three kinds of dried fish, viz., silver bream (*kekek*) and two varieties of horse-mackerel (*talang* and *sĕlar*), may not be eaten with a cough of any kind.

The Kota Bharu *bomor* says, further, that owing to the strong belief of man in jin the influence of these

demons is very persistent in human affairs, especially
when external jin ride upon the wings of the wind.
According to a certain school, the explanation of this
is that when internal jin have weakened a man by loss
of blood, by windy coughing, or by dyspepsia, his
condition is intensified by the co-operation of the
external jin, who come either with a hot wind, dry or
damp, as the case may be, or with a cold wind, which is
either dry or damp, but always prejudicial to the sick
man. Similar beliefs are prevalent in Montenegro.
The external jin appear to be identical with " the
loathed things that rove through the land " of Indo-
Germanic origin. In arriving at these ideas the *bomor*,
a man capable of observation, and of reasoning from
observation, seems to be influenced by the meteoro-
logical conditions of his country ; for instance, the
relative recurrence and high mortality of prevalent
bowel complaints, such as Asiatic cholera and the
typhoid and dysentery groups, when hot, dry winds are
prevalent must have appealed to him, so also pul-
monary diseases, such as phthisis, when hot, damp
winds prevail. Fevers following chills caused by cold
winds blowing on the wet body, and the converse, may
well suggest the idea of external jin being borne by
the winds. Jaundice may have suggested the yellow
spirits of disease. The symptoms of tetanus, hysteria,
infantile convulsions, and delirium may have appeared
to be the work of evil spirits. The clinical manifestations of hæmorrhagic small-pox, gangrene, and perhaps
septicæmic plague, in Kelantan may have strengthened
the idea of black jin.

The following Malay folktale is of interest : it fore-
tells the fact that Asiatic cholera is connected with
subsoil wells, and tends to explain the easy tolerance
of Kelantan natives to the " pinking " or addition of
permanganate of potassium to their wells during

epidemics of cholera. The legend was told me by a
Kelantan Malay (Nik Ismail) on the staff of the State
hospital : " A merchant had seven sons who did nothing
but play the mandoline very beautifully in the streets
all day and all night. This caused all the king's wives
to fall in love with the lads, but the ruler of the country
got very much annoyed and planned their death. He
ordered a well to be dug in his grounds, but concealed
in such a way that no one should suspect its existence.
When this was done he invited the seven minstrels to
play at his palace. As they advanced across the
pitfall they all tumbled into the well together, whereupon the king ordered it to be filled in at once. Not
long afterwards cholera attacked the royal household,
and his Highness, seeking to discover the cause of his
misfortune, called in his *bomor*. After some time the
bomor found that it was due to anger on the part of
the ghosts of the murdered men because no propitiation
had been offered. The seven ghosts eventually agreed
with the *bomor* to leave the country provided a boat
filled with various kinds of food should be launched
and floated out to sea."

The survival of this superstition in launching such
vessels at sunrise is still existent in Kelantan. During
the height of an outbreak of cholera (August, 1920) I
passed a pretty little model of a steam launch, made out
of the stem and leaves of the sago palm, floating empty
down stream. It finally stranded on the river bank
near the mouth of the Kelantan river. Kelantan folk
still think that ghosts devour the offerings (sweets,
cakes, eggs, a few cents, yellow rice) placed on board
these strange craft, and that cholera will, if epidemic,
occur wherever the empty boat happens to get stranded
unless the sacrifice, contributed by public subscription,
is replenished and the little ship again shoved out to
sea by the *bomor*. In Perak the ceremony is rather

different. Mr. A. F. Worthington, of the Malayan Civil Service, told me that during a cholera outbreak in Lower Perak (1902) he assisted in launching one of these boats. It contained a crew made of three neat little wooden dolls, each about three inches high. The *bomor* told him that the offerings were intended for the crew, and he gathered that the idea was that of the " scapegoat." On this occasion the little boat was launched in the evening on the ebb when the tide served. Tobacco was put among the offerings. A full description of these spirit boats is given by Skeat in " Malay Magic."

The memory of the seven brothers is preserved in an ancient charm intended as a cure by magic of small-pox. It is given in Chapter III. In addition, To' Bomor Ĕnche' Harun contributes the following information about small-pox. It is taken from one of his ancient manuscripts on Magic : " A nameless tree grows on the banks of the *Sungai Neil* (? the Nile), a river whose water flows to heaven. This tree bears fruit once a year, and when there are many fruits on any one side of the tree, small-pox will occur in the subjacent country. In days long ago, the Prophet once summoned the leaders of the small-pox demons, who are, *Mĕring Tanu* for the male group, and *Mĕring Tandok* for the female group. Muhammad told them to put the disease on his body, so that he might experience the pain of small-pox. They did as he commanded, and when the Prophet realized the pain he read a passage from the Koran calling on Allah to drive out the disease. When the group leaders *Mĕring Tanu* and *Mĕring Tandok* heard the inspired words as the Prophet read and spoke them, they said they would avoid any-body who should ever repeat them ; moreover, if a sick man with small-pox suffered very much, that they would leave him on hearing these prayers to God."

To' Bomor Ĕnche' Harun says there are 199 demons connected with small-pox ; each has a fantastic name and each operates on a selected part of the body. There is *Sĕri Bĕrdĕngong* (His Lordship Buzz) for the ear ; *Sĕri Gĕmpa* (His Lordship Earthquake) for the roof of the mouth ; *Sĕri Gunting* (His Lordship Scissors) for the genital organs ; *Sĕri Pasak* (His Lordship Peg) for all joints ; *Raja Bĕsawan* (The Epileptic King) for the nose ; *Sĕri Bĕrgantong* (His Lordship in Suspension) for the chin ; *Sĕri Chahaya* (His Lordship of Lustre) for the right cheek ; *Sĕri Balek* (His Lordship in Reverse) for the left cheek, and so on. The demon for small-pox on the tip of the tongue is *Maut,* so named from the Arabic word for death. The *bomor* says that if a pock should occur on the tip of the tongue, one will always be found at the *meatus urinarius,* and the prognosis is bad.

Special reference has been made to cholera and small-pox, because these are the diseases most dreaded by Malays—especially small-pox, which by Malays is euphemistically called *pĕnyakit orang baik,* or " the disease of good people " ; but it has completely lost its old terrors in Kelantan owing to voluntary vaccination, which is now carried out successfully by the *bomor* who has been taught to appreciate its value. The barbarous practice of direct inoculation with small-pox virus, introduced to the Far East from Persia, and used by the Kelantan *bomor* as late as 1904, was made a penal offence by the late Sultan in 1905, when the principle of vaccination was explained to him in Council by his Adviser, Mr. W. A. Graham.

An account of the work of the *bomor* in relation to clinical medicine would be incomplete without reference to *taboo* in the sense of quarantine. The *bomor* sometimes forbids any one to enter the sick-room, or even to approach the dwelling by a particular path. A

string with coco-nut fronds hung on it is generally
drawn across the path as a notice of *pantang* or pro-
hibition. Fines are levied by the *bomor* for trans-
gression of his taboo. Two forms of native quarantine
were in force in Kelantan in 1910 during an epidemic
of cholera. One was the village quarantine called
pupoh kampong, and the other was house quarantine,
called *pupoh rumah*. The former was established for a
period of thirty days, either in favour of the outsiders
to an infected village, or in favour of the inhabitants
of a village that had escaped infection in an unhealthy
area. A string called *tali pupoh* was stretched across
the main path entering the village, and twists of leaf
depended from the string. At either side of the path
was stuck a bamboo, the upper end of which was split
into a bowl-like shape, and contained a young coco-nut,
and to the stem was tied a fold of betel and a native
cigarette. These were not, as might be thought,
offerings to the evil spirits of disease, but a sacrifice
to other spirits called up by the *bomor* to combat the
evil spirits of cholera, who are not always to be recognised. In one village the *hantu raya*, an incestuous evil
spirit of great power and treachery, had been raised in
order to assist the *bomor*. On the near side of the string
a hollow bamboo clapper was hung, and all persons
wishing to enter and pass through the village had to
beat at the clapper and wait for the *bomor* to admit
them after a muttered incantation and the scattering
of a handful of rice over the passengers. As the *bomor*
was not in constant attendance, a troublesome delay
was often caused to travellers. Passers-by are not
permitted to stay the night in a village under this form
of taboo. The fee payable to the *bomor* by anybody
found to have disregarded it is rather heavy : two
silver dollars and twelve and a half cents in cash ; one
and a quarter pounds of rice cooked with turmeric ;

two and a half yards of white cloth and three skeins of
white thread are demanded.   House quarantine lasts
for three days only, and excludes all outsiders from the
infected house.   This *taboo* is of value to Government in
preventing the spread of epidemic disease, more especially Asiatic cholera ;   the *bomor* generally agrees to
extend the period of quarantine from three to five days.
The idea of magic in the use of a *pupoh* line is apparently taken from Hindu mythology.   To' Bomor Ënche'
Harun said, when referring to the great epic poem
" Ramayana," where the hero Rama is described as
protecting his bride Sita from Ravana, that " they fled
with Laksamana into the jungle and hid there in a hut.
Sita asked her husband to gather some fruit, but begged
him not to stay away a long time.   As he did not
return quickly, she asked Laksamana to search for
him ;   Laksamana drew lines in the form of a square
round the hut, in order to prevent any harm coming
to Sita during his absence."   The magic encircling line
drawn by magicians is generally called *baris laksamana ;*
but the Kelantan *bomor* uses the word *tali* (a line) for
baris.

Dr. Charles Singer, in an address on " Early English
Magic and Medicine " read before the British Academy,
when referring to the doctrine of elf-shot, says : " The
Anglo-Saxon tribes placed these malicious elves everywhere, but especially in the wild uncultivated wastes
where they loved to shoot at the passer-by.   There
were water-elves, too, perhaps identical with the
nixies of whom we learn so much from Celtic sources.
Such creatures were perhaps personations of the deadly
powers of marshes and waterlogged land."   It is
therefore of great interest to find that the Malay *bomor*
attributes ague to the evil spirits of water, and not to
those of bad air.   In a pagan myth recorded by Skeat
and Blagden concerning the attempted creation of

man from seven leaves, one of the seven demons who
subsequently tried to overthrow the seven guardians
of a mountain formed himself into a band of mosquitoes
and then attacked the guardians who had carelessly
fallen asleep (Ref. 13). Furthermore, Skeat affirms
that Malays considered that malaria (*dĕmam kura*,
" spleen fever ") was caused by mosquitoes. This is
of great interest, since we know definitely, through the
work inaugurated by Sir Patrick Manson, that malaria
is spread by certain of these insects. It is too much to
say that the work of the *bomor* in clinical medicine is
merely fanciful ; he endeavours to prepare a *pĕnawar*,
that is to say, a " neutraliser," for every kind of
poisonous principle ; this idea of neutralisation distinctly anticipates modern science. His knowledge of
local materia medica is often profound, and, after all,
some of his theories as to the etiology of tropical
diseases are conceptions now known to modern science
in the form of animal parasites (protozoa, spirochætes,
etc.), which are invisible except under the high powers
of the microscope. Then, again, the spirit-raising
bomor, when engaged in casting out devils, does his best
to restore the sick man to health ; in fact, he gives
himself entirely up in striving to " reach the mystic
source of things, the secrets of the earth and sea and
air." Those who would dismiss his spiritualism as
worthless imposture and his belief in possession by
spirits as fantastic credulity should remember that the
village *bomor* pins his faith on the animistic belief of his
forefathers where fear and curiosity predominated.
It would be unfair to damn him as " an accursed
sorcerer who poisons honest folk to gain his private
ends," and more generous to regard him as one of the
" dealers in destiny's dark council."

REFERENCES

(1) BREWER, E. C. " Dictionary of Phrase and Fable." 1923.
New ed., " Jinn," p. 612. London : Cassell.

(2) BROWNE, E. G. " Arabian Medicine." 1921. Cambridge
University Press.

(3) BURNE, C. S. " The Handbook of Folk-lore." 1913. London :
Folk-lore Society. No. LXXIII.

(4) CLIFFORD, Sir HUGH. " East Coast Etchings." 1896. Singapore : Straits *Times* Press.

(5) DENNYS, N. B. " A Descriptive Dictionary of British Malaya."
1894. London.

(6) GIMLETTE, J. D. " A Bee Bomor." *Jour. Malay. Br. Roy.
Asiat. Soc.* (Singapore). 1926. Vol. IV., Part III., p. 421.

(7) GOLLANCZ, C. " The Book of Protection." 1912. London :
Oxford University Press.

(8) MARETT, R. R. " Psychology and Folklore." 1919. London :
Methuen.

(9) MAXWELL, Sir GEORGE. " In Malay Forests." (Appendix).
1925. London : Blackwood.

(10) McNAIR, Major F. " Perak and the Malays." 1878. London :
Tinsley.

(11) RIDLEY, H. N. " List of Malay Plant Names." *Jour. Straits
Br. Roy. Asiat. Soc.* (Singapore). 1897. No. 30.

(12) SKEAT, W. W. " Malay Magic." 1900. London : Macmillan.

(13) SKEAT and BLAGDEN. " Pagan Races of the Malay Peninsula."
1906. London : Macmillan.

(14) SINGER, C. " Early English Magic and Medicine." 1920.
London : Oxford University Press.

(15) SWETTENHAM, Sir FRANK A. " Malay Sketches." 1921.
London : Lane.

(16) WILKINSON, J. R. " A Malay-English Dictionary." 1903.
Singapore : Kelly and Walsh.

(17) WINSTEDT, Dr. R. O. " An English-Malay Dictionary."
1917. Singapore : Kelly and Walsh.

(18) WINSTEDT, Dr. R. O. " Shaman, Saiva and Sufi." 1925.
London : Constable.

(19) YEATS, W. B. " Irish Fairy Tales." 1900. London : Unwin.

CHAPTER III

CHARMS AND AMULETS

THE Malay language is replete with charms and spells which bear the Brahmanistical name of *mantĕra* and the Arabic name of *doa*; numbers of them have been translated and explained by Winstedt, Skeat, Blagden, and several other authors. Winstedt, in his " English-Malay Dictionary," differentiates charms to engender love, beauty, and courage ; to protect against ghostly and material hurt ; to silence enemies ; to counteract poison, etc. ; to terrify ; to cause forgetfulness ; to hinder a girl from marrying a rival ; to obtain good business ; to secure from lust and thieves ; to shatter a rival's weapon, and charms hung on fruit trees. The charm hung on fruit trees is to make the fruit disagree with any one who steals it. Skeat gives many more in his " Malay Magic " : his are magic rites connected with the several departments of Nature, *e.g.*, charms for wind and weather ; bird charms ; beast charms ; vegetation charms ; mining charms ; reptile charms, and so on.

Kelantan Charms.—Reference will be made only to a few Kelantan charms, which are mostly of interest in regard to poisoning and disease, and to a few odd love charms. They are the special wealth of the *bomor* and have come down to him orally from generation to generation of " medicine-men," and later have been recorded in illiterate transcriptions. The *bomor* uses them in *jampi-jampi* before he finally blows his breath on the patient with the idea of blowing the disease out of the body. Offerings of food are sometimes put into

special basket-trays (*anchak*). If the offerings are
intended for forest demons they are hung from a tree,
if gnomes are to be conciliated they are buried in the
ground, or they may be fixed to seaward on a fishing
stake.

Sometimes Kelantan Malays erect, of their own
accord, stems of bamboo (*sakok* or *sangkak*) about
four feet long, to make homely sacrifice to the spirits
of disease. These bamboo " cressets " are stuck in the
ground near any one's dwelling-place ; the free end is
split in several places, so as to form a receptacle in
which a young green coco-nut is placed overnight.
During an epidemic it is considered very unlucky to be
without a *sakok* in the garden. This custom is common
in Kota Bharu ; when cholera was prevalent (1920) a
sakok was quietly and unobtrusively set up in the
garden of my quarters by somebody unknown, but
such proceedings are not specially sanctioned by the
bomor.

As a practical man the *bomor* is well aware of the
value of ceremony, of mystery, and of peculiar elocution
in his pose as a magician or wizard. Powerful incantations that are difficult to understand are essential ;
he uses many Sanskrit and Arabic words and sometimes rigmarole. A formula given me by an old *bomor*
in an up-country district of Kelantan is one mainly
intended to neutralise the power of forest demons and
other black jin dwelling " beyond the mountain's
farthest purple rim," but it may be used also as a charm
for practically any disease. It is one long threat, but
the Malay is corrupt and is untranslatable in places :—

Peace be with thee ! Forest Lord and Jungle Chief,
Whose realm is the World !
Prince whose sway is over this jungle land !
Well know I whence thou art sprung.
Harken to the tale of thy birth !
Child of the Darkness thou ! I of the Sunshine !

> Sprung art thou from unsubstantial sand,
> I of sturdier clay and older far than thou !
> Hail ! all ye Spirits of these mountains,
> Of this forest and district !
> Mark well my words, else are ye accursed of the gods of old,
> Whom eye cannot see or tongue describe.

It is of peculiar advantage to a timber contractor to get a *bomor* to secure rich profit to him by reciting this charm just before he commences felling, especially if he intends to set up a shed for coolies in thick jungle. It is recited seven times over a piece of benzoin ; after the recitation the benzoin is burnt, and its sweet scent, charged with the message of the *bomor*, is considered a fitting sacrifice for the disturbance made by felling. Another lengthy charm deals with ghosts in the form of black jin. It is intended to cure a man of small-pox and is recited by the *bomor* over a draught of water, which is afterwards given to the sick man to drink.

> Good folk ! I know your beginning,
> Ye did dwell formless in the depths of hell,
> And issuing from the depths of hell did visit the children of
>   Adam and take on visible form.
> Seven brothers were ye in all ;
> Born of black exudings, of black pores, of black skin,
> Of black flesh, blood, veins, and sinews, of black bones.
> Not mine this charm but that of the Dewa Sang Samba,
> Not mine this charm but that of the Dewa Bĕtara Narada,
> Not mine this charm but that of the very dregs of hell.
> Well versed am I in all poisons,
> And can quench fiery pains :
> Poison do I charm away, fiery pains I quench,
> Efficacious am I, yea successful by my teacher's help.

The demons of early Christianity also, like those of the Mesopotamian system, were often grouped under the mystic number seven.

Other illnesses attributed to evil spirits are mentioned by different authors, especially Skeat and Blagden. Sir Hugh Clifford describes the *pĕnanggalan*, a horrible, partially disembowelled wraith from the lying-in room who comes to torment little children. There are many others. Skeat describes an evil thing called the *polong*, who is always attended by a familiar in the shape of a grasshopper. This familiar is described as the plaything of the *polong* and is called the *pĕlĕsit*. The *pĕlĕsit* appears to be similar to the *nigget* of Essex. A writer to *The Times* of September 3rd, 1915, gave an account of a witch who died within forty miles of London in 1915. Among other unnatural things, this old woman kept *niggets* or " creepy-crawly " things that she fed with little bits of grass all chopped up. She sat and played with her *niggets*. The *pĕlĕsit* is very well known in Kelantan and Kedah. It is acquired by a special process in Black Art from the corpse of an infant, the first-born child of first-born parents. The creature becomes the owner's servant and obeys her in all things ; its chief use, however, is to inflict sickness and death upon persons who are disliked by its patron. The owner of a *pĕlĕsit* is always a woman, who plays with it and feeds it on her blood and is supposed to keep it in a bottle. She can be recognised by her failure to meet the eye, by her refusal to take a bit of pinang nut, still pinched in the scissors of the betel chewer's outfit, or by becoming momentarily deranged (*latah*) if a frog is popped under a coco-nut shell and put behind her back. The *pĕlĕsit* can be exorcised by the following formula :—

> Vampire, well do I know thy origin,
> Begotten of the after-birth,
> Engendered of the discharge of unproductive blood,
> *Kĕmang* thy name !
> Gazing skyward thy vomit be blood,
> Bending earthward thy vomit be ordure.
> In the name of Allah and in the name of His Apostle !
> With the blessings of Allah and the Prophet !

A short time ago the wife of a Chinese dispenser to the State Hospital, Kelantan, became delirious with fever and refused either to take any English medicine or to be treated by her husband. She was a middle-aged Chinese woman. In despair, her husband, Eng Siong, called in a male Siamese *bomor*, who said a *pĕlĕsit* had got in from outside and was sucking her blood. The *bomor* declared he could exorcise the *pĕlĕsit* provided the *pĕlĕsit* revealed, through the Chinese woman, the name of its real owner. The *bomor* commenced by chanting a formula, constantly asking *mu 'nak royat tidak ibu bapa-mu* (" will you reveal the name of your parent or not ? "). The patient made no reply ; he then threw yellow rice at her, but without effect. He next took an onion and some black pepper which he pounded together, and placed part in one scrap of cloth and part in another. He then tied one of these bits of cloth round the woman's left thumb and the other round the great toe on the same side, at the same time pinching the muscles of her thumb and redoubling his question : *mu 'nak royat tidak ibu-mu.* At last the *pĕlĕsit* squeaked through the dispenser's wife *lĕpas-lah! lĕpas-lah!* (" let me go, let me go "), but the *bomor* squeezed the harder until the climax came, when the woman, again speaking for the *pĕlĕsit*, squeaked *aku 'nak royat* (" I want to tell."), and mentioned the name of a certain woman in the town.

In difficult cases a dry chilli is put over a fire made with charcoal in a brass bowl ; this is held near the patient's face while the *bomor* blows the pungent fumes into the mouth and nostrils, or, in very obstinate cases, he chews the onion and the black pepper and then spits a mouthful into the face of the sick person. When a *pĕlĕsit* will confess nothing, the sick man is said to rave in anger and then to die. An alternative formula for the exorcism of the *pĕlĕsit* is given in romanised Malay in Appendix I, but the Malay is so corrupt that no English version can be given. It is of a very abusive character.

Some time ago the Ĕngku' Said Husain, of Kota Bharu, told me that his small son had been attacked by a *pĕlĕsit*. The child was delirious with fever. His father was sure about the *pĕlĕsit* from the expression on his son's face ; he also heard a noise like the sough of the wind when it flew into the child's bedroom. A *bomor* was called in at midnight and the evil thing exorcised. It had come in from next door, and was declared to be the familiar of 'Che Lumat, an elderly woman who lives across the way. 'Che Lumat earns her living by weaving silk cloth. She told me afterwards that she had been blamed on account of some unpleasantness which had occurred at the time between herself and the youngest of the Ĕngku's wives, owing to an incident not uncommon in Malay life.

When charms fail, it may be thought necessary to drive out an evil spirit by smoking over a fire, as was done only a few years ago. A full account of the tragedy, with a warning to the ignorant, was published on February 16th, 1923, in *Pĕngasoh*, a Kelantan newspaper printed in Kota Bharu. I am indebted to the Hon. Mr. H. W. Thomson for the romanised Malay version which is given in Appendix I, and for the following translation : " A woman aged about 19, named Meh Mas, daughter of Meh Lumat of Kampong Pasir, Pĕnambang in the township of Kota Bharu, was recently confined of a male child—her first. On the morning of Monday, December, 26th 1922, she began to feel the pains of labour. The midwife arrived at 11 in the morning. When the child came down for birth, the mother would not strain herself to hasten delivery, nor would she sit crossways, but had to be held by others. About 11.30 the child was born, perfectly formed, and the mother was unconscious for a while. When she came round and began to talk, the words came pouring out of her mouth incoherently,

and she took no notice of the child, and when it wanted
the breast she refused it. As she appeared to be quite
fit, and as the after-birth all came away quite clean, it
was evident to the *bomor* and midwives that she was
possessed by the spirit known as *Miriam,* which always
attacks the newly-confined. So each of them started
saying incantations, till they foamed at the mouth—
" You wouldn't have believed the noise they made (all
on account of the evil spirit)," said the old woman in
charge of the incantations. Next they took four
black peppercorns and gave them, one each, to four
strong men who pressed the peppercorns with all their
might into the bases of the nails of her thumbs and big
toes. When they pressed, she screamed ; and the
more she screamed, the harder they pressed. All grew
more and more astonished at the obstinacy of the
wicked spirit which refused to come out of the woman
in spite of such pain, and they said : ' Wait till to-
morrow, and then you shall suffer for this.'

" The whole day was spent in this way, and the
night of Tuesday began. One of those present said
that in cases of child-birth such as this it was customary
to take 45 (male) coco-nut shells and light candles in
them. So they got the coco-nut shells as he advised ;
but the woman remained as before, and would not have
the candles lit. When this was so, they said ' She must
be fumigated with smoke ; but it is no good doing it
from far off in an obstinate case like this.' Accordingly
they built an open-work dais, about 18 inches high,
and put the woman on it. Then they burnt the coco-
nut shells and got the live embers from them and put
them into a receptacle, into which they added rotten
and pungent ingredients, such as stinking sulphur,
dried pepper, black pepper and the like. They put
all this under the dais just level with the face of the
woman, and they turned her over on her stomach so

that her face looked into the fire. When the pungent and stinking fumes rose up, the woman struggled; but they held her tight and pressed her down so that she could not struggle. When this happened her language became more and more wild. Then the person who was driving out the evil spirit said, ' See how obstinate it is ; don't let go until it comes out.' While this was going on, a man came past who was a *guru* (teacher) in the neighbourhood, and told them to stop. But they replied ' This is not a teacher's business ' ; and when a lot of other folk told them to stop, they said ' You don't understand.'

" When daylight came, they saw that the woman's face was all scorched and her breasts slightly so. When they saw this, for the first time they began to be rather frightened, especially her mother and her husband, although they had previously approved of the treatment. What more is there to be said? The woman grew more and more exhausted, and at noon on Wednesday she died. The child survived seven days and then followed his mother. Let this be a warning to all not to follow any advice which reason cannot accept."

The newspaper report refers to the evil spirit as *hantu polong*, a malignant thing well known to all Malays (see pp. 47, 103). The *polong* is thought to be the instigator of many different diseases.

Some Malays, misguided in religion like these Kelantan villagers, apply the treatment of smoking over a fire to their sick children. Ridley records that a quantity of chewed sugar-cane, dead leaves, and other roadside rubbish is boiled and the child is bathed in the decoction, and is then smoked over a fire made with a weaver-bird's nest (*sarang burong tĕmpua*), the skin of a bottle gourd (*labu*) and a piece of wood which has been struck by lightning (*Agric. Bull., Straits & F.M.S.*, 1906, Vol. V., No. 6, p. 195).

A soothing charm chanted by the *bomor* in cases of snake-bite, the stings of centipedes and scorpions is this :—

> Peace be with you !
> OM ! Potent this charm !
> Fain would I charm this into the flesh,
> The veins, the sinews,
> Charm this into the bones !
> Charm given of Allah, given too of Muhammad,
> The Apostle of God.

The medicine given with this charm is " liquid opium with the ashes of a cat's whiskers ! "

The aid of the Hindu man-god Krishna is said to be invoked as an alternative in Kelantan, only to be used for snake bite and the stings of scorpions and centipedes. Krishna is said to be referred to as " Lambu " :—

> Ya Lambu tu ! Lambu yu !
> Lambu nuk ! Lambu tu ! Ya Lambu !

This rigmarole is to be recited for three mornings over any seven leaves from any kind of tree, three times over each leaf, after which each of the seven leaves is drawn gently downwards over the painful spot.

During the wet weather of November a Kelantan Malay, Nik Ismail (vaccinator and travelling apothecary on the State hospital staff), was bitten between the toes by a non-poisonous snake at Kampong Banggor. He called in a village *bomor*, who was able to relieve the acute pain. The *bomor* grasped Nik Ismail's leg firmly above the knee and chanted a song in some language unknown to Nik Ismail, and then blew with his breath down the limb. He then applied an anodyne made in the form of a poultice from two jungle roots. This was a friendly service, otherwise a fee of a Straits dollar (2*s*. 4*d*.) would have been charged. The self-reliance of the *bomor* and his sublime belief in his calling does much towards the cure of a credulous patient by means of charms. An ancient formula intended to neutralise any kind of poison was given me by To' Bomor Ënche' Abu Bakar, a very old *bomor* now living in the jungle, but formerly for many years a vaccinator on the hospital staff. It is the 190 charm, so called from the supposed 190 bones of the human frame, the 190 veins, the 190 kinds of human blood, the 190 diseases, the 190 forms of insanity, and so on :—

> The charm! the mighty charm, that of the hundred and ninety!
> The charm is not mine, but that of the fair-faced Dato' Mĕngkadom,
> Springs its virtue from the white roc,
> And the white elephant!
> White blood, white bones, and a white (sincere) heart.
> With it have I charmed away salt from the sea,
> Yea! and thee too will I charm!
> I pray that my charm may charm away venom and quench the burning.

A spell for neutralising the effects of poison was given in confidence, by the late To' Bomor Ënche' Abdullah, formerly one of the chief " medicine-men " to the royal household. Fresh coco-nut water is used as an antidote along with it, but the coco-nut water has to be obtained from *nyiur puyoh*, a dwarf coco-nut palm allied to the golden *nyiur gading*, a tree " that may be planted only in princes' gardens " :—

> *OM !* this is a powerful charm !
> The charm of the hundred and ninety.
> Not my own spell, but that of all that is deadly !
> Born of the green and deadly berry !
> Fain would I charm thee out of this body !
> Obey not and I will curse thee with the cursings of Jesus, father of the charm.
> In the name of Allah !

The coco-nut water is placed in a bowl ; juice from the red sugar-cane is added, and then the *bomor* blows three times into the bowl, muttering his spell at the same time, and finally administers his remedy. If the

jaws are clenched, the To' Bomor told me that the
mouth must, if necessary, be forced open with a stick.
Much the same kind of formula is sometimes used in
some parts of England, when a dock leaf is applied to
relieve the sting of a nettle :—

> Out fire, in frost,
> I wish it in the name of the Holy Ghost.

Similar spells are still woven within sound of the
rumble of London's motor omnibuses. A writer to
The Times (1919) refers to the magic of a London
herbalist who blows with his breath three times after
chanting a rhyme. This " breathed spell " is very
similar to some of the *jampi-jampi* of the Malay
" medicine-man."   As the winds have blown the
disease to the sufferer, so does the *bomor* by the might
of his song blow it from him :—

> Here come I to cure a burnt sore.
> If the dead knew what the living endure,
> The burnt sore would burn no more.

The scene is the little shop of a herbalist in the East
End. A mother brings her child, whose leg has been
scalded by boiling water spouting from a kettle. The
herbalist, an old man with a white beard, blows his
breath three times on the blisters of the scald. The
action of blowing as a common accompaniment of
Nordic magic is recorded by Dr. Charles Singer, whose
words I have paraphrased above to suit the Malay
" medicine-man."   It is also recorded that " medicine-
men " among the tribes of the north-west Amazons
work their cures by means of " breathed charms " ; in
this case sometimes the " medicine-man " will " breathe
on his own hand and then massage the affected part."

One of the special prerogatives of the old Malay Rajas
is summed up in the phrase *tikam ta' bĕrtanya* (" to slay
without having to ask leave "), and the idea of this

ancient right is still preserved in the exultation of a
blood-curdling spell, showing how real the belief is in
regard to precautions that must be taken against evil
spirits. The spell is a Kelantan one, supposed to cure
a man who has become dazed by the will-o'-the-wisp
or jack-a-lantern flashing past him in the gloom :—

> Peace be with thee, O Jin son of Jan !
> O Satan son of the Sultan Pharaoh,
> Know that I am lord,
> I slay blindly without having to seek leave,
> Slay without being guilty of crime,
> I, in sooth, am Lord of all living things !

The evil spirit here referred to is *jin lintasan,* a restless,
ever-wandering spirit that haunts groves at nightfall.
It is supposed to resemble the human form, but to
dart about like a will-o'-the-wisp. Winstedt gives the
pedigree of the evil spirit " Jin the son of Jan of the
line of the Pharaohs " as being founded on the Arab
notion that the last king of the pre-Adamite jinn was
Jan the son of Jan, and that he built the Pyramids "
(Ref. 16, p. 35).

The rendering of Kelantan charms into English is
exceedingly difficult, and I am greatly indebted to one
of my brother officers who was in the Kelantan service
for his help. The original texts from which they have
been translated are given in Appendix I. Spoken
charms form an important part of the armentarium of
the *bomor ;* they seem to be vehicles for the operation
of sympathetic magic.

An empirical prescription, used by the *bomor* in the
treatment of yaws, contains the bones of a dugong, a
mammal which is often connected with Malay love
charms. The prescription is as follows : " Take the
knee-cap of a tiger (Felis tigris) ; a bone from the
dugong (*duyong,* Halicore duyong), a bone and a horn
from the rare wild mountain goat (*kambing gĕrun,*

Nemorrhædus sumatrensis) ; the horn of a stag (*rusa*, Cervus unicolor), and a red sulphide of arsenic (*bĕlerang bang*, realgar) ; some dark red wood from Java (*chĕn-dana janggi*) and the root of a jungle plant (*mempasi rimau*, unidentified). Rub the horns and bones down on a stone placed in boiling rice-water. Add a small amount of ashes from the hearth to scrapings made from the other ingredients, and then give the con-coction by the mouth." The dugong, a sea mammal, rare in Malayan waters, gave rise to the conception of the treacherous mermaid, " the fair pretty maid with a comb and a glass in her hand." It is mentioned both by Dr. Winstedt and Sir Frank Swettenham in con-nection with love charms ; the former writer gives the charm of the dugong in verse, to be recited thrice on waving a kerchief towards the setting sun. The dugong is asserted by some to be the remains of a pig off which Muhammad himself dined before he pronounced pork to be the accursed thing ; its bones are used by the *bomor* as an antidote for poisoning by cyanide of potassium. In Kelantan the dugong philtre is made from the lachrymal secretion (*minyak ayer mata duyong*) of this shallow-water sea mammal. It is prepared in the following way : Pick a young coco-nut so growing that it is facing the sun ; express the oil carefully in the usual way ; add only a very few tears from the dugong's eyes. Hide it and keep it constantly about the person in a very small bottle ; when a favourable opportunity occurs, smear it on the skin or on the apparel of the fair one as a love stimulus.

In 1913 I saw a Kelantan charm (*tangkal*) in actual use as an antidote to native poisoning. The charm was lying at the bottom of a brass bowl half full of water ; a bit of the heart of the nipah palm (Nipa fruticans, Linn., Palmæ) was floating on the top of the water, while an imperfect specimen of a " fossilised " crab and another " fossil " were lying at the bottom of the bowl. The talisman was a collection of nine curiously shaped pebbles cleverly strung together by means of silver wire in the form of a barbaric necklace. A man and a boy had been poisoned the night before by thieves with a wild yam called *gadong*. An old crone, the grandmother, was giving her son and grand-child sips of magic water out of the brass bowl. The old woman said that the charm had been in her family for many years, having been bought a long time ago from an Arab for fifty dollars. The " fossilised " crab had been borrowed from a friend for the occasion. The name of the other " fossil " was unknown ; it was purchased by her husband many years ago from an uncle of the late Sultan for seventy dollars. In colour and appearance it somewhat resembled a piece of candied angelica. She said the charm was a sovereign remedy for sterility if used in the same way, *i.e.*, by steeping the stones in cold water ; but she subse-quently admitted that this magic diluent was of no value without a powerful incantation on the part of the *bomor*. It is curious that such an immaterial specific should be credited with such potency.

Another curious charm used in Kelantan by the credulous is a metal bowl (*batil azimat*). It is moulded in brass, about the size of a small pudding basin and somewhat similar in shape, but a central knob, like a boss of a miniature buckler, projects inwards from the bottom of it ; this knob, as well as the whole bowl, is covered with symbols and texts from the Koran, cut with a file on the inside and on the outside, as well as on the rim of the bowl. The *batil azimat* is rare in Kelantan and is much prized by Kelantan Malays. It is placed in a water jar and the water is given to a patient, especially a sick child, to drink or bathe in ;

or water is put into the bowl itself and the charmed water from it is taken internally. Nik Woh, a Kelantan woman of good family living at Kampong Banggor, told me that she derives much comfort from this enchanted water whenever she happens to be feeling out of sorts. Nik Woh is the fortunate possessor of a *batil azimat* that has been in her family for generations, and was originally brought from Mecca. At Mecca these brass bowls are merely used as drinking cups for children who are being taught the Koran ; the bowl itself is made in Persia, where it can now be bought for a trifling sum of money. In the " Adventures of Hajji Baba of Ispahan," by James Morier (1824–28), the diviner uses " a brass cup of a plain surface, but written all over with quotations from the Koran, having reference to the crime of stealing, and defrauding the orphan of his lawful property."

At times the ministration of a *bomor* smacks of artful trickery. This happens when medicinal rubbing is resorted to in certain cases of illness ; the patient is rubbed with a round stone, an egg, or a ball of dough made of rice, for three consecutive mornings, suitable charms being repeated each morning. A fee of one silver dollar is charged for this " sucking charm " (*bĕralin*). Sometimes the faith-healing cure is confirmed by picking a red hair or two, or a spicule of bone, out of the dough ball ; these will be recognised as the property of some evil *hantu* or jin. An incident relative to this is recorded because it also shows how little attention to orthodoxy is paid when a Malay intends to attain the full sense of complete satisfaction. Sitti Hawa (Eve), a relative of the Mufti, the official expounder of the Muhammadan religion in Kota Bharu, came to the out-patient room in 1912 complaining that while stitching she had pierced her left hand and the sewing needle had broken off short in the centre of the palm. Nothing could be seen or felt, and she, perhaps wisely, declined surgical exploration, but she was not satisfied and decided to consult a notorious *bomor* who had just been sent to prison. This *bomor* had a great reputation for skill in extracting broken needles by magic and without pain. He was a Muhammadan Siamese, called Ali Siam, imprisoned a second time for cheating; but a relative of the Mufti had no difficulty in obtaining from the Inspector of Prisons, who happened at the time (1912) to be one of the late Sultan's uncles, permission to enter the Central Gaol for the express purpose of consulting the convict Ali Siam. The *bomor* first bandaged her hand, next drew a rough diagram of a human being on a piece of notepaper, muttered something over it, then burnt the notepaper and threw the ashes into a plateful of water. He bade her put her hand into the water, and after a short interval removed the bandage; a piece of broken needle was in the plate, and Eve was satisfied.

Bezoar Stones. — Bezoar stones are endowed by Malays with magic properties. They are called *batu guliga*, and are well differentiated; a list of those derived from the animal and vegetable kingdoms is given by Winstedt in his " English-Malay Dictionary." It comprises bezoars from the rhinoceros, snake, seaslug and dragon; from the coco-nut, jack-fruit and bamboo, as well as petrified dew (hydrate of silica). The curious *batu guliga* of the bamboo is " bamboo manna " or *tabashir*, a siliceous compound found in the stem of the plant (Sanskrit, *tabakshira* or " barkmilk "). The substance referred to by Dioscorides and Pliny as sugar is supposed to be *tabashir*. Tengku Chik Pĕnambang, the Inspector of Prisons referred to above, told me as a remarkable incident that he once found a *batu guliga* in the body of a certain spider in Kota Bharu. A genuine oriental bezoar is formed in spheres like a calculus in concentric layers round a nucleus ; it is generally hard and brittle, smooth, round or ovate, and olive-green in colour, but occasionally light like the rare concretions (*tabashir*) found in the joints of large bamboos, inside coco-nuts and in certain fruit trees. The bezoar of organic origin, as distinct from a mineral bezoar, was first discovered in the stomach of the pasang or Persian wild goat (Capra ægagrus), but it does not appear to have been found in the domesticated goat (Capra hircus). Similar stones are found in the stomach, intestines, and bladder of ruminants, such as the ox, and in the horse and gazelle. A large collection is contained in the museum of the Royal College of Surgeons of England (Ref. 1).

> Gall stones from women, men and apes,
> Enteroliths from cows and snakes ;
> Vesical stones from cats and dogs,
> And calculi from boys and hogs.
> Oat-hair concretions found in man,
> Bezoars from wild-goat, calf and ram ;
> Ægagropiles of many styles,
> From women, girls, and crocodiles.

In the East the bezoar is generally found in the intestines and gall-bladder of small animals, such as the long-tailed monkey (Semnopithecus), especially in the chestnut-red langur of Borneo (S. rubicundus). A soft brown variety is found in porcupines. The core is often a piece of dart which has broken off short when a young animal, such as a wild pig, though wounded, has reached maturity, but the calculus may be formed by accretion round any other foreign body, *e.g.*, a chip of wood or a bit of straw which has become embedded in hairs that the animal has licked from its skin. These stones are highly esteemed by Chinese as an antidote to poison and as a medicine. The Pharmacopœia of the Royal College of Physicians of England, 1746, contained a prescription which is worthy of the *bomor;* it was " probably of great virtue, because it reads like an exorcism " (Ref. 1).

> Pulvis e chelis cancrorum compositus,
> Jus viperinum, vin. viperinum,
> Chalybis rubigo preparata,
> Pil. saponacea, pulv. bezoardicus.

Malays endow the *batu guliga* with the power of motion and believe that it feeds upon rice much in the same way as their breeding pearl. The Malay test for a good *batu guliga* is to place a little lime or chalk in the hand and rub the stone against it, when, if it be a genuine stone, the lime becomes yellow. It has long been regarded as efficacious in preventing infection and the effect of poison. In " Malay Magic " Skeat says the ceremony of applying the *guliga* charm generally takes the form of grating the stone (*asahkan buntat*), mixing the resulting powder with water, and drinking this water after the following charm has been recited by the *bomor* :—

> The upas loses its venom,
> And poison loses its venom,
> And the sea-snake loses its venom,
> And the poison-tree of Borneo loses its venom,
> Everything that is venomous loses its venom,
> By virtue of my use of the Prayer of the Magic Bezoar Stone.

Bezoar stones are worn as amulets against disease and evil spirits, and are considered to possess wonderful medicinal virtues, but their principal value is founded on reputation. They are supposed to be powerful aphrodisiacs. The bezoar is wrapped in a piece of cloth and worn on the navel, or water, in which the stones have been steeped, is swallowed in all good faith, when they are desired to act in this way (Ref. 7). The bezoar stone is also called *buntat* in Malay, and when deemed to possess talismanic properties it is known as *buntat gĕmala*. A stone of this sort, the *gĕmala naga*, is said to have luminous properties, and to be used by dragons to light their way in the dark at night. Another, the *gĕmala ular*, gives luminosity to the head of the black cobra. A piece of holy wood from Mecca, *kayu raja naga*, is sometimes carried about as a precaution against snake bite ; it is light brown, friable and hygroscopic, and is applied to the punctures.

Snake-stones.—A mineral bezoar is used also as a " snake-stone " ; it is an amalgam of gold, silver and tin, called *buntat raksa* (Ref. 9). The *bomor* also uses a black stone (*batu ular*) as a " snake-stone " ; it is supposed to have been vomited by the snake and to possess luminosity in the dark. The Malay practice of using " snake-stones " is similar to the conjuring tricks of Indian snake-charmers. Castellani and Chalmers describe " snake-stones " as highly polished, very light black bodies said to consist of calcined animal bones soaked several times with blood and calcined after each soaking. The stones are very hygroscopic, and when applied to a wound cling to it and suck up fluids, and perhaps some poison. The word *nurbisa* (an antidote to poison) is applied by Malays to this kind of charm. The use of the *batu guliga* by Malays as an amulet is similar to that of an ancient amulet worn in Cyprus to protect the wearer from the bite of venomous animals. In Malta special amulets consisting of certain small stones, which are supposed to be shaped and coloured like the eyes, liver, heart or tongue of a viper, are still in use as an antidote to poison. These Maltese amulets are found in the clay of the traditional caves of St. Paul's Bay, and are steeped in wine which is subsequently given to the sick man to drink (Ref. 10).

The black stone called *batu ular* is sometimes worn by Malay thieves as a protective charm. A belt found by the Kelantan Malay police in 1917 on the dead body of a robber contained, among other stones, a so-called *batu ular*, wrapped up, with a wild boar's tusk, in a piece of white cloth which was covered from top to bottom with Siamese drawings, letters and numerals. The belt was described by the police as an amulet commonly worn by thieves ; at the inquest Kelantan peasants described the stones as *buntat*, or stones found in the bodies of animals supposed to contain usually, but not always, talismanic properties. The chief interest in this police exhibit centred on a charm that was wrapped up also in the belt and was declared by the police to have come from the neck of a wild boar. Superstitions about the wild pig recorded by Skeat in " Malay Magic " are fully believed in by Kelantan folk ; they do not seem to recognise the fable of the " wild boar's chain " with its links of magic iron, but pin their faith on a kind of hair necklace (*chĕmara babi*), which they say the boar is very particular about keeping clean. A lucky man may find it near a jungle pig's wallow when the beast takes it off preparatory to rolling in the mire. In Kelantan the *chĕmara babi* charm consists of a collection of stiff, dark fibres, each about a foot in length, apparently obtained from a palm tree, such as the palmyra, or perhaps the coco-nut. It is thought by many to be a very valuable protective charm against the charge of a wild boar. Others say it is very useful to burglars because it keeps people in a sound sleep (*sĕkot*). The *chĕmara babi* charm is said to protect the skin of the wearer from hurt or harm from any kind of weapon. Some say it comes off the hairy leg of the evil spirit known as *hantu raya*. The high priest of the Siamese community in Kelantan told me that the numerals and letters on the white cloth wrapper of the belt had been taken haphazard from the sacred books of Siam, and that the diagrams represented Buddha as a central figure, surrounded by crude drawings of a child in different stages of uterine development and at term. He drew particular attention to the wild boar's tusk, which he stated to be solid throughout, and said that another like it could not be found among a thousand wild pigs (Ref. 6).

A turquoise finger ring is said to be of value in warding off poisonous snakes in Kelantan, much in the same way as a necklace of blue beads is said to ward off bronchitis in England. The *chinchin wafak*, a gold ring engraved with astrological and other symbols, is also worn as a talisman, but the most important ring in regard to Malay poisons is the finger ring fashioned out of the beak of the solid-billed hornbill, which is much treasured for use in the emergencies of native poisoning. In June, 1913, a Malay noble, a descendant of the Prophet, was conducting an experiment (strongly suggestive of " salting " a mine) with cyanide of potassium, used in counterfeiting coin, with the idea of turning an oxide of iron into an oxide of tin. During the course of his experiments a fowl pecked at the cyanide, spun round, and apparently died. It was, however, saved by the mother-wit of a young princess, the wife of the noble, who used a ring of the kind mentioned above. She rubbed her ring down in water and gave a mouthful to the fowl, making it vomit. This lady's ring is much worn by friction from use on other similar occasions. The supposed virtue of this antidote rests on the unknown properties of a solid yellow wax-like stuff from which these rings are made ; this stuff forms the solid casque on the beak of this particular bird (Rhinoplax vigil, Forst., Bucerotidæ). It is sometimes carved into love charms. Brooches and buttons are made from it in the form of amulets ; they are supposed to turn to a livid colour when the wearer is threatened by the approach of poison. Spoons for the detection of poison in food are also made, but cups such as the mediæval " poison cups " do not seem to exist. This superstition is well known in Kelantan. The country people think that such a ring, that turns green, is kept by the Tĕngku Bĕsar Tuan Soh, an uncle of the late Sultan of Kelantan, but the Tĕngku says that he has no ring of this kind in his possession.

This rare species of hornbill is almost peculiar to Malaya, and is nicknamed by Malays " the bird that felled the house of its father-in-law," in accordance with a very old, oft-told legend. The very peculiar note of the bird gives the point to the story : " It commences with a series of whoops, uttered at intervals of about half a minute for five or ten minutes ; then the interval between each whoop grows shorter and shorter, till the *whoop, whoop, whoop* is repeated very quickly ten or a dozen times, the bird ending up by going into a harsh, quacking laugh." The birds are confined exclusively to deep jungle. The Kelantan version of the legend as told by a *bomor* is as follows : " Once upon a time there was a poor man who earned an honest living by growing vegetables for sale ; he lived alone in a jungle hut with his wife and daughter. In due time, a youth came to seek the daughter's hand in marriage, and at length the father gave consent ; but soon after, the happy couple began to quarrel with their parents. The son-in-law was idle and too lazy to do anything but sleep. They all began to quarrel so much, that at last both the son-in-law and his wife took axes and made ready to cut down the wooden supports of their father's house. The poor peasant said, ' If you cut down the posts, I will curse you, so that both of you will turn into birds.' But the young people paid no heed to his words and proceeded to chop the posts until down crashed the hut ; then and there they laughed in their folly. Then and there each of them was turned into a hornbill, that called *torok* or *burong tĕbang rumah bapok mĕntua* (' the bird that felled the house of the father-in-law ').

Henceforth they were condemned to imitate for ever the peculiar cry of this jungle bird : *Kong-kong, kong-kong, kong-kong ; bĕrok, bĕrok, bĕrok ; Ha! Ha! Ha!*— which thus perpetuates the legend ; for *kong-kong, kong-kong* suggests the chop, chop, chop, chop of the axes, *bĕrok, bĕrok, bĕrok* pronounced quickly, somewhat as ' bro ') gives the crash of the falling timbers, and then follows their wicked laughter, Ha! Ha! Ha! "

Just as in English tradition certain plants and trees, such as the bay tree, mistletoe, wood betony and true-love, are protective against the malice of demons and witchcraft, so also Malays think that certain old trees, tombs of saints, graves, rocks, and even some animals possess wonder-working charms. This must be a survival of a very old belief. With regard to the bay tree (Laurus nobilis), Dr. Parkins (1814) says : " And I am mistaken if it were not Mizaldus [1] who saith that neither witch nor devil, thunder nor lightning will hurt a man where a bay tree is." Again, we have the oak as the abode of Thor, the Thunder-God, and the wild ash as Yggdrasil (Igg'-dra-sil'), or the " Tree of Life," of Scandinavian mythology ; many minor ailments can be cured by ash twigs, notably snake bite. In England as well as Scotland the rowan tree is especially protective against demons, witches, and the envious and evil eye :—

> Black luggie, hammer-head
> Rowan-tree, and red thread,
> Put the warlocks to their speed.

Malays use a bracelet made of black silk threads (*gĕlang bajang*) to protect their babies from a male vampire in the form of a civet-cat (*bajang*), which is supposed to be generated from the blood shed in child-

---

[1] *Mizaldus.* Mizauld Antonio, an early writer on meteorology and weather forecasting.

birth. A ligature made of a woman's hair is supposed, in Kelantan, to be a magic antidote to the wound made by a cat-fish. Skeat describes the ceremony of marking the forehead of the new-born child with certain ashes in a certain way to protect it against evil spirits and convulsions (Ref. 9).

There are curious ideas about foot-prints ; in some places a tiger with one foot-print smaller than the others is a *rimau kĕramat,* or " ghost-tiger." The magic five-pointed star (pentacle) is the foot-print of King Solomon. This mystic figure is worn as a defence against demons ; it resembles the five-pointed star-fish. The foot-print of a girl is often referred to in Malay love charms ; for example, one quoted by Dr. Winstedt is : " Take sand from her foot-print or her foot-bridge or from the front of her house-door. Take a black jacket, oval at the neck ; put the sand in the jacket ; tear it right and left and make it up like a doll ; fold it in two and tie it with threads of seven colours. Turn the doll round every morning and evening, at mid-day, at midnight." The most common Malay amulet is the *azimat,* or written talisman, worn for good luck. It generally takes the form of written texts from the Koran, with or without Arabic figures. The magic writing is preserved in a cover, made either of gold, silver, zinc or other metal, or simply of cloth, according to the means or the fancy of the wearer. The *azimat* is a personal charm, and is obtained on request, for all legitimate purposes, from the local resident saint (*To' Wali*), by whom it is blest. One of the most common is the *azimat sawan,* folded into the form of a triangle and incased in a triangular metal or cloth cover with a base of $1\frac{1}{2}$ inches. These are worn round the necks of children to afford protection from convulsions. A similar protective charm takes the form of a piece of holy thread, perhaps imported from Mecca, either black or of the royal yellow colour, tied round the child's right wrist. A good deal seems to depend upon the way in which the Malay amulet is worn. Some charms to keep the devil away and the *azimat sawan* mentioned above are worn round the neck covered up under the clothing ; others, such as charms to invoke pity (*azimat orang tengok kasehan*), charms to terrify (*azimat pĕnggĕrun*), and charms to make a man invulnerable (*azimat pĕnimbol* or *kĕbal*) are generally worn round the waist. Sir Hugh Clifford, however, when describing the death of a " principal Moor of Malacca " who was wounded during an engagement at sea with Dalboquerque in 1511, refers to a *kĕbal* charm worn as an armlet—" they found on his left arm a bracelet of bone set in gold, and when they took this off his blood flowed away and he expired " (Ref. 4).

The wife of the Malay storekeeper at the State hospital, Kota Bharu, a Kelantan woman, wears a charm called *azimat mĕnjauhkan Shaitan*, which is intended to keep the devil away. It is made of about 18 inches of neatly twisted cord, in the pleats of which five small scrolls of texts from the Koran are made secure. Each is incased in a 2-inch roll of thin zinc. When 'Che Bah goes to market from the hospital she is accustomed to smoke her talisman over a piece of burning benzoin and then tie it round her waist, underneath her skirt, knotting it behind. Charms to deter devils from getting into a house take the form of texts from the Koran with Arabic figures, either written or carved on the lintel of the main door, or above the doors leading to the bed-chambers in houses of the well-to-do. Malays use nothing like our Devonshire charms for fits, such as the gruesome baked frog hung round the neck in a little silk bag, the stone charm for toothache, or the tooth charm for dentition.

Some of the Malay written talismans are by no means

texts from the Koran ; one, for example, which comes
from Malayo-Javanese literature, and which is expected
to drive away a bullet, is this :—

> Peace be with thee !
> *Nabi Jankia* is thy father's name,
> *Nabi Rabbana* is thy mother's name,
> *Sang Mabok* is the name of thy gunpowder,
> Great Dragon [1] is the name of thy bullet,
> *Jala Patah* is the name of thy voice.
> Lo ! I am *Radin Aria Misan Sĕkar*, thy son of this terraqueous
> globe.

This particular talisman can be obtained from a
bomor ; it is worn round the waist and firmly believed
in by some Kelantan people. The magic rests in the
charm, not in the *bomor*. The story connected with it
shows that the *bomor* knows exactly the origin of the
influences at work and everything bearing upon them.
This is one of his main ideas when practising magic and
the Black Art. " Once on a time a certain king of Java
was preparing for the circumcision of his son, and
ordered his ministers to procure a cannon to be fired
at the ceremony. A little prince, called *Radin Aria
Misan Sĕkar*, was playing with the king's son at the
time, and overheard the royal command. He went
straight to the king and said he would find the cannon.
The king said : ' Find the cannon in seven days and
you shall be a Minister to the Crown Prince ; if you
fail I shall kill you.' The little prince *Sĕkar* agreed to
this and went to his home. When his father and mother
knew about it, they were very sorry to think that their
son would soon be killed. They set out for a certain
cave, telling him to come in seven days' time. In the
cave they fasted and prayed in silence that they might
be turned into cannons so that their son might live.
On the seventh day they became cannons. When the
little prince found them he went at once to tell the king

---

[1] *Naga Umbang.* The great sea-serpent, the monstrous dragon of the sea.

that two cannons were ready. The king ordered a number of men to go and bring the cannons from the cave, but they came back to say that they could not lift them. Whereupon the king ordered the little boy to bring them and threatened to kill him if he should fail. The little prince easily dragged the two cannons from the cave by himself and placed them in front of the king. The king then told *Radin Sĕkar* to make one of the cannons go off by itself, and so the little boy went to the one that was formerly his father and asked according to the king's command : the cannon fired and frightened half the countryside ; all the ministers fell into convulsions, and half the earth itself trembled. When the disturbance had subsided the king gave the same order for the other cannon and the same thing happened again."

A more modern printed charm circulated in the early part of the last century is given by William Marsden in his account of the inland Malays of Korinchi : " They commonly carry charms about their persons to preserve them from accidents ; one of which was shown to us, printed (at Batavia or Semarang, in Java) in Dutch, Portuguese and French. It purported that the writer was acquainted with the occult sciences, and that whoever possessed one of the papers impressed with his mark (which was the figure of a hand with the thumb and fingers extended) was invulnerable and free from all kinds of harm. It desired the people to be very cautious of taking any such, printed in London (where certainly none were ever printed), as the English would endeavour to counterfeit them and to impose on the purchasers, being all cheats." A collector would be poor withal without any love charms made by the pagans or other peoples of Malaya. The rarest and most potent of the pagan charms is the *chĕnduai* love charm. It is a rootlet with a fragrance which is said to

be stronger than that of the durian, and is usually
carried in a pouch attached to the girdle.

But the Kelantan *bomor* who is a specialist in love
charms can supply many strange things : Arabic
figures on a piece of paper to be worn inside the round
velvet Malay cap (but not, of course, inside the little
white cap, shaped like a jelly mould, worn by holy
men) ; Arabic figures written on an egg, to be buried
by the lover beneath the bed-chamber of his heart's
desire, or underneath the steps of her house ; Arabic
figures written on a thin sheet of lead to drop into a
well to cause her to think of him when she quenches her
thirst with the enchanted water ; Arabic figures written
on paper to hang on a high tree, when she will think of
her lover as the love charm is blown about by the wind ;
or a girl's name with Arabic figures written on a
" lemon." The last charm may perhaps be intended
to act by telepathy ; the *bomor* must, however, be
aware of the phenomena commonly attributed to " the
long arm of coincidence," though the essential condition of his knowledge of the girl's name might
suggest the possibility of collusion. Any lemon with
a bit of the stalk attached will do ; the *bomor* jots
down the girl's name and the magic Arabic figures on
it either with a penknife or a stout needle. The lover
suspends the lemon by means of thread from the top
of his mosquito net in such a way that it hangs exactly
over the region of his heart ; he then sets it spinning,
thinking of his sweetheart the while, until sleep over-
takes him. In order to be really effectual the lemon
should spin for three nights in succession. The old
bomor (To' Bomor Enche' Harun) who gave me this
charm said it was a very old one, and remarked with
a charming naïveté that it might be ineffectual in these
modern days.

REFERENCES

(1) BLAND-SUTTON, Sir JOHN. "Attic Salt for Gall Stones." *Brit. Med. Jour.* (London). 1924. November 1st, p. 795.

(2) CASTELLANI and CHALMERS. "A Manual of Tropical Medicine." 1919. 3rd ed., p. 277. London : Baillière, Tindall and Cox.

(3) CLIFFORD, Sir HUGH. "In Court and Kampong." 1927. 2nd ed. London : Richards.

(4) CLIFFORD, Sir HUGH. "Further India, being the Story of Exploration from the Earliest Times in Burma, Malaya, Siam and Indo-China," p. 58. 1904. London : Laurence and Bullen.

(5) GIMLETTE, J. D. "Some Superstitious Beliefs in Malay Medicine." *Jour. Straits Br. Roy. Asiat. Soc.* (Singapore). 1913. No. 65.

(6) GIMLETTE, J. D. "A Curious Kelantan Charm." *Jour. Straits Br. Roy. Asiat. Soc.* (Singapore). 1920. No. 82.

(7) KEHDING, F. "Extracts from Notes on the Sultanate of Siak." *Jour. Straits Br. Roy. Asiat. Soc.* (Singapore). 1886. No. 17.

(8) MARSDEN, W. "The History of Sumatra." 1811. 3rd ed., p. 323. London.

(9) SKEAT, W. W. "Malay Magic." 1900. London : Macmillan.

(10) SKEAT, W. W. "The Past at our Doors," p. 48. 1911. London : Macmillan.

(11) SINGER, C. "Early English Magic and Medicine." 1920. London : Oxford University Press.

(12) SWETTENHAM, Sir FRANK A. "Unaddressed Letters," p. 217. 1898 (ninth impression, 1928). London : Lane.

(13) TYAN and MAITLAND. "The Book of Flowers," p. 260. 1909. London : Murray.

(14) WINSTEDT, Dr. R. O. "Malayan Memories : A Raja of Dreams," p. 5. 1916. Singapore : Kelly and Walsh.

(15) WINSTEDT, Dr. R. O. "An English-Malay Dictionary." 1917. Singapore : Kelly and Walsh.

(16) WINSTEDT, Dr. R. O. "Shaman, Saiva and Sufi." 1925. London : Constable.

CHAPTER IV

BLACK ART IN MALAY MEDICINE

THE language used by exponents of Kelantan sorcery is a medley made up of many elements; besides illiterate Malay it includes corrupt Arabic, broken Siamese, mutilated Javanese, debased Sanskrit, words from the spirit language, and words from a so-called "pre-natal" language. The belief in devils, familiars and ghosts, with its attendant fears, is so common among Malays that it is not very surprising to find certain people still practising as specialists in the Black Art using his or her knowledge to advantage, and, in the case of the *bomor bĕlian*, perhaps trading on the family reputation of a bygone age.

The Malay spirit-raising *bomor* is a type of the wizard-priest similar to the Shaman of Siberia. Many Malays of this kind, both men and women, still practise in Kelantan: among them are the *bomor bĕlian*, the *bomor mambang* and the *bomor gĕbioh*, the *bomor mok pek*, the *bomor putĕri* (Kelantan, *pĕtĕri*), the *bomor mindok*, and the *bomor bĕrbagih*. In Kelantan the expression *bĕrmain pĕtĕri* is used of any kind of incantation or magic séance. Occasionally the Kelantan *bomor pĕtĕri* travels to Johore and other places. In Perak the *bomor* practises the sorcery of *bĕrhantu*, although rarely nowadays, while the *bomor bĕrjin* and the *bomor orang bunian*, or the wizard of the good fairies in the forest, earn their living in Pahang.

The *bomor bĕlian* is perhaps the chief of all Malay "medicine-men," and in the villages is generally a Siamese woman, who exorcises evil spirits by means of dancing and incantation. It is said that when she is operating in any district all other " medicine-men " are disqualified for the time being. The evil spirit that is raised by the *bomor bĕlian* is generally the tiger spirit (*hantu rimau*) ; but she also deals with the wild man's lullaby (*anak Pangan dadong*), the young cut-throat (*bujang sĕmbĕleh*), the swaying child of the plain (*anak lenggang padang*), the ghost of the argus pheasant (*hantu kuang*), the ghost of the stone cave (*hantu anak gua batu*), the ghost of the sea (*hantu sĕmar laut*), the ghost of the heir apparent (*hantu Raja Muda*), and the old black jin, who is the most powerful (*Dato' jin hitam*). She calls up the ghost of the pig-tailed monkey to help her in her sorcery, and utters her incantations to the accompaniment of the tambourine (*rĕbana*). The male *bomor bĕlian* is a personage found among the pagan races of the Malay Peninsula : he deals exclusively with the tiger spirit and is accredited with the power of becoming a " were-tiger " ; his title is the only one in which heredity asserts itself. The mysterious doings of the tiger-spirit man have been described by Skeat in " Malay Magic " (Ref. 3).

The *bomor mambang,* as well as the *bomor gĕbioh,* concerns himself mainly with the fairies known as " Celestial Beings," such as the water-nymphs and the elves. These two wizards work with the tambourine and small drum ; their witchcraft is similar to that of the *bomor mok pek,* except that in his sorcery, which is known as *pĕrmainan mok pek,* or *main mok pek* for short, the *bomor mok pek* uses no musical instrument.

Main Mok Pek.—The help of the *bomor mok pek* is sought to cure sick people, to discover lost or stolen property, and to find out if anything pertaining to witchcraft has been buried underneath a house. There is only one performer, the *bomor mok pek* himself, who operates with a small bundle of canes, using them as divining-rods. The bundle I have handled was made up of seven pieces of rattan, each about two feet long, evidently selected and polished with care, and tied together at one end. The *bomor mok pek* first smears coco-nut oil on his hands and on his canes ; then he holds them over burning incense and utters an incantation over them. After a while his hand begins to shake violently and the canes to rattle ; and if he has been engaged in order to find lost property or hidden objects pertaining to witchcraft, the rods are supposed to lead him to the place where the articles in question can be found. When he reaches his goal his hand points to the place and the rods cease to rattle. During the performance of *main mok pek* the *bomor* behaves as if he were no longer master of himself, and appears for the time being to be possessed of supernatural powers. He is generally looked after by his friends and restrained, for instance, from getting down a well ; but if he makes for the river he is left to his own devices. If he is engaged in the cure of a sick man he approaches his patient with the oscillating rods and makes a careful survey of the man's body ; when they cease to rattle he strikes gently with them on some part of the patient's body as a sign that he has located the place in which the evil spirit of the disease is hiding. In Kelantan villages a bundle of sprouting stems from young areca palms is sometimes substituted for the rattan canes. The Kelantan practice is somewhat different from that employed in Perak and described by Swettenham in " Malay Sketches " : " Yet another plan is to place in the hands of a *pawang*, magician, or medium, a divining-rod formed of three lengths of rattan, tied together at one end, and when he gets close to the person ' wanted,' or to the place where anything stolen is concealed, the rods vibrate in a remarkable manner " (Ref. 6). It has been suggested that the wizard of the divining-rods may

be self-deceived by muscular fatigue causing a change
of position in his hand.

Main Gĕbioh.—The performance of *main gĕbioh* is
almost similar to that of *main mok pek*, except for the
presence of a drummer and the substitution of a bunch
of green twigs for the divining-rods made of rattans.
The leaves of these twigs (*daun sĕmĕru* or *kĕmantu*) have
a pungent smell, especially on bruising. Mr. I. H.
Burkill kindly identified *sĕmĕru* botanically from a
specimen sent to him from Kelantan as Clausena
excavata, Brum., Rutaceæ. *Main gĕbioh*, like *main
mok pek*, is generally a village performance.

Malays sometimes trade on the fears and superstitions
of others by means of hidden objects of evil portent.
For example, in 1910 a handful of earth was sent by the
Kelantan police for investigation ; it contained some
small bones, probably those of a goose, a bit of wax
candle, a sprinkling of broken shells, and a rusty nail :
these had been put into an old metal bowl and buried
under the bedchamber of the late Sultan to act as
witchcraft against the Sultanah. A *bomor* from the
interior was implicated, and some anxiety was displayed
as to whether he had employed the bones of an animal
or those of a dead child. A lady of the palace, impelled
by jealousy, is reported to have persuaded the *bomor* to
cause annoyance in this way. A similar procedure
(*talamatai*) is carried out in Melanesia, in which a parcel
consisting of a dead man's bones, or part of an arrow
which had killed a man, is wrapped in leaves and placed
in the path of the man it is desired to injure. A piece
of hide from a buffalo that has been killed by lightning
stroke, with certain Arabic figures traced upon it, can
be bought from a certain *bomor* in Kelantan and buried
beneath the ladder of a sick man's house with the same
object in view.

The *bomor pĕtĕri* and the *bomor mindok* work together

to the sound of the Malay viol (*rĕbab*) and the tabour (*rĕdap*). A great noise is made during their performance by the frequent beating of this devil drum. The *bomor pĕtĕri* deals with the *hantu raya*, a very powerful evil spirit, with the black jin and the yellow jin among many others, while the *bomor mindok* is more especially interested in the spirits of the hills, those of the clouds and winds, and in the ghost of the faded lotus (*hantu tĕlepok layu*). Some of these particulars come from Pahang : they are given to show the extent of the art practised by the *bomor ;* many more might be quoted, *e.g.*, the special *hantu* belonging to Malay royalty. Doubtless the same spirits occur under different names in different places.

Main Pĕtĕri.—A general idea of the Black Art as it is commonly practised in Kelantan may be obtained from an account of a village performance called *pĕrmainan pĕtĕri*, or *main pĕtĕri* for short. This is performed for various reasons, *e.g.*, primarily to cure the sick, but also to punish an enemy, to discover stolen property, to cause an abatement of epidemic disease, to obtain proof of the infidelity of a wife, or to win the love of a woman. *Main pĕtĕri* is a much more serious matter than *jampi-jampi*, or the mere employment of verbal charms. The *bomor pĕtĕri* proceeds by way of friendly pact with the devil and the leaders of his legions, with many apologies to the Almighty for his action, to set one class of spirits against another, either for the purpose of exorcism or of revelation. His faith in the unseen teaches him that he deals with some non-human agency which, from preconceived knowledge, he has under his control. His faith seems to cure by imparting a similar faith to the sick man. Supplication and propitiation play an important part in *main pĕtĕri*, and the formulas used are of as great importance as were those of Babylonian-Assyrian medicine, which was also based on the theory that disease is due to the entry of a demon into the sick man's body.

Main pĕtĕri usually takes place at night in a room specially decorated for the occasion with flowers, especially the sweet-smelling Indian jessamine (*bunga mĕlor*), which is said to possess a special attraction for spirits. A canopy of yellow or other cloth is put up from which garlands and wreaths of various coloured flowers are suspended. The performance lasts from dusk to dawn in a village, but ends in a town at 11 p.m., in accordance with the terms of a Government " pass " issued by the police. An extension of time is allowed by the chief police officer for the last night's perform-ance. A plate containing a little cooked rice stained yellow with turmeric, an egg, three small skeins of white thread, a little ground rice stained yellow with turmeric, betel ready for the chewing, six *kĕndĕri* of money (about 19 cents), and a candle made of bees-wax are suspended in a swing support made of rattan, either from the canopy or from the wall of the room. These offerings are the *pĕngĕras guru*, or honorarium to the chief performer, *i.e.*, the *To' bomor pĕtĕri*. Another tray or dish filled with the same things, but augmented by a little rice toasted in the husk and a pancake, together with a cup of fresh water, is placed on a white mat under the canopy. This is the *kĕndĕri* or sacrificial offering to the spirits that are about to be called up.

The chief actor is, of course, the *bomor pĕtĕri ;* but he is powerless without the support of his colleague, the *To' Mindok* or *Juru Rĕbab* (the fiddler). The *To' Mindok* plays a three-stringed viol (*rĕbab*) ; there are also two other musicians—the *orang palu batil*, who beats a brass bowl with two pieces of bamboo, and the *orang palu rĕdap*, a drummer, who slaps the goat-skin head of his drum with his right hand and strums with his left as he supports the hollow end of the drum on his knee. The *To' Mindok* sits facing west exactly underneath the plate which contains the honorarium intended for the *bomor pĕtĕri;* the drummer sits on his right and the other musician on his left. The following things are placed near the band for use during the performance : a plate of bananas of different kinds, a cupful of scented water, a plateful of toasted *padi* (rice in the husk), a young green coco-nut, a brazier, and a pillow. Later on the fruit will be eaten by the *bomor pĕtĕri;* sometimes he or she may distribute some of it to the onlookers ; the toasted rice will be thrown about during the performance ; the scented water will be sprinkled over the *bomor;* the brazier, filled with burning incense (benzoin), will be placed in front of him when he starts to play, as well as the pillow with a little parched rice upon it. He will drink the water of the coco-nut during the stage of *main pĕtĕri* when he becomes possessed of the spirits from time to time.

When all is ready the first thing that the *bomor pĕtĕri* does is to take some of the sacrificial offering (*kĕndĕri*) prepared for the spirits and spread it on top of a banana leaf ; he then sits cross-legged, facing east opposite to the *To' Mindok,* and proceeds to recite a very long prayer of invocation.

THE SACRIFICIAL PRAYER OF THE To' BOMOR PĔTĔRI.

O God save me from the accursed Devil !
In the name of God, the Merciful, the Compassionate,
I humbly make this sacrificial offering,
Yellow rice, a pancake, parched rice, a drop of water, a quid
    of betel.
That it may reach our mother on Earth and our father in
    Heaven,
Our first parents, our original teachers,
Living at ease on holy ground,
Reclining against the two pillars
Of the holy graves at Mecca and Medina,
The House of God.

Teachers four [1] and wise men three [2]
May sins both small and great be forgiven,
I beg a blessing for . . . (the patient).
If (his disease) be acute I pray you blunt its sharpness,
If it be heavy, lighten it,
If painful, ease it,
If hot, cool it,
(?) In the twenty Attributes [3] and the twelve worlds,[4]
(?) In the seven Senses [5] and the four (?),[6]
Earth, Water, Fire and Air, the four Elements.
I pray you prolong his stride, extend his life,
Let his daily bread be plentiful.
O Spiritual Teacher keep well my secret,
I am a physician,
I am the *Bomor*,
And this sacrifice is offered to the four Shaikhs,[7] and the seven
    Miracle-Workers.
O Shaikhs, ye control the four corners of the Earth,
And seven countries, with eight provinces.[8]
From the rising sun to the setting sun,
From pole to pole,
Under the canopy of Heaven and on the face of the Earth
Ye control the frontiers and the districts,
Ye control the river reaches within this village.
O Wonder-working Seven ! Receive my humble salutation,
Wonder-Workers, growing, created, magical,
I pray you take the yellow rice, the pancake, the parched rice,
    the drop of water, and the quid of betel
As a token of my confiding request.
If I be in the wrong, O Miracle-Workers,
Correct me, curse me, spurn me.

[1] The Archangels, according to the Koran : Gabriel, the angel who reveals ; Michael, the angel who fights ; Azrael, the angel of death ; Azrafil, the angel of the resurrection.

[2] The three friends of the Prophet : Abubakar, Omar, and Ali.

[3] The *bomor pĕtĕri* (To' Drahman) explains that the twenty attributes are the seven senses, the twelve worlds and the mountain *Sĕtong*, which is symbolical of the human head.

[4] Worlds : the words given in explanation by the *bomor pĕtĕri* (To' Drahman) are apparently artificial, hopelessly corrupt or derived from a forgotten tongue ; some seem to be Arabic, but used in other senses : *zabrut* (the first stomach or rumen of ruminants), *lokuk* (length), *habir* (the third stomach or omasum of ruminants), *isla* (liver), *jisin* (heart), *jirin* (lungs), *naksud* (tongue), *rahamani* (brain), *laukuk* (bile), *lauhar* (neck), *mĕlukut* (windpipe), and *jismani* (flesh at the top of the chest—? thymus gland).

[5] The seven senses are given as : *zakar* (feeling by male organ—? animation), *tangan* (feeling by hand), *kaki* (feeling by foot), *mulut* (taste), *mata* (sight), *tĕlinga* (hearing), *hidong* (smell). Speech is omitted in favour of feeling by foot.

[6] ? four stages.

[7] Shaikh Abdulsaman, Shaikh Abulkadir, Shaikh Bantalok, and Shaikh Abdulajar.

[8] The *bomor pĕtĕri* (To' Drahman) explains that the earth is divided into seven countries, each with eight provinces.

I pray you restore him (the sick man) to his former self,
Restore him fully to his previous health.
Now that I have addressed the seven Miracle-Workers
I approach the low-lying Earth,
To entreat the Raja Jin,
Father of all Jins, chieftain of all Jins,
He who lives a hermit in the pen of the Black Cow,
The Pillar, the Prop, the Fanner, the Leveller, the Mover, and
    Shaker of the Earth.[1]
(?) Left by Ina Jagak wrapped in the Rainbow,
(?) Ancestor of Jin Dohor, of a thousand skin diseases, the seven
    spotted.
I conjure thee to recall thy thousand and forty followers from
    the Earth,
Restrain them from mounting guard over the body of this son
    of Adam . . . (the name of the sick man).
Recall all thy followers from village, field, jungle, sea and land.
Call them back from the four corners of the Earth,
The hundred thousand Jin and the hundred thousand Dewa,
And any Jins not already mentioned,
The *Bomor* and the *Mindok* will tell of them.
I pray you accept this sacrificial offering,
It is not my sacrifice, but that of the learned Akmal Hakim.
Hail! First of the *Mindok*,
Hail! Earliest of the *Pětěri*.

Having recited this the *bomor pětěri* gives the sacrifice
to anybody sitting near by, who places it on the ground
outside, close to the house, and puts one lighted candle
of beeswax near it. The *To' Mindok* now starts to
fiddle and sing the *běrtabek*, a kind of introductory
apology, during which he scatters handfuls of toasted
rice about the room, and may even put some of it into
his mouth. The full band strikes up. The *běrtabek* is
sung in a plaintive tone ; it is a very lengthy incantation of more than 130 lines. Although probably
wearisome to the casual reader, it is given in full, so
far as is possible, as well as the other incantations, in
English and in romanised Malay (Appendix I) to
serve as a record of a peculiar performance that has not
hitherto been described by other observers.

[1] The Black Cow lives under the earth ; her legs form the pillars and the
props ; her tail is the fanner ; her body is the leveller and the shaker, and her
mouth is the mover.

The Introductory Song of the To' Mindok.

In the name of God !
Ere the pen was made,
Or the ink ground,
The tablet of Fate not yet written,
The beginning (of time) not yet laid down,
And the End not yet fixed,
The Earth not yet spread,
The arch of Heaven not yet created,
And the Sea not lowered down,
In perfect darkness and gloom before Creation.
Jins and Dewas still unborn,
Satan not yet created,
The Prince of Darkness not yet created ;
First came God and then the Apostle,
First the Apostle and then the Prophet,
First the Prophet and then Adam,
First Adam and then the holy Saints,
First the holy Saints and then the Miracle-Workers,
First the Miracle-Workers and then the Witnesses,
First the Witnesses and then Myself.
I bow my head to the Earth,
In remembrance of my Mother on Earth,
And I gaze up to Heaven,
In remembrance of my Father in Heaven.

. . . .
. . . . . .

Keep well my secret, when I became a physician and a doctor of
 the learned.
In remembrance of Shaikh Abdulsaman,
Who lives a hermit in the East,
Shaikh Bantalok the orator, a danger to his foe,
Who lives a hermit in the West,
Shaikh Abdulkadir and Shaikh Abdulajar,
Who live as hermits (?) at the opposite poles,
The Shaikhs who control the four corners of the Earth.
In remembrance of the Miracle-working Seven of the Earth !
Who hold the frontiers, the districts and the reaches.
Having interviewed the Seven Miracle-Workers,
Now I shall take a short cut across the point and cross the river
 reach ;
If it be far, I will make it near,
If the way be tortuous, I will go direct,
To address the hundred thousand and the thousand and forty
 jin in their lair on Earth.
The physician (*To' Bomor Mindok*) is not going to offer prayer
 to the village spirits.

Nor is the physician going to offer up a sacrificial feast,
Nor is he paying tribute,
The physician (*To' Mindok*) seeks (blessings) upon . . . (the
    sick man).
Restore him fully to his previous health,
Restore him to his former self,
Sang Gana (Ganesha), king of the village,
Taga Gana, warrior of the orchard,
Langjuna the Sage who encircles the village,
Luk-lik in the village,
Daeng (the *Hantu Raja*) in the village,
Awang the length of a stride ; of the free swinging arm, the bald
    temples ; the curly hair ;
With red eyes, teeth dipped with white, broad breast and
    discoloured hands and feet !
Ye seven gnomes of the village !
Approach not this sick man.
Now I address Mamuk, the Black Spirit of the thunderbolt,
And the Yellow Jin of Ranjuna's bow,
The western lightning of the New Year,
Do not sit chuckling and laughing at . . . (the sick man).
Now I address the four Sultans,
Sultan Ahmad, Sultan Ajimat,
Sultan Ponggok, king of the village,
And the Raja Muda of the village ;
The Phantom of the village,
The Young Bachelor of the Orchard ;
The Seven Princesses of the village,
With black wings of misfortune,
At the four corners of the village,
Do not sit chuckling and laughing at . . . (the sick man).
Now I address the seven children of the Dewas, the head of the
    village ; the live coals of fire ; the security for death ; the
    one who passes through fire ; the scraping drift-net ; the
    render of the shroud ; the yawning grave,
Also Irun Dana the well of blood.
Ye children of Jins on the lofty fort !
Awang with the red moustache,
Awang with the curly moustache,
Awang of the thicket.

.   .   .   .   .   .
.   .   .   .   .   .

Spectre Huntsman with seven faces facing the sky,
Ghost of the forest clearing,
If my patient be guilty,
Recall all your attendants,
The warrior Panglima Mansur of the crooked chest,
The Pari Jin, ghost of the Sea,

(?) Child of Mansur, King of the jelly-fishes,
Children descended from Sultan Bahar, soldiers of the Sea,
Ye warriors Ipoh, Jĕpoh, Bagos and Bugis,
Children descended from Ton Teja Kuda Pila,
Dwelling on rocks and sands and herded beside lakes and meres,
If any offence through want of tact by my patient has occurred,
I pray thee recall all thy followers to the setting sun ;
The Young Jin, Fire Axe, the Handy Hatchet, the Turning
    Chisel and the One who passes through fire ;
The descendants of the Golden Sultan, sheltered by the wind,
Mamuk of the sunrise, the black spirit that darkens the sun,
The yellow jin of sunlight rays ;
The descendants of Shaikh Bara Api,
The black spirit, Gelumbong Ajar,
The red spirit, Gahna's bracelet ;
All the leaders of rutting elephants,
Whose drivers are crazy ;
The black spirit of dense fog,
The yellow spirit of the trailing gloom,
One foot at the gates of Heaven,
One foot at the door of Earth ;
The descendants of Sang Nyanya,
Ajal Jin, Death's Commander,
Prince of Pestilence, Pharaoh's grandchild,
Chief of Misfortune throughout Creation,
The thousand and forty Jins of the world,
Messengers of Balang Ajar, the Prince of all Evil,
The Dato' Peg, an only uncle of the young Jin,
Sarakal Api, Kĕpiat Api,
Mĕlalu Api and Pĕlatong Api,
The entire golden party of the King of the Ghosts,
The whole hundred and forty-eight,
The seven layers in the sky,
The seven layers on the earth,
Those living at sea and those on land,
The earthly Jin and the Celestial Beings,
The ancestors Sang Sĕnohong and Sang Kaki,
And Siva the Destroyer (Bĕntara Kala).

The *bomor pĕtĕri* now sits on the white mat facing the
To' Mindok, smears coco-nut oil on his hands, body
and head, and covers himself up in a yellow or other
coloured shawl : he puts the brazier with the burning
incense in front of him and mumbles some words that
cannot be heard, calling on the good spirit that is
subsequently to help him, *i.e.*, the *pĕnggawa* or control

spirit : he is in a state of amnesia and is known now as the *Orang Lupa,* literally the " man who forgets " ; for all intents and purposes he has become a *pětěri* spirit. The *To' Mindok* then commences to fiddle briskly preparatory to singing his second song, which is called the *Gěrak Orang Lupa.* His idea is to put some life into the " man who forgets " and to quicken the calling up of the control spirit. The band plays furiously with this object in view.

The Bestirring Song of the To' Mindok.

First the King (*Pětěri*) lay sleeping upon a small bed,
Then he got up, took a small kettle and washed his face,
Took a veil and faced the setting sun,
Reciting the profession of Muslim faith,
Praising God and praying to the Prophet,
After praying to the Prophet,
He sat down cross-legged and reached out for a small betel box.
Chewed betel twice or thrice then ceased,
Then he took a small box of mother-of-pearl,
Took a cloth of shot silk from Sind,
And donned it as a sash above his shoulder,
Wearing also a yellow flying coat of the Dewas,
The coat fitted closely to his tender skin,
He took the (?) golden oil and smeared it on his hair,
Then he faced a burning censer :—
I want to rouse the original King and the old-time Dewa,
Sulong Nurdin leader of the King's procession,
Sulong Sayang leader of the Dewa's procession,
Sulong Gětar leader of the warrior's procession,
Sulong Taman Sari leader of the Jin's procession,
I want to rouse a King of the Mountains, a Dewa of Heaven !
Mamuk of the Garden, and the warriors of the Upper Hall,
Awake ! with the four Kings,
Raja Běrsawan, Raja Měndara Raib, Raja Měndara Lelang,
And Sěri Maharaja, the Wind of Tanar the renowned.
Awake ! Wind of Descent and Wind of Heredity,
Descended from the father, and inherited from the mother.
Awake ! ye four supporters,
Ye four warriors, ye four nobles,
Awake ! ye four helpers,
Abubakar, Omar, Osman and Ali,
Awake ! Wind Sharěat of human hair and skin,
Wind Hatěkat of flesh and blood,
Wind Tarěkat of sinews and bones,

Wind Ma'rifat of life and seed,[1]
Four winds within,
Four winds without,
Four on the right, four on the left,
Four below and four aloft,
Awake ! Go out by the door of Desire,
By the door of Faith, the door of Longing,
And the door of Perception.
Where is the heart that you do not pity ?
Where is the heart that you do not crave for ?
Where is the heart that you do not grieve for ?
Where is the heart that you do not love ?
Twisting and turning, bending in confusion,
Like a bough playing in the wind,
Like an owl in love with the moon,
Like the argus pheasant singing her little ones to sleep,
Like an elephant swaying his tusks.
Now Mamuk ;   driver of the Green Horse, Awake !
Awake ! Jĕlumung Dewa ; get ready the steed and chariot.
The Princess (*Pĕtĕri*) waits only for the propitious day and the
     lucky hour.
Umbrella-bearers get ready the umbrellas,
Spearsmen get ready your spears of State.
At length the King springs up, faces the East, takes three strides
     and swings his arms three times.
The mountain is split by the sound of the royal drums,
The umbrellas revolve
The great dragon . . . to the cave
The King takes a short cut across the point,
Shaping his course to the Twelve Worlds,[2]
Along the bridge of the Seven Doors,[3] along the Nine Roads.[4]
To the Mountain Sĕtong,[5] the Water-way of Life.

Presently, when the *To' Mindok* has finished his
chant, or even before he has done so, the *bomor pĕtĕri* is
seen to nod and shake his head, and he soon begins to
roll it round and round in the most violent manner (if a

---

[1] Sharĕat is for Ar. *Shari'at,* " law (of Islam) " ; Hatĕkat for *I'tiqād,* " belief,
faith " ; Tarĕkat for *Tariqāt,* " the way (*i.e.* of purity) " ; Ma'rifat, " knowledge
(of God)."
[2] The Twelve Worlds (also referred to in the sacrificial prayer of the To'
Bomor Pĕtĕri) are said to be symbolical of the contents of the human body.
[3] The Seven Doors are given as : *kĕhĕndak* (wishes), *atĕkat* (faith), *chinta*
(longings), *rasa* (perception), *hawa* (affections), *nafsu* (desires), and *angan-angan*
(thoughts).
[4] The Nine Roads are given as : *mulut* (the mouth), *hidong* (the nose), *mata*
(the eyes), *tĕlinga* (the ears), *ubun-ubun* (the fontanelles), *pusat* (the navel),
jubor (the anus), *kĕmaluan* (the genitals), and *pĕgangan* (the hand-grasp).
The mountain *Sĕtong* is said to be the head of the *Pĕtĕri.*

woman is officiating, her long black hair twirls and swirls in unison) : his eyes are closed ; every now and again he clears his throat as if about to speak and claps his hands to emphasise the consecutive coming and going of the individual helping spirit. These possess him one at a time until he has chosen the one that he desires to retain. This goes on until the *bomor pĕtĕri* reaches a state of frenzy, the musicians, with true comradeship, playing unceasingly. At last when he is so dizzy that he can no longer continue, he raises both hands as a signal for the *To' Mindok* to stop singing and for the band to cease playing. He is dazed—he swoons—he is in a trance. The stage has now been reached when he (" the man who forgets ") is actually in possession of the helping spirit whose aid he has invoked, and now he is regarded as representing a *pĕtĕri* spirit in whatever he says or does ; he is acting, in fact, as a medium.

These *pĕtĕri* spirits are all good spirits ; they are divided into two classes. One class contains the princesses of olden days who became good fairies, such as the *hantu pari* referred to in the introductory song of the *To' Mindok*, as well as the *pĕtĕri Sakdom* and others. The second class consists of the *pĕnggawa* or control spirits, good spirits who are summoned by the *To' Bomor Pĕtĕri* to help him in casting out the evil spirit or spirits that may have got into the sick man's body. Among these good helping spirits are *Budak Kĕchil Kuda Kuala ; Budak Kĕchil Telur* (the lisping lad), who are males ; and *Pĕtĕri Mayang Mas* (the princess of the golden palm blossom), who is a female spirit. There are many others. The *bomor pĕtĕri* claims that with the help of the *bomor mindok* he can draw evil spirits, but only one at a time, out of a sick man, and for this purpose he regards himself as actually becoming a *pĕnggawa* spirit for the time being. The spirit-raising *bomor* is generally a hard-featured man or woman of good physique. In Kelantan he or she is also called the *tukang eleng,* or the " head shaker."

When the performance of *main pĕtĕri* is being given in order to cure the sick, the *bomor pĕtĕri* is instructed by the *To' Mindok* to find out first of all if the illness is being caused by disease, or if it is the work of a demon. He is then, as the case may be, required to cast out the disease or to suck the evil spirit or spirits out of the sick man's body by drawing their essence into his own body (*isap akan uap sĕrta angin jin di-dalam itu*). As soon as the " man who forgets " (now a *pĕtĕri* spirit) is in the trance, every one is expected to keep quiet ; but when he seems to be coming round he is subjected to a number of questions ; they are put to him only by the *To' Mindok.* The queries begin with " Who is he ? " ; and the name of a *pĕnggawa* spirit is given in reply. It may be considered unsuitable. The *To' Mindok,* for instance, may think that a more powerful spirit is required, and in this case he will say that another must be called up. The singing and fiddling recommences and continues until the *bomor pĕtĕri* is again brought into a trance. Several false starts of this kind may be made. Eventually the *To' Mindok* tells the *pĕtĕri* to find out for certain whether the sick man's illness is due to disease or to the work of a devil.

The *pĕtĕri* takes a lighted candle, gazes at the flame, throws two or three grains of toasted rice at it, and finally extinguishes it as a sign that he now knows exactly what the cause of the illness is. He reports accordingly to the *To' Mindok,* and is directed to set to work ; but a good deal of coaxing is required of the *To' Mindok* at this stage before the *pĕtĕri* actually begins to operate. At last the *pĕtĕri* crawls towards the sick man, who is reclining near by, and sucks, or pretends to suck, about the body of the patient until he has located the

seat of the disease. Sometimes he puts the great toe of
the sick man into his mouth and really sucks it. As
soon as he has located the site of the affliction by means
of this leech-craft he chants an incantation or spell
called the *bangkitan,* by which either the demon will be
exorcised or the disease itself will be cast out.

THE EXORCISM OF THE TO' BOMOR PĚTĚRI.

O Universe the World of Adam!
Earth was made from a clod taken from an eddy of Heaven,
Water from Heaven's river,
Fire from the fumes of Hell,
Air from the four elements,
From *Di* came first human skin and hair,
From *Wadi* came flesh and blood,
From *Mani* came bones and sinews,
From *Manikam* came life and seed,
Human skin and hair were created by the Archangel Gabriel,
Flesh and blood by the Archangel Michael,
Sinews and bones by the Archangel Asrafil,
Life and seed by the Archangel Azrael.
Where is this jin lodging and taking shelter?
Where is he lodging and crouching?
Jin! if thou art in the feet of my patient
Know that his feet are moved by God and by the Prophet,
If thou art in the stomach of my patient
His stomach is God's sea, the sea too of Muhammad,
If thou art in the hands of my patient
His hands pay homage to God and also to the Prophet,
If thou art in the liver of my patient
This is the secret (place) of God, the secret (place) too of His
    Prophet,
If thou art in the heart of my patient
Know that the heart is Abubakar's palace,
If thou art in the lungs of my patient
Know that the lungs are Omar's palace,
If thou art in the spleen [1] of my patient
Know that it is the palace of Ali,
The heart, the lungs, the spleen and the gall-bladder,
Are the homestead of Life,
They are not the homestead of Jin or Devil,
Nor are they the homestead of sickness and suffering.

---

[1] The word *limpa* is used for spleen. The *bomor pětěri* (To' Drahman)
explains that the spleen is only called *kura* when it becomes enlarged by repeated
attacks of ague, because the spleen then resembles a tortoise (*kura*) in shape
(*děman kura,* fever with ague).

Ho, there ! O Jin ! thy origin was in the fumes from the " flame-
tongue " of smokeless Hell !
I know the origin of *Harijin* thy father.
Thy mother's name was *Marijin*,
Thy child's name was *Narijin.*

The *pĕtĕri* now returns to the mat and either stands
or sits in front of the *To' Mindok*, holding out his hands
for the band to stop playing. He is again questioned by
the *To' Mindok*, who asks " Who is he ? "—to which
the *pĕtĕri* replies either that it is a jin, or perhaps a
familiar, or merely a disease. He is asked how the jin
(if it be a jin) got in and by whom sent. Sometimes no
reply is given to the last question, but, in any case, a
good deal more coaxing by the *To' Mindok* and promises
of food, etc., is required before the *pĕtĕri* gives any
satisfactory reply. He is asked to keep the jin out of
the way in future, and so on, until the *To' Mindok*,
having exhausted all his questions, recommences to
play, as also do the other two musicians. The *bomor
pĕtĕri* shakes his head about again for, perhaps, five
minutes, then suddenly stops and holds out his hands
to the *To' Mindok*. The *To' Mindok* asks if the jin
has been taken out of the sick man's body by the
pĕnggawa spirit or, as the case may be, if the disease
has been cast out ; and the *pĕtĕri* replies in the affirma-
tive. The jin, if it be a jin, that has been causing all
this trouble is now supposed to be in the body of the
bomor pĕtĕri, who is again made to shake his head as
described above until he falls into a fresh trance. He
now has to cast the jin out of his own body by the aid
of the *pĕnggawa* or helping spirit. When the *pĕtĕri* can
assure the *To' Mindok* that all the spirits have left
him, the *To' Mindok* says that the performance may
stop for the present, and the *To' Bomor Pĕtĕri* is
himself again.

The *To' Mindok* is the right-hand man of the *To'
Bomor Pĕtĕri*, and if any hitch should occur in choosing

the correct *pĕnggawa* or helping spirit the *bomor* might
have to go on shaking his head indefinitely ! At an all-
night performance that I witnessed at Kampong Kota
in 1913 a Malay woman officiated as the *To' Bomor
Pĕtĕri.* Gravity and decorum prevailed throughout on
that occasion ; but occasionally the male *bomor* calls
up either *Pĕtĕri Mayang Mas* (the princess of the golden
palm blossom) or any of the other female control
spirits. He then impersonates a woman in his gait, and
by arranging his dress to suit the part, etc., is said to
cause amusement to the spectators.

Sometimes when the *bomor pĕtĕri* is dealing with evil
spirits an extra turn, as it were, is given in the performance of *main pĕtĕri;* he may inform the *To'
Mindok* that the mischief is not the work of one jin,
and say of his own accord that *Nenek Jin Hitam* (the
grandfather of all the black jin) must be called up to
give an explanation. This being decided, the *To'
Mindok* sings and fiddles, the band plays, the *bomor*
shakes his head, and again goes into a trance. Now,
for the time being, the *pĕtĕri* is *Nenek Jin Hitam*, and
as he can represent only one spirit at a time, the
pĕnggawa spirit has left him for the moment. *Nenek
Jin Hitam* is. critically cross-examined by the *To'
Mindok*, and is asked why he has black followers as
well as those of lesser devils to cause all this trouble,
and who told him to do so. *Nenek Jin Hitam* replies
(through the medium, *i.e.*, the *pĕtĕri*) that he has
joined forces with the other devils because an in-
sufficient sacrifice has been offered. At this stage the
To' Mindok has to use a great deal of coaxing and may
promise anything with intent to deceive the " grandfather of the black devils," until at last, to everybody's
relief, *Nenek Jin Hitam* agrees to withdraw. On these
occasions the *To' Mindok* may sing the following
song :—

THE FAREWELL SONG OF THE TO' MINDOK TO NENEK JIN HITAM.

> Go ! and wait at the end of the Earth,
> With all thy hungry followers,
> From the four corners of the Earth,
> Receive tax and tribute.
> Gather together all the jin,
> Evil spirits, devils, goblins and ghosts,
> From Land and Sea, from Jungle and Valley,
> From Hill, Mountain and Village,
> Go ! eat the feast offered.

The cost of a special performance for the cure of a sick man or woman is about sixty or seventy Straits dollars ; but the ordinary village performance in Kelantan generally comes to only about twenty-five dollars. The village performance is popular because the occasion is taken to show hospitality to friends from near and far. When *Main Pĕtĕri* is performed with the idea of winning the affection of a girl, the *pĕnggawa* spirit acts as " love's messenger " and a bunch of jessamine is given to the lover to keep in his bedroom. In the case of stolen or lost property, a substantial reward must be offered to the *pĕtĕri*, and even then his information is often both vague and ambiguous.

The detailed description of *Main Pĕtĕri* given above was related to me by word of mouth in 1921 by *To' Bomor Ēnche' Drahman bin Muhammad Ali* of Pasir Mas, a well-known *bomor pĕtĕri*, employed on occasions by the late Sultan of Kelantan. *'Che' Drahman*, now retired on pension, was formerly a police sergeant. The incantations were dictated by him from memory to the chief clerk of the Medical Department, an educated Singapore Malay, who is his son-in-law, and who wrote them down at the time in romanised Malay. *To' Bomor Ēnche' Drahman* knows no English ; with simple gravity he said that he was ready to defend in Malay the doctrine of the introductory songs, but requested that the *To' Imam* (President of the Mosque) should not be told that he had divulged the *bangkitan*

Photo : Kuan Weng of Kota Bharu, Kelantan.

A KELANTAN SPIRIT-RAISING BOMOR.
To' Bomor Ĕnche' Drahman—Pasir Mas.

which is his final song in the performance of *Main
Pĕtĕri*. In this curious *bangkitan* incantation which I
have referred to as an exorcism, ideas as to embryology
are mentioned ; these occur in the incantations of
other Malay sorcerers : three separate elements (*di*
and *mani* and *wadi*) of the spermatic fluid (*manikam*)
are supposed to create an embryo without the need of
an ovum.

I am not qualified to deal efficiently with the translation of the incantations in *Main Pĕtĕri ;* my crude
version is open to much criticism from Malay scholars.
The simple and literal rendering that I attempted in
1921 with the help of *To' Drahman* himself and one
of my brother officers was greatly improved by the
kindness of Winstedt and Blagden. A very curious
dialect is spoken in Kelantan which differs considerably
from the Malay in the western and southern states of
the Peninsula—*e.g.*, *sangkak* becomes *sakoh*, and
pangkah, *bakoh*. Moreover, Malay charms always
contain many corrupt or obsolete words handed down
from pre-Muhammadan days through the memories
of illiterate peasants which makes translation exceeding
difficult. Dr. R. O. Winstedt, who reviewed the
second edition of " Malay Poisons and Charm Cures "
in 1923, says, with reference to the " Sacrificial Prayer "
of the *To' Bomor Pĕtĕri* (see p. 80, footnote 4) : " Most
of the words, at any rate, are Arabic and are used of
' worlds ' in the scheme of the Muslim mediæval
cosmogony, for which To' Drahman again found
' seats ' (*makam ; astana*) in the animal world. *Zabrut
= 'alam jabarut*, the world of almightiness, wherein lie
hidden the processes of the Divine nature intimated in
the attributes and names of God ; *mĕlukut = 'alam
malakut*, the invisible intelligible world. According to
a Javanese account, quoted by Kraemer, the *'alam
nasut* is situated in the eyelid or in the *'akl*, the *'alam*

malakut in the white of the eye or the *ruh*, and the
'alam lahut, the divine spiritual world, in the light of
the eye or in the *rahsa !* " Crude pantheism, which
finds in man the microcosm of the universe with all the
"worlds" that philosophers and mystics have invented,
identifies these with different parts of the body ; and
hence To' Drahman's explanations (R.O.W.). Some
of the "worlds" (*'alam*) are explained in Nicholson's
" Studies in Islamic Mysticism " (Cambridge, 1921).

The reader is referred to Winstedt's book " Shaman,
Saiva and Sufi " for much further information about
the Malay shaman (Ref. 14, Chapters VII and VIII) ;
to his paper " More Notes on Malay Magic," which
contains also an account of *Main Mok Peh* (Ref. 13),
and to his article " A Malay Pantheist Charm "
(Ref. 12), in which he has skilfully unravelled part of
the " Bestirring Song " of the *To' Bomor Mindok*.

Main Bĕrhantu.—The *bĕrhantu* of Perak and
Selangor is similar in many respects to the *pĕrmainan
pĕtĕri* of Kelantan. *Bĕrhantu* has been described by
Sir Frank Swettenham in his book " Malay Sketches,"
p. 153, the patient in this case being a reigning Sultan
of Perak. Mr. W. W. Skeat has also described it as
practised by a *bomor bĕlian* on an ordinary citizen in
Selangor, and Mr. J. R. Wilkinson gives an interesting
summary of the two accounts in " Papers on Malay
Subjects " (The Incidents of Malay Life), p. 45 (Ref. 8).
Dr. Winstedt has written of a *bĕrhantu* he witnessed on
the Perak river (" Malayan Memories " : A Malay
Séance) (Ref. 11). *Main pĕtĕri* is always played for
three nights in succession, sometimes for seven nights,
and then the patient is left to take care of himself. If
his condition improves, the same performance is gone
through again, after a lapse of one or two weeks ; but if
no improvement is noticeable, nothing further is done.
In the event of an obvious recovery, a final performance

(*malam bĕrjamu*) is given ; this is a special sacrificial offering to all the spirits concerned and conducted in a small shed or out-house. It is an elaborate proceeding.

The model of a square platform with four posts and five stories is made out of bamboo or of stems of the sago palm and decorated with coco-nut palm leaves. A miscellaneous collection of every kind of food for which ghosts and spirits are believed to have a passion is placed on each story. In addition to the sacrificial offering, already referred to as the *kĕndĕri*, the following things are put upon the platform : fish—a bit of skate, of shark, a crab, a prawn ; flesh—pieces of chicken, duck, goat and beef, both cooked and raw ; vegetables —various, both cooked and uncooked, boiled rice of seven different colours ; two kinds of intoxicating liquors (arrack and toddy) ; some bananas, various kinds of cakes, the blood of a fowl, and some parched rice. Each of these is put into a separate little container made of banana leaf (*tĕmilong*) and placed in the proper order from the basement to the top story. One silver dollar is placed on each floor, making a total of five dollars. This money is intended for the *pĕtĕri*.

The same collection of things, in miniature, is placed on a square mat made out of coco-nut palm leaves, and called *peng*, as well as one silver dollar ; a similar collection with another silver dollar is also put into a kind of basket shaped like a cradle, also made of coco-nut palm leaves, and called the " prince's hall " (*balai Raja*). One beeswax candle is put at each of these places. Three plates are placed on the ground, one containing some yellow rice, another holding three small skeins of white thread, and the third containing twelve and a half cents (*pitis sa-kupang*). This is the *pĕkras guru*, or honorarium to the *To' Bomor Pĕtĕri*. Four jars full of water are also placed on the ground, three of them containing the coloured leaves of crotons

and dracænas which are commonly seen as ornamental
shrubs in European gardens (*puding mas* and *puding
perak*, Codiæum variegatum, and *andong* or *jĕjuang*,
Cordyline terminalis), while the fourth water jar is a
copper pitcher with a round bottom and a smallish
circular neck. The neck of the pitcher is covered with
three pieces of white cloth by means of white thread,
and it is inverted so that it may contain *ayer songsang*,
or " topsy-turvy " water. Twelve and a half cents
are placed on each of the four water jars. A bamboo
with the free end split so as to form a kind of basket is
stuck into the ground and a young green coco-nut with
a silver dollar on the top of it is placed in the receptacle ;
underneath the green coco-nut, and about the middle
of the bamboo stem, a small platform made of bamboo
is arranged and decorated with coco-nut palm leaves.
A tiny and third collection of all the foodstuffs, including another silver dollar, is placed upon this little
platform.

After playing all night in the manner already
described, the devil eventually enters the *bomor* about
three or four o'clock in the morning ; the candles are
then lit and the *pĕtĕri* proceeds to taste, or pretends to
taste, the sacrifice. He commences first with the
offerings displayed on the small mat called *peng*,
proceeding to the four-post platform and ending at the
basket cradle called *balai Raja*. He is finally dis-
possessed about daybreak, and now the *To' Bomor
Pĕtĕri* performs the concluding ceremony of *Main
Pĕtĕri*. This is called *pĕlĕpas*, and by it the sick man
is released from all machinations by evil spirits. A
cup containing ground rice in the form of a thin paste
(*tĕpong tawar*) and a number of strips of palm leaf
tied with slipknots in the form of a bow (*lĕlĕpas*) are
placed in readiness ; he takes the rice paste and marks
a cross (*pangkak ;* Kelantan, *bakoh*) on his own fore-

head and on the foreheads of those (especially the children) who happen to be near him, and then pulls the bows to pieces. The sick man bathes in the water of the three jars containing the yellow croton and deep red dracæna leaves, and the ceremony of *pĕlĕpas* is ended by the *bomor* making a ring out of each small skein of thread, which he passes in turn over the head of the patient, drawing each slowly over the body down to the feet. The performance is now over ; the platform is taken to the neighbouring jungle and left there, but the small mat called *peng* and the cradle are kept in the village for a few days. The " topsy-turvy " water in the copper pitcher is to be drunk by the sick man after a lapse of seven days, or he may be allowed to bathe himself with it. The use of water by the Malay " medicine-man " is of interest because it also figures largely in the medico-magical practices of Anglo-Saxon medicine (Ref. 5).

I have known the mental distress of two native patients relieved in Kota Bharu by the performance of *pĕrmainan pĕtĕri :* one was the wife of my gardener, 'Che Lima, a Kelantan woman who invited me to witness the night-long performance ; the other was a Portuguese Eurasian, wife of a Government clerk, who suffered from hysteria following forcible massage used by Malay women to procure an abortion. 'Che Lima had suffered a long, indefinite illness following a confinement, and had been treated as an out-patient at the State hospital for some time. It is not improbable that the cure in both these cases was due to suggestion. 'Che Lima was one of those who " likes to take medicine."

The demoniac theory of medicine is of very ancient origin. It is derived largely from the civilisation of the Tigris and Euphrates. Dr. Charles Singer, in an address to the Royal Academy (1920) says : " Besides the original stratum of demonism in Greek medicine which was presumably drawn more directly from Babylonian sources, much new belief concerning demons has been introduced into the Greek system by Christianity, and has been propagated from an early date by the spread of that religion in the West. The pathology of the New Testament is mainly demoniac and many of the miracles of healing are exorcisms. There were devils of blindness, dumbness, madness and epilepsy, and Luke the physician regarded the ' great fever ' of Simon's wife's mother in the light of a demon, for Jesus, he says, ' stood over her .and rebuked the fever ; and it left her.' So also the infirmities of Mary Magdalene were of the nature of seven evil spirits—the demons of early Christianity, like those of the Mesopotamian system, were often grouped in sevens—and Peter considered that all those whom Jesus healed had been ' oppressed of the devil ' " (Ref. 5). The constant grouping of seven in Malay demonology is noteworthy, also the Malay idea that evil spirits may account for the frailty of womankind.

In Kelantan, as in other Malay States, the highest circles affect the practice of Black Art, and to please the people in accordance with ancient custom the late Sultan gave a public performance of *pĕrmainan pĕtĕri*, lasting for seven nights, during the cholera epidemic of 1920 in order to remove the calamity (*tolak bala*). The idea was to exorcise the demons that were causing the epidemic and so cause its abatement. When the performance is given by royalty, or commanded by a reigning Sultan, the final ceremony is a very elaborate affair. A white buffalo is slaughtered for the occasion. The Kelantan ceremony is, however, much less costly than the *bĕrhantu* carried out, on rare occasions, in the far richer State of Perak. In Kelantan a special shed is built and the model of a forty-pillared hall takes the place of the four-post platform of the village performance. This forty-pillared hall is a model built of wood, bamboo, and branches of the sago palm, and is adorned with plaited coco-nut palm leaves so arranged with trailers (made by cutting diagonally to the mid-rib) as to bear a fanciful resemblance to a long-legged centipede. Pieces of tongue, liver, heart, and stomach of the white buffalo are added to the miscellaneous collection of food already mentioned as part of the sacrificial offering in the village performance : one dollar is placed on the first floor, two on the second, and so on until seven on the top floor makes a total of twenty-eight dollars. In addition to the arrangements made in the shed for the ordinary performance a young green coco-nut is put on the ground at each corner of the building, and four plates, each containing fifty cents, are slung up in little swing platforms attached to the four walls. This money is in addition to the nineteen cents of the *kĕndĕri*, or sacrifice made to the spirits by the *To' Bomor Pĕtĕri* at the opening of the performance.

In days gone by the old-established custom of *tolak bala* (lit., repelling misfortune) used to fall heavily on the peasants, because the village headmen collected the money from them by force to pay for the white buffaloes and the rest of the very elaborate performance ; but the old idea of *tolak bala* is still existent, as may be seen from a letter written to me by one of the late Sultan's uncles on April 25th, 1920. After compliments : " I beg to inform my friend that I intend having a *pĕrmainan pĕtĕri*, and to slaughter a white buffalo to cast out misfortune, as is the custom, once in every three years. It is now more than ten years since this has been done, owing to the difficulty in raising money. Formerly, the sum of twenty-five cents was collected from every house in the vicinity of *Kampong China*, as far as the rivers *Kĕladi* and *Tikat*. The performance then lasted for seven days and seven nights ; but I am now going to do it only for three days and three nights. Therefore I hope my friend will please arrange with the Government to grant me any reasonable amount that he may think fair."

Main Bĕrjin.—The *bomor bĕrjin* and the *bomor orang bunian* deal with elves and fairies of the forest who are descended from the fallen angels ; they use no music, and, like the *bomor mambang*, mostly concern themselves with the spirits known as " Celestial Beings." The *bomor bĕrjin* specialises in the *mambang* spirits that are personified in the golden sunset clouds, such as *hantu mambang bulang*, the enwinding spirit, and *hantu mambang kuning*, the yellow spirits. The term *mambang kuning* is used idiomatically when, after a rainy day, the sunset seems to give a yellow tinge to everything. This tinge is believed to be the work of evil spirits and to bring disease in its train. The *bĕrjin* spirit-raiser also calls up the " old man of the sea " (*Dato' Sĕmar Laut*) and *Dato' Gayang*, the " vacillating dotard," as well as evil spirits connected with blood-poisoning (*hantu bisa*) and those of blindness and deafness.

Main Orang Bunian.—The performance given by the *bomor orang bunian* is similar in many respects to *main pĕtĕri ;* but the *bomor* dresses in white, he does not shake his head about like the *bomor pĕtĕri*, and he names his fee before crawling towards the sick man.

Main Bĕrbagih.—*Pĕrmainan bĕrbagih* is adapted from a shadow-play. It is a good example of Hindu beliefs which have survived in Malaya. Many of these survivals have been traced by Dr. Winstedt, who has found much evidence to prove that Malay magic came from India, from which he concludes that India left an

ineffaceable influence on Malay life and thought long
before Islam came to Malaya from India (Refs. 9 and
10). In Kelantan *main bĕrbagih* is performed with the
idea of curing the sick, of discovering the spell-bound,
and of finding lost or stolen property by means of the
Black Art. The *bomor bĕrbagih* borrows a few grotesque
figures of the Hindu demi-gods that are used in a
shadow puppet play called *wayang kulit*. He chooses
seven of them to help him in his witchcraft ; three are
yellow figures and the others are painted black. They
are cut out of raw cow-hide, with a small chisel, in the
shape of hand screens, jointed and supplied with
strings to cause movement and represent Hindu
deities. In the hands of the *bomor* they are supposed
to have a benign influence, but to the ordinary mortal
their appearance is singularly repulsive. The most
important of the puppets is the black Sĕma or Dewa
Sang Tunggal ; he is always, and perhaps exclusively,
used by the *bomor bĕrbagih*, most of the others being
brought on only in the last night's performance. The
yellow *dewa* are : Bĕtara Ikĕrma Jaya, Radin Inu
(the " hero prince "), and Sang Sĕnohong or Bĕtara
Guru (Siva as the supreme teacher) ; the black and
more important ones are : the Sĕma or Sang Tunggal
referred to above, Bĕtara Narada, Narada Truas, and
Bĕtara Kala, who is Siva the destroyer. Sang Tunggal,
Narada Truas, and Radin Inu only are brought out
during the preliminary performance.

The ground work of *main bĕrbagih* is similar to that
of *main pĕtĕri ;* but it is played in the sick man's house,
which is not decorated for the occasion, and no music is
employed. There are three performers : the chief, *i.e.*,
the *To' Bomor Bĕrbagih*, is called *Orang Lupa*, or the
" man who forgets " ; his right-hand man, who corresponds to the *To' Mindok* or the " fiddler " in *main
pĕtĕri*, is known as the *To' Dalam*, or the " Lord of the

Interior "; while another man, called the *pĕngateng*, assists generally and sprinkles water over his chief. The honorarium to the chief performer in *main bĕrbagih* consists of a plate containing rice, with two dollars and fifteen cents and a skein of white thread ; a saucer containing yellow cooked rice and a boiled hen's egg is placed on the top of the plate. The sacrificial offering to the spirits consists of yellow cooked rice, a pancake, parched rice, a quid of betel, a cup of cold water, and a beeswax candle, which are placed on a brass salver. The brass pedestal tray and the plate are placed near the *To' Dalam* and the *pĕngateng*, who sit together. The *Orang Lupa* sits in front of them with a plate of yellow rice, a plateful of toasted rice, a candle, a cupful of scented water, and a censer of burning benzoin in front of him.

When everything is ready the *To' Dalam* opens the performance by making a long speech similar to the sacrificial song of the *To' Bomor Pĕtĕri*, after which the sacrifice is dealt with in the same way as in *main pĕtĕri*. The *Orang Lupa*, sitting in front of the *To' Dalam* and facing the east, holds the puppet *Sĕma* over the burning incense and waves it about while he slowly chants a lengthy magical hymn ; he then shakes his head about until he falls into a trance. The *To' Dalam* asks him to cure the sick man : when he has agreed, he crawls towards his patient and waves the *Sĕma* puppet several times over the sick man's body, but does not pull the strings.

Main bĕrbagih lasts for two or three nights ; if recovery ensues, a final performance is given, but this is often not performed until two or three weeks have elapsed. The stage property is much the same as in *main pĕtĕri*, but differs in a few minor details : the model of a wayside resting-place takes the place of the four-post platform, there are two bamboo " cressets " and two pitchers of " topsy-turvy " water, seven water jars, which contain the blossoms of the coco-nut and areca palms in addition to the croton and dracæna leaves ; and there is a small boat which is made out of the spathe of the areca palm blossom and fitted with a paper sail. One pitcher of " topsy-turvy " water is placed in front of the *To' Dalam* and the other is put at the back of the room. The little boat is launched in the river when the performance is over and the tide serves. A similar miscellaneous collection of food as is used in *main pĕtĕri* is put in the model of the wayside resting-place and is reserved for the exclusive use of the *Dewa Bĕtara Kala* (Siva the destroyer), while the food in the two bamboo " cressets " is for the other *Dewas* as well as that on the little mat called *peng*. The cargo on board the small boat and the contents of the basket cradle called " the prince's hall " is also intended for them.

The craft of the *bomor* is not always employed in healing the sick ; for instance, when it is desired to attribute the sickness of a friend to the witchcraft of an enemy, the services of a certain *bomor* are available who will undertake to arrange, for remuneration, that the opprobrium is fixed on the victim of a plot. A few years ago, with this spiteful object in view, a small bamboo cylinder containing an addled egg and some porcupine quills was buried in the path leading from a sick man's house to the river at Temerloh, in Pahang, and doubtless if a familiar such as the *bajang* spirit had been available it would have been included in the bamboo cylinder.

The *bajang* is allied to the *pĕlĕsit*, which is said to be the pilot of the evil *polong*. When not an inheritance the *polong* can be acquired by means of special witch-craft. It is lured from the corpse of a newly buried still-born baby by means of incantations. This black witchcraft is carried out at the dead of night by standing over the grave and coaxing the *polong* out of its lair. Hayes Marriott relates the story of a Malacca *pawang* or *bomor* named Musa who was said to earn his living by bewitching children and causing their death by the aid of a familiar called the *polong*. There seems to be little doubt that this sinister *bomor* traded on his reputation ; so many children died that it was not a difficult matter for such a fellow to get travel-money and proceed to another village (Ref. 2).

The *bomor* cannot rival the " Leech of Folkestone " (" Ingoldsby Legends ") in his witchcraft, but some Malay " medicine-men " who are accomplished in the Black Art of spirit-raising claim to be able to catch the souls of the women they love in the folds of their turbans, and then go about with the souls of the beloved in their girdles by day and hide them under their pillows by night, and can teach others how to abduct souls for evil purposes (Ref. 7). The idea of neutralising the spell of a " black witch " by piercing the dried heart of an animal, such as a sheep or cow, with needles and pins, as described by Mr. Edward Lovett in the *Morning Post* of August 23rd, 1918 (" A Modern White Witch of Exmoor "), would not appeal to Malays. The spirit-raising *bomor* is prepared to go far in black witchcraft.

Skeat records how the *bomor* makes a waxen image the length of a footstep to represent a corpse. Then if blindness is desired the eye is pierced, piercing the waist makes the stomach bad, death is caused when the head is transfixed with a palm twig, then the image is enshrouded and prayed over as if it were really a corpse ; burial follows in the middle of the path which leads to the dwelling of whomsoever is to be be-devilled when he steps over it. Sometimes the *bomor* or *pawang* repeats a formula protesting that it is not he but the Archangel

Gabriel that is arranging the burial of the victim. At other times he says, " It is not wax I slay, but the liver, heart, spleen of So-and-so," before he finally buries the image in front of the victim's door (Ref. 3). The Kelantan *bomor* of to-day generally, I think, leaves such proceedings to his Siamese colleagues. Examples have occurred, however, in Perak in which waxen images of white men in high places have been designed and pierced with pins by Malay sorcerers within recent years, but without any dire results.

REFERENCES

(1) MARETT, R. R. "Psychology and Folklore." 1919. London : Methuen.
(2) MARRIOTT, Sir HAYES. "Malay Witchcraft." *Jour. Straits Br. Roy. Asiat. Soc.* (Singapore). 1903. No. 39, p. 209.
(3) SKEAT, W. W. "Malay Magic." 1900. London : Macmillan.
(4) SKEAT and BLAGDEN. "Pagan Races of the Malay Peninsula." 1906. London : Macmillan.
(5) SINGER, C. "Early English Magic and Medicine." 1920. London : Oxford University Press.
(6) SWETTENHAM, Sir FRANK A. "Malay Sketches." 1921. London : Lane.
(7) "The Encyclopædia Britannica." 1927. 13th ed. London.
(8) WILKINSON, J. R. "Papers on Malay Subjects : Life and Customs." 1920 Part I, p. 45. Singapore.
(9) WINSTEDT, Dr. R. O. "Hindu Survivals in Malay Customs." *Jour. Fed. Malay States Museums* (Perak), p. 81. 1920.
(10) WINSTEDT, Dr. R. O. "India and Malay Beliefs." *Jour. Straits Br. Roy. Asiat. Soc.* (Singapore). 1921. No. 83, p. 88.
(11) WINSTEDT, Dr. R. O. "Malayan Memories." 1916. Singapore : Kelly and Walsh.
(12) WINSTEDT, Dr. R. O. "A Malay Pantheist Charm." *Jour. Straits Br. Roy. Asiat. Soc.* (Singapore). 1922. No. 86.
(13) WINSTEDT, Dr. R. O. "More Notes on Malay Magic." *Jour. Malay Br. Roy. Asiat. Soc.* (Singapore). 1927. Vol. V, Part II, p. 342.
(14) WINSTEDT, Dr. R. O. "Shaman, Saiva and Sufi." 1925. London : Constable.

CHAPTER V

SPELLS AND SOOTHSAYING

THIS chapter is based, for the most part, on notes made from an old Kelantan manuscript on magic. Although it has no connexion with Malay poisons and their cure by charms, it is given to show the curious conceptions of the Malay mind when engaged in circumventing Muhammadan tenets. The old book was lent to me by Nik Ismail, of the Kelantan Medical Department ; the script was partly translated by the help of Mr. A. F. Worthington, British Adviser, Kelantan, and has been further revised and checked by Dr. Winstedt, who discerns that a knowledge of Arabic is shown by the copyist. Some of the Arabic words used in the charms seem to be used in special technical senses, and an intimate acquaintance with Sufism would be necessary to exactly define their meaning. The book is incomplete ; some pages are missing, and a good deal of it seems to be inexplicable. Nik Ismail told me that it belonged to his father, who is now a very old man. The manuscript appears to be not so much a work on soothsaying as notes on Islamic magic made as an aid to memory. It assumes a knowledge of the Koran, and a general acquaintance with the Black Art. Some explanations of the text were given to Mr. Worthington under promise that nothing which might enable an unscrupulous person to profit by its teaching should be published, because many persons are reputed to have some knowledge of the Black Art, but few have as much as is contained in this work. Many details are omitted in consequence.

Dr. Winstedt, however, suggests that probably the real reason for this secrecy is that the tract contains an unusually good exposition of the magic charms which made a crude form of Sufic pantheism so popular with the Indian and Malay. Such charms are always hedged around with profound secrecy, not merely to enhance their monetary value, but to avoid attacks by the orthodox ; for the doctrines of the Muhammadan mystics known as Sufis were often heretical. Two famous heterodox pantheists, Hamzah of Barus, in Sumatra, who relates that he visited Pahang, and Shams al-Din of Pasai, flourished in the sixth century. " The interests of these men for us lies in the fact that the doctrines of which they were the inheritors and exponents attracted the Peninsular Malay, with a bent for religion, at least as far back as the middle of the fifteenth century, when Sultan Mansur Shah sent an embassy from Malacca to Pasai to propound a Sufi problem " (Ref. 3). Students of Malay pantheism should read Winstedt's " Shaman, Saiva and Sufi," his chapter " Magician and Muslim " is partly based on the study of Nik Ismail's old manuscript (Ref. 4, Chapter X, p. 155). Sufi mysticism teaches the doctrine that the soul is the subject of ecstasies of Divine inspiration in virtue of its direct emanation from the Diety ; it is associated with the idea that the soul is imprisoned in the body and that death is the return to its original home. These mysterious views are contrary to the fundamental article of the Muhammadan creed which exalts God as a being passing all comprehension. Among interesting items contained in the manuscript under review is the idea of a " prenatal " language. This occurs in two protective formulas. One of them, intended to protect the owner from being stabbed, runs as follows : *ak mak sman tapal mak nak aak ak kak ja pak nal ak tik ak kak jemak nak ak tak aa ak.* An intelligent and well-educated Kelantan Malay told Mr. Worthington that these words belong to the language we speak before birth, and gave him, in explanation, a curiously literal equivalent in Malay of a verse in Wordsworth's ode " Intimations of Immortality from Recollections of Early Childhood " :—

> Our birth is but a sleep and a forgetting ;
> The Soul that rises with us, our life's star,
> Hath had elsewhere its setting,
> And cometh from afar :
> Not in entire forgetfulness,
> And not in utter nakedness,
> But trailing clouds of glory do we come
> From God, who is our home :

The origin of the formula has been forgotten ; even in Kelantan no information of what the words or sounds mean could be obtained. A Perak protective formula is : " When you meet your enemy face to face, stare hard at him until you see written on his forehead *ya ilah ilahi* (O God ! O Divine One !) Continue staring until you can rub the words off again, and you will subdue his will." According to Islam, each man's fate is writ large on his forehead. Hamzah of Barus says, " Between the two eyebrows that is the spot where the servant meets his God." (Ref. 3). The pre-natal language occurs for the second time in a spell to prevent anyone quarrelling with the maker of it. This spell consists of a very rough drawing of the human figure on a piece of banana leaf. The figure is enclosed in two squares of unequal size, the smaller square being placed diagonally within the larger one.

Pre-natal language is written in the four corners. Three of these have to be made and given, one a day, to a buffalo to eat. The buffalo thus consumes the suspected person's possible malignancy and so protects the owner. The way in which the banana tree is used by Malays in preparing a vindictive spell is described by Begbie. It is known as the *Tuju Jantong* or " Aiming at the Heart " ceremony : " The cordi-form top of a newly-opened bunch of bananas is tied to the accompaniment of a prayer (or rather charm) and the point is then burnt. This communicates with the heart of the intended victim, causing excruciating pain. Eventually the top is cut off, the victim's heart drops from its proper situation : he vomits blood and expires " (Ref. 1).

A few paragraphs of Nik Ismail's old manuscript are devoted to describing how to find out by divination if one will die during the current Muhammadan month. In one, the seeker after knowledge by occult means looks at the bright background ; in another, he shuts his eyes and then looks at the moon ; in another, he looks first at a lighted lamp and then at a bowl of water. Special days and certain hours must be chosen for each month, and special passages from the Koran must be recited, either ten or nine times, as the case may be. In the first month if the moon looks black he will die. A full translation of these paragraphs is given by Dr. Winstedt (Ref. 4, p. 158).

Looking at the moon is a common practice among native races, who consider it a means of communication between two possible distant lovers (the moon forming, as it were, a looking-glass in which each can see the other). When dealing in " Malay Magic " with directions for abducting another person's soul, Skeat relates that one is told to go out on the fourteenth night of the lunar month and repeat a charm of the following sense :—

> When you look up at the moon, remember me,
> For in that self-same moon I am there.

The head-cloth has to be waved in the direction of the moon seven times every night for three successive nights. Reference is also made by Skeat to the connexion between " shadow " and " soul," the shadow being supposed by Malays to embody, or at least represent, the soul. In the Kelantan manuscript the notes on the shadow are rather abbreviated, *e.g.*, during a certain month " if you see your shadow you will die." The explanation given by intelligent Malays is that if you see your whole shadow you will not die, but if the shadow leans to the right or to the left you will be ill, more or less seriously. If you see only a certain part of your shadow you will die. It also contains a protective formula against the act of God (loss by lightning, shipwreck, etc.), with the sound, if terrifying, advice that, unless every word is accurately remembered, it should not be used, as a single mistake will involve an immediate and very unpleasant death. The words are : *Tebat, Tobati, Tobat, Tobat, Tobati, Tohidak, Tebat, Tobati, Tomazat; Tebat* and *Tobat* might equally well be read as *Tebata* and *Tobata*. These words may be mere abracadabra, or perhaps a perversion of some religious formula in Arabic. As Skeat suggests, *Tobati* might be *Taubat-i* (" my repentance ") and *Tohidak* possibly *Tauhid-ak* (" thy faith "). If *Tebat* stands for *Tobat*, the latter word (for " repentance ") would have occurred seven times. They are certainly not Malay words, and are either corrupt Arabic or just the gibberish every charm-book proffers.

Among methods given for divination, one is to be used by chiefs before going into battle to foretell victory or disaster : " Take wax, and weigh it into equal portions ; take threads of different colours and make them into two wicks, of seven or nine threads, but each alike, and make two candles. Hold them over the smoke of burning benzoin and read the following words over them, *ak saton rangka jak*. Raise them above the head, and call upon Allah, the Arch-

angels, and the Sheikhs, to declare the future. Name
one candle for oneself, and one for the enemy ; stand
them on the edge of a white cup and light them. The
candle of the destined winner will burn brightly and
outlast the other." Apart from the consultation of
crude books on necromancy, Marsden gives another
mode of divining used by the Bataks of Sumatra
(1811) : " Before going to war they kill a buffalo or
a fowl that is perfectly white, and by observing the
motion of the intestines, judge of the good or ill fortune
likely to attend them ; and the priest who performs
this ceremony had need be infallible, for if he predicts
contrary to the event, it is said that he is sometimes
punished with death for his want of skill."

A simpler method obtained in Perak : " Take a deep
breath, and expel the breath through the nostrils. If
the current by the right nostril is the stronger, success
is certain." This Perak device is parallel to a method
of divination which forms the most interesting part
of Nik Ismail's book. It, again, is attributable to
the crude pantheism common among the Malays of
the Archipelago, especially in the sixteenth century.
Briefly the idea is this : Certain celestial powers dwell
in every human body, viz., Muhammad the Prophet,
with his favourite daughter Fatimah and his son-in-law
Ali, his followers Abubakar, Omar and Osman, and the
four Archangels Gabriel, Michael, Azrael and Azrafil
(see p. 89). Each has his or her seat in the body
and egress to the outer world through the nostrils. To
call up one or other of them the soothsayer draws in
breath through his nose and expels it in the same way ;
the answer comes as the breath leaves his nostrils. It
is, of course, quite easy to feel whether the main current
of air follows one nostril or the other ; but it requires an
expert to say whether it clings to the outer or inner side
of the nostril. After the soothsayer has learnt the

exact location of the issuing spirit, he has further to distinguish the manner of its going—for example, whether it goes out "like a needle" or "like a string of beads." It follows, naturally, that only a few people can be endowed with such power!

The manuscript then goes on to explain the portent of certain signs given by the answering spirit. At first sight the information to be obtained seems quite innocent; but much might be turned to bad ends. If your friend is out fishing, and you want to know before he returns what luck he has had, you can find out not only what he has caught, but in what part of the fish's mouth the hook took hold. You can find out also whether he is asleep or awake, and what part of the house he is in. It is possible to find out also how long it would be before the owner will awake or somebody will pass by. Another instance of this kind of divination given in the book shows whether your neighbour's wife is to bear a boy or a girl. A certain answer means that the baby will be a girl, but endowed with conspicuously masculine qualities; the terse phraseology of the manuscript is: *jika orang běranak ka-pada Abubakar, anak-nya pěrěmpuan tětapi nasir - nya laki-laki juga* ("if the woman bears a child to Abubakar, it is a girl, but for all that with the character of a boy"). Such an amazon daughter was evidently at one time greatly desired. Acquaintance with these charms seems to be confined nowadays to a very few. Some Kelantan Muhammadans look upon the knowledge of them as good or bad, according to the use to which they are put, and say that if the charms were used for bad ends the celestial powers would change their modes of egress and so lead an evil-doer astray. The strictly orthodox condemn them all.

Much that is written in this old Kelantan tract is

unfit for reproduction owing to its grossness, especially where the teacher is dealing with protective procedures and those relative to the maintenance of chastity. Two formulas are given for " shielding a woman's chastity " ; especially in the second, the reader will think of the modern treatment by " suggestion."

(1) " Recite these words : *man ya rasu sa ; lam ya rasu sa ; bia rasu sa ; man ya rasu sa ; lam ya rasu sa,* thirty times ; then breathe over her from head to foot and wish." These words should be repeated on three consecutive nights. Regrettably, however, it appears that this invocation is not irrevocable, for it may be undone thus : " Take a cup of cold water and recite over it certain passages from the Koran, thirty times, and then give it to her to drink."

(2) " Recite the following over her thrice when she slumbers :—

> *Kum fikum !* when you sit talk of me only,
> *Kum fikum !* when you sleep, let me only be the breath of your life,
> Else shall your body be as a pillar of the firmament.
> These words of mine are the words of the True God.

Now slap her so as to awaken her ; then question her."

Mr. W. W. Skeat tells me that the Arabic words contained in the first formula are corrupt beyond all possibility of recognition. He says that, although the manuscript is evidently based on Arabic, the charms, so far as they can be made out, are so corrupt that one wonders if they were copied by a Malay enthusiast who did not really know Arabic grammar (as the mistakes are in some cases quite childish) or the real meaning of what he heard.

The wiles of a would-be evil-doer may be nonplussed by the following spell which is to " prevent people doing mischief to us," but which is too crude for repetition in a literal translation.　Draw the figure of a man on the ground with the toe.　Vilify it both at mouth and on breast.　Both feet should be placed on the figure's shoulders.　Having done this, stand up and announce in detail how you have besmirched the figure.　This is to be done every day for seven days.　A diagram of the figure interposed here is taken from Nik Ismail's book; the red lines seem to indicate the legs and feet.　The features are curious and perhaps partly masked.　Draw again the same figure with the toe in the middle of a road; turn on your heel on the figure's navel, and announce that you are twisting the man's heart.　Next take a stick and stab the figure through the heart, and then beat it with the stick.　This must be done three times a day.　When stabbing and beating the figure the following words are to be repeated : —

Ittaku pattaku pachi ak asal měnanti.

This jargon is a jumble of Malay and corrupt Arabic. The practical value of the spell is not very clear.　No indication of any personal enemy seems to be given against whom it is directed, and no particular location for the drawing of the figure, such as near the enemy's house, etc., is mentioned.

Earlier in the book a charm is given for waking heavy sleepers.　It is the " Charm for Waking," and is intended as a protection against burglars.

Heigh!　O Scribes of Solomon!　I must sleep; do you watch; if any one, good or bad, comes here, do not hide or seek cover, but call me with all speed.—" There is but one God and Muhammad is His Prophet ! "

Repeat it to your pillow three times, slap your pillow three times, breathe over it three times, and go to sleep.

King Solomon, " the master of all wisdom and of all demons," had power over the spirits and the animal

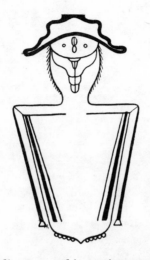

A diagram used in casting a spell.

kingdom ; his name is intimately bound up with the
lore of the magician in Semitic and Muslim literature.
Another charm, " The Fortress of the Unity of God,"
from the old book is translated and explained by Winstedt (Ref. 4, p. 177). In Perak the usual form of
divination is by means of cards. This kind of fortune-
telling, which is much older than Sufism, is easier
to learn, and no doubt has also been introduced from
outside Malaya.

Sometimes for the purpose of making a diagnosis the
Malay wizard (*pawang* or *bomor*) resorts to divination by
means of omens taken from the position of coins thrown
into a water jar, and from toasted rice floating upon the
water's surface. Another method of " water-gazing "
is by looking into a cup containing saliva produced by
chewing betel (Skeat's " Malay Magic " : Medical
Rites). On other occasions this form of divination is
practised by means of omens taken from the smoke of
the burning censer. These methods are elaborate in
technique ; they are fully described by Skeat. Swettenham gives methods of divination for the discovery
of thieves (" Malay Sketches "). Skeat and Blagden
narrate many examples of divination, exorcism, and
spells used by the primitive people of the Malay
Peninsula (" Pagan Races.") Skeat gives the inter-
pretation of several magic squares (" Malay Magic ").
A few " mystic squares " occur in the old book now
under review. One of them consists of sixty-four
squares, like a single chess-board, with writing in each
square. The bearer of it is protected against spear,
kris and bullet, and all kinds of sickness. If placed
at the bow of a boat, it ensures the boat against sink-
ing. If dipped in water, which is then given to a
woman to drink, it ensures her chastity. This charm
must be written when certain stars (*bintang akrab*, the
zodiacal sign of Scorpio) are not visible ; the ink must

be made with rose-water, saffron, and musk, and when it is being written certain words, *lakad ja akom*, must be repeated seven times in the morning and seven times in the evening.

The constellation of the Scorpion is known to be inauspicious.   Dr. Parkins, the author of " The English Physician " (1814), includes two plants under the sign of Scorpio in his astrological and pharmaceutical discourse on various herbs not included in Culpepper's " British Herbal."   Both are used in the treatment of diseases of women.   One is the " Stinking Arrach " of dunghills, and the other " Garden or Sweet Bazil."   Concerning the latter, the author says : " Being applied to the place bitten by venomous beasts, or stung by a wasp or hornet, it speedily draws the poison to it. *Every like draws its like.* Mizaldus affirms, that being laid to rot in horse-dung, it will breed venomous beasts.   Hilarius, a French physician, affirms upon his own knowledge, that an acquaintance of his, by common smelling to it, had a scorpion breed in his brain.   Something is the matter, this herb and rue will never grow together, no, nor near one another ; and we know rue is as great an enemy to poison as any that grows.   To conclude ; it expelleth both birth and after-birth ; and as it helps the deficiency of Venus in one kind, so it spoils all her actions in another.   I dare write no more of it."

In the " mystic square " are the Arabic names of the constellations, which Mr. Worthington surmises were written on each square of the original diagram in the order of the knight's move.   The diagram is not coloured as in some magic squares, because in Malay chess the queen always stands on the right of the king, so in this case no colours are required ; but as there are eight possible starting points for the knight's first move, and at least two ways round the board for each, it is essential to know the key. The great variety of ways in which the knight's tour may be accomplished and the harmonious order of its march is described in Falkener's " Games Ancient and Oriental " (1892). There is another diagram in the old book of sixty-four squares with one square blank, one of 256 squares, and one of forty-nine squares with weird figures for each day of the week. A series of scribe's errors would naturally render these inscriptions unrecognisable and tend to distort them into " mystic " figures for the benefit of magicians and impostors who adopted the squares as charms to suit their own purposes.

A chart drawn in the form of a compass, used by the Kelantan soothsayer (*nujum*) at bull-fights is described by C. C. Brown : " if, for instance, the fight is on a Saturday, the bull should face north and should then take so many steps eastward, until he is facing north-east, the correct station (*dukok ka-ulu adap serong ka-mata-hari naik, baharu bĕtul*), and so on." The Kelantan gang-robber also consults the soothsayer's chart before embarking on a venture (Ref. 2).

REFERENCES

(1) BEGBIE, Captain P. T. " The Malayan Peninsula." 1834. Madras : The Vepery Mission Press.
(2) BROWN, C. C. " Kelantan Bull-fighting." *Jour. Malay. Br. Roy. Asiat. Soc.* (Singapore). 1928. Vol. VI, Part I, p. 74.
(3) WINSTEDT, Dr. R. O. " Some Malay Mystics, Heretical and Orthodox." *Jour. Malay. Br. Roy. Asiat. Soc.* (Singapore). 1923. Vol. I, p. 312.
(4) WINSTEDT, Dr. R. O. " Shaman, Saiva and Sufi." 1925. London : Constable.

PART II

CHAPTER VI

POISONS OBTAINED BY MALAYS FROM FISH

CAT-FISH

The Ikan Kĕli.—Curious scaleless fish known as cat-fish are very commonly found groping their way about in the mud of *padi* swamps throughout the Malay Peninsula. Maxwell says : " Members of the family may be found in swamps, pools and roadside drains and many of the fresh water varieties will make considerable journeys overland to find new pools or streams. They are found in all our rivers and most species may be caught miles out at sea " (Ref. 9). Many of the cat-fish (Saccobranchus) have a breathing sac by means of which they can remain alive apart from water for a certain length of time ; some, such as the Bagarius yarrelli of Java, may exceed 6 feet in length, and are among the ugliest fishes in existence.

The *ikan kĕli* (Clarias magur, Dunker and Rowell ; C. batrachus, Max Weber and de Beaufort—Siluridæ) is a source of poison among Kelantan Malays : the gall and the slime from its skin are said to be combined with datura, opium, and Indian hemp for internal administration. This particular fish, reputed to be the least poisonous of the Malay Siluridæ, has an evil reputation like the peacock, as it is held to be unclean, and some Malays will not eat it. It is, however, quite commonly cooked and used as food throughout Kelantan. Young ones are kept for years in glass bottles as pets by Chinese.

Poisoned wounds may be caused by the slender
pectoral spines of this fish ; whether the poison is
inoculated from the mucus or slime covering the body,
or, as in the case of the spiny dog-fish, derived from a
definite poison gland at the base of the spines, has not
yet been determined. It is believed in Kelantan that
if the brain of the *ikan kĕli* be removed and rubbed into
the wound made by the spine, the poison will be
neutralised and the wound will heal. Fishermen in
Malayan waters say that this unpleasant-looking fish
mews like a cat when it is hooked ; but the popular
name is really given to it in allusion to the long barbels
or feelers about the mouth, which have been compared
to the whiskers of a cat. The " miaw " may be caused
in sac-gilled cat-fish by expulsion of air from the
breathing sac when the fish is in peril.

The Ikan Sĕmbilang.—In addition to the *ikan kĕli*
there is a far more dangerous cat-fish, called the *ikan
sĕmbilang* by Malays (*ikan* means a fish). It is Paraplotosus albilabris (Cuv. and Val.—Siluridæ), and
is the most dangerous of this genus in Malayan waters.
The *ikan sĕmbilang* is much dreaded by Malay fishermen, because it can inflict very serious envenomed
wounds with the serrated spines of both its dorsal and
pectoral fins. These enlarged bony rays are provided
with definite poison glands. Other even more poisonous species, the *sĕmbilang karang* (Plotosus lineatus,
Bleeker ; P. anguillaris, Bloch) and *ikan kĕlara* or
gemang (P. canias), occur in the estuaries and sea of the
Malay Peninsula and Archipelago. Wounds made by
live fish of all the genus are equally dreaded, but
all are valuable as food and widely consumed. The
poisonous secretion is pressed mechanically into the
wound by contact with the spine. Van Leent cites the
case of two Dutch sailors in which lock-jaw followed
pricks on the foot from the *ikan sĕmbilang*. Coutiere

quotes another in which a prick from P. anguillaris on the finger caused pain like the sting of a hornet, lasting for two hours (Ref. 11).

Paraplotosus albilabris is described by Cantor ; it is about 6½ inches in length, dangerous in a similar way to the Synanceia.   It is common in the sea and estuaries of Penang : the dorsal spine is half the length of the head, and only a little shorter than the first ray ; the pectoral spines are more slender and slightly exceed half the length of the head.   This fish cannot eject its venom until the barbed spine is broken, because the poison apparatus of the fins is entirely closed.   When the fin is erected the skin is stretched and the spine bursts through.   In this respect it is similar to the *ikan Shaitan*, or the Satan fish of Java, and differs from many of those spiny dog-fish (Ancanthopterygii) in which the poison apparatus communicates with the exterior.   A toxin has been located by Kabeshima in small cystic distensions of glands at the base of the spines in Plotosus anguillaris ; he found two active principles—a " spasmin " and a " hæmolysin " ; the toxin is destroyed by exposure to boiling and X-rays, and by gastric and pancreatic digestion.   The *ikan sĕmbilang* does not appear to be administered as a poison in Kelantan, but, curiously enough, it is used as a cure for baldness induced criminally (see section TORTOISES AND SNAKES).

CARP

A small fresh-water fish, the *ikan siya*, belonging to the carp tribe (Cyprinidæ), genus Puntius, is used as a poison by Kelantan Malays.   It is said to be administered internally in combination with the galls of globefish (*ikan buntal ;* Tetrodon sp.), and common toad (*katak puru ;* Bufo melanostictus, Cantor—Bufonidæ) and the fresh sap of the upas tree (*pokok ipoh ;* Antiaris toxicaria, Bl.—Urticaceæ).   The gall of the fish is dried by toasting over a fire, then powdered, and mixed with the upas sap. This poison is given in the form of a powder which is concealed in food and is said to cause death. To act as a poison the sap of Antiaris toxicaria must be fresh. The gall of the *ikan siya*, if mixed with the juice of *rotan tawar* (a rattan or climbing palm, unidentified) and taken internally, is said to cause unconsciousness. The *ikan siya* is a pretty little silvery fish found in clear jungle streams at the foot of hills, where it hides amongst the rocks and stones ; it is so elusive that it can only be netted with difficulty. It is about 4½ inches in length when full grown ; the dorsal fin contains a sharp bony spine, which is said by natives to cause poisonous wounds. Though used for food, pregnant women do not eat it in Kelantan, because it is said to bring on uterine hæmorrhage. The family of Cyprinidæ is represented by over a hundred existing genera, arranged under two sub-families, and of these Maxwell refers to more than a hundred species in Malayan rivers (Ref. 9).

GLOBE-FISH

Among the Malayan species of the genus Tetrodon are the smooth " banana-like " globe-fish (*ikan buntal pisang;* T. lunaris), the " stone-like " globe-fish (*ikan buntal batu;* T. fluviatilis and T. oblongus), the rough " thorn-like " globe-fish (*ikan buntal duri;* T. reticularis), and the " porcupine " globe-fish (*ikan buntal landak;* Doidon hystrix). The poisonous properties of the globe or parrot fishes are well known in different parts of the world. The genus contain sixteen species, of which about half are known to be poisonous. The danger of being poisoned by eating globe-fish depends a good deal on season, and on the age and sexual development of the fish. Although the degree of virulence varies very much in different species, it is always most

pronounced when the adult fish is spawning. While
most of the poison occurs in the big roe, other parts
of the fish are known to be harmful. Most of the tetrodon have a peculiarly offensive smell and flavour.
When prepared for food by Chinese, the head is cut off
at once and the entrails entirely removed, but with the
exception of *ikan buntal pisang* (T. lunaris), which
is eaten by Malay fishermen, the other species are
seldom eaten except by the very poor. Greshoff
records the use of T. oblongus as a poison in Java :
the gall is roasted and mixed in food and this causes
" stiffness of the tongue and mouth and hardening
of the abdomen." Referring to T. immaculatus,
var., virgata, Bl., Sch., he says, " the gall when eaten
is narcotic, and causes vomiting and speedy death "
(Indian Poison Reports. The Royal Colonial Institute, Amsterdam). In Kelantan the gall of the local
species (T. fluviatilis and T. oblongus) is used as a
poison. It is generally combined with the decayed
fruit of *rengut* (see p. 185), and other reputed gastro-
intestinal irritants, such as pounded glass ; but, as
seen under section " CARP," it may be used with upas
sap.

In addition to its poisonous properties when taken
by the mouth, the globe-fish frequently attacks
bathers and others who have occasion to enter the
water. It bites by means of a sharp-edged beak,
or cutting-plate, formed by the union of the teeth in
each jaw, and inflicts wounds, generally on the genital
organs of the male, that are similar to, and may be as
serious as, those caused by the saw-edged belly of
the *Piraya* or *Caribe* of the Guianas and South America ;
but at evening time bathers in the Kelantan River
have been known to be bitten on fingers, toes and
thighs. How the more serious effects of the bite
arise, whether from the anatomical position of the

wound, from the presence of poisonous mucus in the mouth of the fish, or by the liberation of venom, is not yet known. Severe constitutional as well as local symptoms occurred in the case of a Turk who was bitten on the genital organs by one of these " puffer-fish " in the Kelantan River in 1910. He was the captain of a Government oil launch and was bathing late in the evening. The fish bite was a very nasty one ; a piece about the size and shape of a sixpence was bitten clean out of the scrotum, the parts became much swollen, and the wound soon sloughed. He was in hospital for many days before he could walk about, but eventually made a good recovery, except for a depressed scar. In June, 1920, Enche' Ahmad, a Kelantan forester, was bitten on the glans while bathing in the evening ; a small piece was bitten clean out, causing profuse hæmorrhage, which could only be controlled by pressure. He, on the other hand, made a rapid recovery, and was discharged from hospital in a week's time.

Specimens of scaleless, but rough-skinned globe-fish caught in the Kelantan River and sent from Kota Bharu to the British Natural History Museum were identified by Professor G. A. Boulenger as Tetrodon fluviatilis and T. oblongus. T. oblongus is closely allied to T. scleratus which is found in the Indian Ocean and the greater part of the Pacific. The *ikan buntal* is a shallow-water fish and easily caught ; when one is captured, or alarmed or touched, it inflates a portion of its œsophagus by swallowing air or water until it resembles a toy balloon. This manœuvre renders the Tetrodon proof against attack ; most species have rough skins provided with numerous erectile spines of various sizes, hence the popular names " sea-hedgehog " and " sea-porcupine." The sharp teeth, by means of which the animal can even

eat its way out of the belly of a shark, are also designed
for the purpose of defence. When inflated with air
this grotesque fish sometimes floats passively, upside
down, with the currents. On returning to its normal
condition it expels the air from its œsophagus through
its mouth and gills with a report as if it had burst.
Another time it may eject a stream of water from
its mouth with a sound which has been described by
McNair as " something between a grunt and the hoot
of an owl."

In certain parts of the Malay Peninsula, the smooth-
skinned *ikan buntal pisang* (T. lunaris) is said to be
used by native children as a football ; it is easily
caught in its inverted position (Ref. 1).

Globe-fish may be readily avoided, as they are said
not to attack objects in motion. Scheube says in
regard to T. fluviatilis (Indo-China) that the poison
teeth on the palate are much the same as those of the
conger-eel (Muræna helena, Linn.) and Stomias boa,
Risso, a dangerous fish found in the Mediterranean
Sea. As a local anodyne, the *bomor* uses the young
leaves of the " black " variety of the datura plant
for the treatment of *ikan buntal* bite ; these are rolled
with chalk or lime in the palms of the hands until
the lime has taken up the juice. The mass is then
applied to the wound.

Poisoning by tetrodon (*fuga* or *fougou* in Japan ;
tinga-tinga or *botete* in the Philippines) is common in
Japan, where there are five poisonous species. According to Scheube (Japan) and Seale (Philippines) symptoms of poisoning begin in three to fifteen minutes after
eating, causing unpleasant dizziness and nausea, pains
in the abdomen, burning in the throat, and severe
headache. If the victim yields to his inclination and
lies down and sleeps, he is soon roused by vomiting,
followed by fainting, collapse and death. The mor-

tality is said to be above 68 per cent., but the symptoms may vary in severity in those who have partaken of the same fish. Death may occur within twenty-four hours. In Japan the globe-fish is said to be used for suicidal purposes. Cases of poisoning and deaths from eating globe-fish have been reported from the West Coast of Africa, the Cape, Japan, Australia, California, the Antilles and Brazil. In some places (Batavia) the sale is prohibited (Ref. 11).

According to Tabara, the poisons of the ovaries and testes are " tetrodonin," a crystalline base, and " tetrodonic acid," a white waxy body, which is the more poisonous of the two principles. These poisons have been studied by several other Japanese investigators and have been extracted recently from the eggs by Ishihara. In its pure precipitated form (" tetrodonin ") the active principle is described by him as a white powder, neutral in reaction, tasteless, soluble in water, very resistant to mineral acids, and readily reducing solutions of copper. The poison of the globe-fish withstands boiling for four hours, but gives way after six to nine hours ; ordinary cooking does not make the fish safe for eating. The physiological effect of injecting the poisonous principles has been described as causing " a fall of blood pressure and slowing of the circulation with cardiac tremor, fibrillation, and finally block. The oculo-motor and sympathetic post-ganglion fibres of the eye are both involved, but the endings remain intact. Death is due to direct action on the respiratory centre and not from interference with the phrenic nerve " (Ref. 2).

STING-RAYS

Certain dangerous fishes called *ikan pari* are used by Kelantan criminals as a poison ; in Malay, *ikan*, a fish, further defined by *pari*, is used collectively for the sting-rays or skates (Trigonidæ), eagle-rays (Mylio-batidæ), and electric-rays (Torpedininæ), which are found at the mouths of Malay rivers and about the sea-coast. The sting of the ray is used as a poison; it is found in most but not in all the species, and is a remarkably venomous weapon of defence in the shape of a large, sharp-pointed, spine, or spines, representing the dorsal fin, and placed near the base of the tail, which, as in nearly all the members of this family is long and whip-like. The common rough-skinned ray of the Red Sea and Indian Ocean (Urogymnus asper-rimus), which may measure as much as 5 feet from head to root of tail, is common about the coast of Kelantan, and is known to Malays as *pari dĕdap*. In this ray the long tail is devoid of either dorsal fin or spine; the flexible tail, about 2½ to 3 feet long, is dotted about with very small sharp, barbed spines. The roughness on the back is due to osseous tubercles between which sharp, conical, dermal teeth are liberally scattered. The tails of *pari dĕdap* are used by Kelan-tan carpenters for files and the skin for sandpaper. Lacerated wounds may be caused by the stroke of the tail, but they are not so serious as those caused by the thrust of the spine. When the spined ray attacks it strikes its tail around some part of the victim and forces the spine into the flesh, causing a deep and jagged wound. On the sea-coast of Kelantan the tail of a sting-ray is not infrequently carried as a switch. In January, 1921, a Malay constable was punished by the court for slashing a leading merchant at the sea-port of Tumpat across the face and neck with one of these switches. The injuries, which consisted of bruised abrasions on the face, neck and forearm, were not of a serious surgical nature.

The far more serious wound caused by the spine has been described as follows : " A Chinaman, aged twenty

years, was attacked, the wound being in the thigh.
When rescued he fainted, and on regaining conscious-
ness had complete numbness and paralysis of the limb
affected. The wound remaining unhealed, he was
brought to hospital a fortnight later, and on admission
he had a peculiar stiff look and unusual glassiness of the
eyeball, extreme weakness bordering on collapse, pallor,
feeble heart, but ravenous appetite. The injured leg
was not swollen, but sensibility was lost. There was a
jagged, irregular, sloughing wound 2½ inches (6 cm.)
deep with a copious, very sickening, fœtid, thin, dark-
grey discharge. With treatment the sloughs gradually
came away, though small subcutaneous abscesses
developed and large parts of the muscles came away,
exposing the bone. Finally granulation occurred,
though meanwhile the same fœtid pus collected in the
knee-joint " (Ref. 2).

The spine of the sting-ray (*sĕngat pari*) is given by
Malay poisoners by the mouth : it is burnt, reduced to
powder, and then mixed with needle crystals (raphides)
of the *rengut* fruit (Epipremnum giganteum, Schott—
Araceæ). In the mode of use of the spine thus prepared, the action can only be magical, and may be
compared to its use as a charm by the ancient Greeks ;
they attached one to the navel of a pregnant woman,
which caused easy labour if the spine was taken from
a living fish which was then thrown back into the sea ;
the spine also when powdered with hellebore was
applied to the teeth to cause painless dentiton. Superstitious Malays believe in the existence of a leviathan
ray which dwells under a gigantic sea-mushroom
(*chĕndawan*). The spines are sometimes known as
sondak pari ; but in Selangor, Kelantan, and on the
east coast generally, they are called *sĕngat pari*.
The former name is probably connected with the west
coast *sondak*, used to designate the spikes or spears of

jungle grasses (Skeat). They resemble a lance-shaped
dart in general appearance, varying in length with the
development of the fish ; the larger ones may be as
long as 8 or 9 inches (about 20 to 22 cm.), being
replaced annually by new ones growing from behind
as the old ones wear out. Consequently an individual
ray may possess two, or more rarely, three or even
four stings, lying side by side, if the old spines have
not fallen off. The sting or spine is attached to the tail
by strong ligaments and some muscles which allow
a slight lateral movement. The existence of a poison
gland in connexion with the serrated spine on the tail
of the sting-ray has been a matter of dispute from the
days of Aristotle down to the present century.

A perfect spine given me by a Kelantan fisherman
measures 7 inches (17.78 cm.) in length ; it is a sharply
pointed, rather narrow, straight piece of bone, serrated
from above downwards on each edge. The sharp
cutting teeth or serrations average up to about $\frac{1}{5}$ inch
(5.10 mm.) as a maximum ; they slant backwards,
and are recurved, gradually getting smaller and indefin-
able as they approach the base of the spine. The under
surface presents two well-defined grooves, one on either
side of the ridge of bone which runs along the spine,
separates the two serrated margins, and becomes
flattened out at the base ; the dorsal surface is smooth
and rounded. The spine lies with its under grooved
surface opposite the dorsal surface of the tail. The
fact that poison glands, protected by a sheath, are
situated at the base of the spine and fill the grooves, and
that the emission of the poison takes place in a very
simple manner, was proved by Porta in 1905 (Ref. 12).
As the spine is thrust into the flesh the sheath is forced
towards the base, compresses the gland, and evacuates
the poison along the grooves into the wound. The
flesh of the sting-ray is not poisonous when cooked for

food ; but the tail, with the attached spine, is invariably removed before exposure for sale in the markets.

There are several species of sting-rays with Malay names. Maxwell has identified *pari kĕlawar*, the " bat " ray, as Trygon uarnak, Forsk. ; *pari bĕndera* or *p. daun*, the " flag " or " leaf " ray, as T. sephen, Forsk. ; *pari lalat*, the " fly " ray, as T. walga ; *pari rimau*, the " tiger " ray, as T. Kuhlii, and *pari dĕdap*, Urogymnus asperrimus, Bl., Schn. The " bishop " ray, Ætobatis narinari, Euphr. (*pari lang*, the " eagle " ray), one of the six species of the Myliobatidæ recognised in Malayan waters, is known to cause severe symptoms of poisoning. Violent pain and faintness precede rapid local swelling about the puncture, which quickly becomes the seat of violent inflammation, and perhaps gangrene. Crevaux has shown that the spines are channelled in South American species and connected with poison reservoirs (Ref. 11). The poison glands of T. pastinaca, a sting-ray which ranges from the south of England westwards to America and eastwards to Japan, have been studied by Muir Evans (Ref. 5). He found that complete sections of the spine showed that " the grooves are occupied in their deepest portion by alveolar connective tissue provided with blood vessels and lymph channels, and separated from the more superficial mass of special epithelial tissue by a pigmented capillary meshwork. This epithelial tissue contains columns of cells in an active state, the secretion of which is discharged towards the lateral dentate margin " (*Brit. Med. Journ.*, October 29th, 1921). That the gland is really a poison organ is further confirmed by the interesting observations of Dr. Lo Bianco, who saw a young man faint after a mere prick by a trygon which he was handling. He also showed that other animals succumb, for in a tank in the Zoological Station at Naples a Trygon violacea attacked a loggerhead turtle. The trygon died, with its sting broken off ; shortly after, the turtle ceased to feed and died on the fifth day, when the spine of the trygon was found still embedded in its muscles, surrounded by septic matter (Refs. 5 and 12). Madame Marie Phisalix describes the results of wounds by Trygon garappa, a species common in Guiana, usually known in the upper reaches of the River Essequibo as T. hystrix (Ref. 11). Schomburg compares the symptoms to those caused by snake-bite and records a fatal case from Demerara (Ref. 5). Dr. Muir Evans says : " I am inclined to think the venom is more of the cobra type than Weever venom (viperine) " (privately communicated).

At Chĕrang Jelor, in northern Kelantan, some Malays with devilish ingenuity fastened a couple of spines to a pole and maliciously stabbed a horse, causing two small flesh wounds. The severity of the pain maddened the animal, which was thought likely to die. The wounds were enlarged and treated with 2 per cent. iodine solution. The Malay stable-boy remarked that the recovery of the horse would not have ensued if the spines had remained in the wounds. Should a portion of a spine get broken off in a wound, it may travel about the tissues by help of the small barbed serrations and contraction of surrounding muscles, until perhaps it eventually causes death. Dr. Rankin bacteriologist to the King Chulalongkorn Hospital at Bangkok, showed me a specimen which had been accidentally swallowed by a Siamese girl and had been removed subsequently from an abscess at the back of her neck. The sting-ray had been boiled with part of the spine left in it. Campbell Highett records a similar case which also occurred in Bangkok. In Kelantan a Siamese once stabbed a Malay in the back with one of these spines which broke off in the flesh; the fragment was successfully removed by Dr. L. H. Taylor at the State Hospital in 1914. The serious nature of these wounds was well known to the ancients. Muir Evans, quoting from Pliny on " Aranæus," says : " But there is nothing more terrible than the sting that arms the tail of Trygon, called Pastinaca by the Latins, which is 5 inches long. When driven into the root of a tree it causes it to wither. It can pierce armour like an arrow, it is strong as iron, yet possesses venomous properties " (Ref. 5). They are mentioned in Lucian :—

> The King of Ithaca, Laertes son,
> I mean Ulysses, 'twas my self that killed,
> And not Telemachus with scate-fish bone.   (Ref. 10.)

The " poisonous trygon's bone " is also referred to in West's " Triumph of the Gout " (Lucian). The present day use of trygon venom by the Bĕnua tribe of pagans in Johore as an arrow or dart poison is referred to under section THE UPAS TREE, p. 191.

REFERENCES

(1) BOULENGER, E. G. " Queer Fish." 1925. London : Partridge.

(2) BYAM and ARCHIBALD (Editors). " The Practice of Medicine in the Tropics by many Authorities." 1921. Vol. I. London : Oxford Medical Publications.

(3) CANTOR, T. " A Catalogue of Malayan Fishes." *Jour. Roy. Asiat. Soc.* (Bengal), p. 265. 1849. Calcutta.

(4) CASTELLANI and CHALMERS. " A Manual of Tropical Medicine." 1919. 3rd ed., pp. 194, 234. London : Baillière, Tindall and Cox.

(5) EVANS, H. MUIR. " The Defensive Spines of Fishes." *Phil. Trans. Roy. Soc.* (London). 1922. Series B, Vol. 212, pp. 1–33.

(6) ISHIHARA, F. " Tokoyo Igakukai Zasshi." *Nitteil. d. Med. Gesellsch. Z.* Tokoyo. December 5th, 1917. Vol. XXXI, No. 23, p. 1. From Review in *Trop. Dis. Bull.* (London), 1920. Vol. XVI, No. 2, p. 120.

(7) KABESHIMA, I. " Nippon Biseibutsugakki Zasshi." *Jour. Japan Protozool. Soc.* January 1st, 1919. Vol. I, p. 45. From Review in *Trop. Dis. Bull.* (London). 1920. Vol. XVI, No. 2, p. 120.

(8) LYDEKKER, R. " The Royal Natural History." 1923. Vol. V.
London : Warne.

(9) MAXWELL, C. N. "Malayan Fishes." *Jour. Straits Br. Roy.
Asiat. Soc.* (Singapore). 1921. No. 84, p. 179.

(10) PHILIPS, J. " The Works of Lucian." (English publication.
1711.) " Tragopodagra, or Gout-Farce." Vol. III, p. 201.
London.

(11) PHISALIX, M. " Animaux Venimeux et Venins." 1922. T., i.
Paris : Masson.

(12) PORTA, A. " Ricerche anatomiche sull' apparecchio venenifero
di alcuni pesci." *Anatomischer Anzeiger.* 1905. 26, p. 232.
Jena.

(13) SCHEUBE, B. " The Diseases of Warm Countries " (English
translation, 1903), p. 344. London : Bale, Sons and
Danielsson.

(14) SEALE, A. Editorial. *Philippine Jour. Sci.* (Manila, P. I.),
p. 289. 1912.

CHAPTER VII

OTHER POISONS OBTAINED BY MALAYS FROM THE ANIMAL KINGDOM

REPTILES

TORTOISES AND SNAKES

JUST as the ancient Egyptians prepared a poison from a roasted centipede (" Anart-Worm ") cooked in oil, and their modern sisters a kind of turpentine oil, to cause loss of hair when applied to the head of the " hated one " in rivalries and harem intrigues, so also, with a similar object in view, Malays prepare a gummy fluid by stewing a tortoise in water and adding the decoction so made to one obtained by boiling a black cobra down in water. This preparation is to be smeared over the head of the person to be annoyed during his or her sleep. The application is said to cause death if untreated by the *bomor*, who uses a cat-fish (*ikan sĕmbilang*) as an antidote, while the priest-leech of ancient Egypt relied upon tortoise-shell, roasted, powdered, and cooked in oil from a hippopotamus hoof (Ref. 9). The common Kelantan land-tortoise is a shy little animal said to be very afraid of thunder. Malays say that if it " bites " it will not let go until a thunder-storm comes on : it is the small hinged tortoise or terrapin (*kura*, Cyclemys amboinensis, spp.) found in rice fields and swamps, also in ponds and streams.

The action of venom from the hooded snakes on the unbroken skin of man is trivial compared to its action on the conjunctiva. Unlike viperine, it can be

swallowed without causing illness. Futile attempts
at homicide in the East are occasionally made by mixing
the powdered head of a cobra with food (Ref. 14).
Greshoff records that in Java the head of a poisonous
snake (*œler walang;* Bungarus candidus, Linn.) is
roasted so that oil exudes with which the natives
poison their weapons (Indian Poison Reports. The
Royal Colonial Institute, Amsterdam). Out of the
130 snakes domiciled in the Malay Peninsula, Flower
lists thirty-four as poisonous (Ref. 5). It is curious
that only the black cobra mentioned above and a
common emerald green tree-snake (*ular puchok,* Dryophis prasinus, Boie—Dipsadomorphinæ) which by
many Malays is held to be non-poisonous, seem to be
employed by Kelantan poisoners. As a poison the
bile of the green tree-snake is used mixed with that of
a tree-frog (*katak pisang*) and that of the jungle-crow.
This preparation, smeared on the gambier which is
used in betel-chewing, is said to cause the appearance
of blood in the urine.

The slender and graceful whip-snake, Dryophis
prasinus also occurs in the Philippines, where it is
popularly supposed to live among the rice stalks
and is known as *dahun-palay.* In the Philippines its
bite is said by natives to be fatal in from fifteen
minutes to half an hour ; it is even believed that the
leaves wither upon which its breath has fallen. Griffin
says, however, when reporting on the poisonous
snakes of the Philippine Islands : " While undoubtedly
poisonous, this snake is one of those in which the fangs
are at the back end of the maxilla, so far back that the
snake would have to stretch its mouth tremendously
to bite an object the size of a man's leg."

The folklore of Malayan snakes recorded by Skeat
in " Malay Magic " is full of fantastic ideas and curious
myths. Two examples only of strange snakes need be

mentioned here, the *ular bĕlerang*, a fabulous red sea-snake, so venomous that a bite from it on the rudder of a boat will suffice to kill the crew, and *ular chinta-mani*, a fictitious golden-yellow snake, the finding of which betokens success in love (Ref. 15).

AMPHIBIANS

FROGS AND TOADS

The use of bile from the frog *katak pisang* with snake bile, has been mentioned above. Two frogs are known as *katak pisang;* one is the bright green tree-frog (Rana erythræa, Schleg.), the other, Rhacophorus leucomystax, a greyish-brown frog with four darker lines along its back, commonly found on banana trees. The skin is glandular, the glands, especially those on the head behind the eyes, secrete a poisonous fluid which serves as a protection when the animal is molested.

The galls of two kinds of toad—(1) *katak lĕmbu* or *bĕrtandok*, a horned toad-frog (Megalophrys nasuta, Schleg., Pelobatidæ), and (2) *katak puru*, the common Malay toad (Bufo melanostictus, Schleg., Bufonidæ)— are used as poisons. The horned toad-frog is curious because of its almost smooth skin : it is brownish in colour and the upper eyelids and snout are produced into large triangular flaps of skin ; it is generally found in hill-country. Under " Our Toads," Pliny refers to the horned toad-frogs : " The biggest they are of all others, with two knubs bearing out in front like horns, and full of poison they be " (Historia Naturalis. Venice, 1469—Translation. P. Holland, 1635. Tome II, p. 434. London). The bile of *katak lĕmbu*, the horned toad-frog, is used by Malays in combination with decayed *rengut* fruit, the pill-millepede, and the bile of the honey bear, also with the land-bug *kĕsing* (which see).

The common bath-room toad, *katak puru*, is similar in appearance to the common European toad; it is dark yellowish or brownish with a number of black ridges or wrinkles and warty protuberances on its back and about the head. The glands at the back of the head are exceptionally large. A larger jungle species, B. asper, has a very rough warty integument. The bile of this common toad is a favourite excipient with Malay poisoners; the most deadly combination in which it is said to be used is mentioned under section CYANIDE OF POTASSIUM.

Speaking generally, toads are shunned: ducks and snakes will not eat them, although both eat frogs; cats and dogs have learnt by experience to avoid them. Malays say that the "bite" of the common toad is poisonous and is deadly. The jungle folk of the Malay Peninsula recognise them as poisonous, as is seen from the following line of the "Toad Song" of the Besini tribe (Ref. 13) :—

> *Krat rengkong fĕtah bul-dah*
> And the body of tue toad exudes poison
> (has slime that is poisonous).

The toad has, in common with most batrachians, two distinct sets of cutaneous glands—(a) mucous, and (b) granular; both have definite poisonous properties (Refs. 2 and 12). The granular glands or protuberances found by the head of the animal are highly developed, and are known as the "parotid" glands of the toad. These glands secrete a creamy, yellowish-white, acid venom. When excited, all toads exude this irritating milk-like fluid from their cutaneous glands; it is called by Malays *susu katak puru*, or the "milk of the puru toad," and is obtained for evil purposes by slicing the "parotid" glands with a knife. The exudation soon becomes sticky, and is said to be used as an external irritant in combination

with the very irritating saps of the *rĕngas* and *binjai*
trees (both Anacardiaceæ) and the waxen bloom of the
ash-pumpkin or white-gourd (Benicasa cerifera, Savi—
Cucurbitaceæ). The mixture is put into a bamboo
tube, kept until it decomposes, and then transferred
for storage to a glass bottle.

Decomposition is hastened by the addition of some
water. This preparation is intended for throwing
at the victim or smearing on his sleeping mat, or on
his skin during sleep. It is said to cause an incurable
eruption like a tinea or ringworm in appearance, and
even, in some cases, death.

The active principle of toad poison was first investigated in 1817 by Pelletier in Europe. In 1873, Casali
and Fornara extracted an alkaloid called " phyrine "
which acted on the heart like digitalis. In 1902,
Faust discovered two poisons, an acid " bufotalin,"
which was the more poisonous of the two, and
" bufonin," a neutral body which was not so active.
Further research by Phisalix and Bertrand shows
that the poison of the toad owes its activity to two
substances, " bufotalin," a resinoid body, and " bufotenin " ; the former is soluble in alcohol, but only
slightly soluble in water, the latter is highly soluble
in both alcohol and water. When injected hypodermically into a frog, " bufotalin " stopped the heart
in systole, while " bufotenin " brought about paralysis
(Ref. 12). Besides being a cardiac poison, this toad
venom was found to act on the respiratory and nervous
systems, causing paralysis, vomiting, and contraction
of the pupil. It is an irritant to the skin and mucous
membrane, and especially to the conjunctival membrane of man. Weiland and Weil (1913) also extracted
" bufotalin " from the skin of toads with alcohol
in the form of colourless crystals. The yield of crude
" bufotalin " before crystallisation averaged 20

grammes from 2,000 toads. Later research by Weiland and Alles (1922) shows that " bufotoxin," a nitrogenous substance, is the primary poison ; it was isolated from the fresh secretion of the " parotid " glands by squeezing them with blunt forceps. The nearly white milky juice procured in this way from 380 toads when dried in a vacuum desiccator gave 4 grammes of a vitreous mass. Weiland and Alles consider that " bufotalin " and " bufotoxin " are allied to bile acids. Minute quantities may be detected by means of a cholesterol test : treated with acetic anhydride and concentrated sulphuric acid successively, " bufotoxin " gives a temporary cherry-red colour which changes to blue and finally becomes a beautiful green. A full description of the chemical properties of these two toad poisons is given by Autenrieth (Ref. 2).

As regards physiological action, the conclusions are that both " bufotoxin " and " bufotalin " exhibit pronounced digitalis action in bringing the frog's heart to systolic stasis ; they also have strong hæmolytic action, and in this respect the two toad poisons behave like saponins (Ref. 2).

The flesh of the toad, so far from being poisonous, is said to afford, in Europe, as wholesome nutriment as that of the frog. In England it used to be considered diuretic and diaphoretic and had a place in old dispensatories. Natives in the Atrato valley in Colombia heat a small species of frog alive over a fire to obtain the skin secretion as an arrow poison ; sufficient venom is collected from a single frog for poisoning more than fifty arrows. Darts are poisoned by South American Indians in the same way ; it is said that a poisoned spear wound will kill a monkey and even a jaguar.

INSECTS

MOTHS

The moth Aloa sanguinolenta, Fab., furnishes a Malay poison in the fine hairs of its larva, which is a black caterpillar called *ulat bulu darat*, or "hairy caterpillar of the land," as distinct from *ulat bulu laut*, "hairy caterpillar of the sea" (Chloia flava). It seems to be the only one among the many hairy caterpillars of Malaya that is chosen by Kelantan criminals for the irritating effect of its fine hairs. Some *ulat bulu darat* were reared in Kota Bharu and the imago identified by Dr. Hanitsch, Director of Raffles' Museum, Singapore, as mentioned above. The urticating hairs are used for internal administration by poisoners, and are said to be combined with bamboo hairs and the needle crystals of the half-rotted *rengut* fruit. A very cruel example of polypharmacy in which they are said to be used is given under section KĔLADI. Under the microscope the dry hairs of this caterpillar can be recognised as slender, black filaments, bearing short, sharply-pointed, alternate barbs.

Stinging caterpillars are a well-known source of dermatitis ; it was formerly thought that mere contact with the hairs caused the injury to the skin, but the irritant is now known to be chemical rather than mechanical. According to Byam and Archibald, an irritating fluid, secreted by tegumentary glands, is injected through hollow hairs. In England well-known sources of urticaria occur in the "woolly bear" caterpillar of the garden Tiger-Moth and in the very hairy larvæ of the Tussock-Moths. Some years ago a curious irritant rash, mostly among children in a village in Kent, was traced to the black and red caterpillar of the Gold-tailed Moth (Euproctis similis

seu auriflua). Potter has reported from America a
peculiar skin eruption caused by "nettling" hairs
from the larvæ of the Brown-tailed Moth (Euproctis
chrysorrhœa) which appeared on parts exposed to
contact with the cocoons of the caterpillar. A break-
down in the formation of the rouleaux of red-blood
corpuscles was observed (*Jour. Amer. Med. Assoc.,*
October 30th, 1909). A peculiar stomatitis has been
caused by the same caterpillar in France, and Phisalix
refers to the ejection of secretion from glands in the
Brown-tailed Moth which dries as a powder about
the hairs, and states that this powder has an urticating effect on the skin. An extremely acute and severe
urticaria may be caused by contact with the powder
from the body or wings of a poisonous moth found
in Japan ; " in the powder were found peculiar micro-
scopic needle-like bodies, in great numbers, with a
pale violet fluid in the lumen " (Ohno. *Jap. Zeits. f.
Dermatol. und Urol.* July, 1919. Vol. XVII, 599—
Summary in German, p. 26). A case of extreme
severity in which urticaria was complicated with acute
nephritis caused by contact with a hairy caterpillar,
has also been reported from Roumania.

Puppies that had eaten couch-grass contaminated
with hairs from the larvæ of the processionary moth
(Cnethocampa processionea) are known to have suffered
from stomatitis in France, and it is said that chicken
and ducks occasionally suffer from enteritis as a result
of eating hairy caterpillars in large numbers (Ref.
12).

BEETLES

The Beetle Dĕndang.—A small green beetle called
dĕndang, resembling the " Spanish fly " (Cantharis
vesicatoria, Lath.—Coleoptera) is used by Malays
both for medicine and poison. As a poison a single

děndang beetle is dried over a fire until it becomes crisp; it is then powdered, and the whole of it is mixed into any kind of native cake. This dose is too small to cause death, and is probably given with intent merely to cause serious illness. The powdered insect is dirty greyish-brown in appearance, with numberless shining green particles. In Kelantan the *děndang* beetle is generally met with in May and June on a fern called *daun paku hijau* (Gymnogramme calomelanos, Kaulf—Filices); at other times it is rather uncommon. This fern is described botanically in " Malayan Ferns " (Department of Agriculture, Batavia, 1908). The under surface of the fronds is covered with a thick white waxy powder (Ref. 1). The *děndang* beetle is greatly treasured by Kelantan Malays when found, and is killed, dried, and generally kept in a bottle to prevent its decay. Malays say that it drops from heaven during the fifth month of the Muhammadan year; they do not recognise the existence of the larva which inhabits the earth. In Kelantan and Kedah the word *děndang* is used for a crow, and occurs in many Malay proverbs.

The Malayan species is similar to, if not identical with, a species of cantharides found in Assam (C. hirticornis, Haag.). This species is black with a red head; it occurs abundantly in Assam, where it feeds on spinach (Amaranthus) and other vegetables. A red-brown species (Illectica testaceæ, Fab.) is also found in Assam during the rains (Ref. 8). Both kinds, black and red are known to Kelantan Malays. The Kelantan insect measures about ½ inch in length, and is about 1½ grains in weight when dry. It is easily recognised by the shining green colour of the elytra or fore-wings, which cover the black membranous hind-wings and soft part of the body. Most of the cantharides beetles have the power of exuding an oily yellowish liquid from their joints when disturbed ; but the active principle, cantharidin, is produced only in the genital organs of both male and female insects (Ref. 12).

Děndang used by Malays as a Medicine.—The *bomor* uses *děndang* in the treatment of chronic gonorrhœa, and as an emmenagogue, but it does not appear to be used by Malay criminals as an abortifacient. For use as a medicine the insect is divided into seven equal pieces, and a piece is taken every day with a quid of betel. I have known a Kelantan woman recover from amenorrhœa by taking *děndang* in this way. As in other parts of the world, aphrodisiac properties are ascribed to the cantharides beetle, but it is stated that almost fatally poisonous doses must be used to obtain such effect. All the cantharides beetles are powerful irritants to the alimentary tract and genito-urinary organs, causing, in over-doses, a frequent irrepressible desire to pass water, which is done only with pain, straining, and the presence of blood in the urine. They cause blisters and symptoms of a violent irritant. Twenty-four grains of powdered cantharides have caused death within thirty-six hours from peritonitis, with collapse, convulsions and coma. Smaller doses have caused serious effects. Sedgwick reports the case of a girl who became dangerously ill after eating one Spanish fly given in a tart (*Med. Times and Gaz.*, 1864, ii., p. 617).

The active principle, cantharidin, is found permeating the trunk and soft parts of the beetle only ; it is present in the proportion of about ½ per cent. (Lyon and Waddell). It is a powerful vesicant. The characters and tests are given in the British Pharmacopœia of 1914 as follows : " Colourless glistening crystals, inodorous. Very slightly soluble in *water, petroleum spirit,* or *alcohol* (90 per cent.) ; more soluble in

chloroform, in *acetic ether,* and in *acetone;* soluble
also in fixed oils. A 0·1 per cent. solution in a fixed
oil raises blisters when kept in contact with the
skin. Melting point 210° to 212°. Slowly volati-
lises at 100°, more rapidly at higher temperatures.
Soluble in *solutions of sodium hydroxide,* the solution
depositing crystals of Cantharidin when acidified.
Gently warmed with *sulphuric acid* it yields a colourless
solution, from which it is separated unchanged when
freely diluted with *water.*" Cantharidin gives a green
precipitate with copper sulphate, and a red precipitate with cobalt sulphate. It can be recovered from
alkaline fluids by acidulation, shaking out with chloroform, and digesting with a few drops of oil, after
evaporation of the chloroform, then testing for vesica-
tion by contact with the skin. " The green or copper-
coloured particles of the insect may be identified in
the stomach or in vomited matter. For the detection
of cantharidin the materials are shaken with acidified
chloroform and left in contact for twenty-four hours.
The chloroform is then separated by a separating
funnel, filtered, and allowed to evaporate spontaneously
in a watch-glass. The residue is taken up with a little
oil and a small piece of lint moistened with it. This
is placed in contact with the skin, and if retained for
some hours the skin will be found reddened, and on
wiping it with chloroform a blister will be produced "
(Ref. 14). From a medico-legal aspect it is well to
remember, also, that when these beetles undergo
putrefaction the elytra or fore-wings resist the process
of decay for a very long time, and this is specially
the case with the red species, in which the elytra are
more densely chitinised. Hence specks of powdered
dĕndang may be detected on the lining of the stomach
or intestines by the aid of a lens many months after
death has occurred.

LAND-BUGS

The Bug Kĕsing.—A dull-grey coloured land-bug called *kĕsing* (Rhynchota), with long four-jointed antennæ and an unpleasant sickly smell, is said to be used as a poison in the country districts of northern Kelantan. Specimens sent from Kota Bharu were identified by the late Major J. C. Moulton, Director of Raffles' Museum, Singapore, as Acanthocoris scabrator, Fab., belonging to the family Coreidæ. As a native poison *kĕsing* is combined with the gall of the horned toad-frog and two millepedes, *tĕlong*, a small dark-red, unidentified millepede, and the well-known pill-millepede. These are carefully dried and reduced to powder. The mixture is said to cause general emaciation and death.

GRASSHOPPERS

The Grasshopper Pĕsan.—The *pĕsan*, as found in Kelantan, has been allocated by Colonel A. Alcock, Professor of Medical Zoology, University of London, under the genus Gryllacris, of the family Locustidæ. It is a long antenna grasshopper and quite uncommon. In Wilkinson's abridged " Malay-English " dictionary (1919) *pĕsan-pĕsan* is identified as a large venomous spider. In Kelantan *pĕsan* has the eerie reputation of giving premonition of death to the person it may bite. No evidence is at present forthcoming whether it has poisonous properties. The Malay word *pĕsan* signifies order, instruction, command, direction.

MILLEPEDES

In Kelantan the juice obtained by crushing millepedes is a favourite excipient for many of the set poisonous preparations, especially those containing the decayed fruit of *rengut*. The large tropical pill-millepede (*pinang kotai bukit*, or *kosai*, Zephronidæ) is stated to

be often used in this way. It is a red-black millepede of thirteen segments, about 2½ to 3 inches (63 to
76 mm.) long, found on hillsides, in damp places under
flat stones, and addicted to rolling itself up into a complete ball when touched and remaining in this state
for a considerable length of time after the manner of a
wood-louse. In this way it protects itself from attack.
A big black worm-like millepede called *jĕlantor* is
contained in a particularly deadly combination mentioned under section RENGUT. It belongs to the genus
Spirostreptidæ, and is one of the largest known millepedes, reaching a length of about 9 inches (228 mm.) ;
it is found in clearings of dense jungle, especially
after rain. In Pahang *jĕlantor* is known as *chalutong*,
and in Kelantan as *ulat bidai chĕrang* (chĕrang, a clearing in the forest).

Most of the genus (Spirostreptus and Spirobolus)
secrete a poison from stink glands with a smell similar
to that of prussic acid, which causes smarting, dis-
coloration, and desquamation of the skin. M. Phisalix sums up the substances secreted by millepedes,
and so far identified, as camphor, hydrocyanic acid,
and quinone. A small red unidentified millepede,
called *tĕlong* or *pĕlong* in Kelantan, which measures
about 2 inches (50 mm.) in length, is not considered
poisonous, but is used, as has been seen, with *kĕsing*,
the land-bug, and *pinang kotai bukit*, the curious little
pill-millepede.

MOLLUSCS

SLUGS AND SNAILS

The Slug Ulat Kĕchar Lotong.—A rare slug, also
called *ulat jĕlutong*, because its colour somewhat resembles that of the adult *lotong* monkey (Presbytes
obscurus) is said to be highly venomous. It seems
to be almost entirely confined to the east coast of the

Peninsula, and in the jungle might be mistaken, at first sight, for the brown Malayan Peripatus. Annandale, one of the members of the " Skeat " expedition of 1900, observed these slugs in the northern States of the Peninsula and remarks : " Both Peripatus and slugs resembling it are said by the Malays to be so poisonous that if a drop of their slime, which is very scanty in the latter, and is, of course, ejaculated from certain large glands in the former, falls on a man's limb it will cause it to rot off.   The slugs are sometimes calcined and their ashes rubbed on the horns of fighting bulls, under the belief that even a scratch from a horn so treated will cause the bull's opponent to fall down dead " (Ref. 4).

Kelantan Malays, who dread the very sight of *ulat kĕchar lotong*, say that if it be trodden upon by the naked foot, it causes an ulceration which will eventually reach the bones.   Here it may be mentioned that slugs of the genus Atopos were found in the stomach of the vicious, but non-poisonous snake, *ular katam tĕbu* (Dipsadomorphus   dendrophilus,   Boie—Colubridæ) taken by the " Skeat " expedition.

Ulat kĕchar lotong has been identified by Mr. G. C. Robson, of the British Museum (Natural History) as Atopos maximus, Collinge, from Kelantan specimens captured at Nibong, Batu Mĕlentang in Kelantan Bharu ; they were found with difficulty among rotten timber on high, shady ground and are said to subsist on crumbling wood and decaying leaves. In life the slug is dark slate-blue with a bright salmon-pink foot-sole ; the colours can be retained by placing the specimen in a 12 per cent. solution of zinc chloride, but it must be killed with the greatest care.   Drowning in water, which takes twenty-four hours, is the most satisfactory method, because during the process of drowning the body becomes fully distended.   One of

the Kelantan specimens, now in the Natural History
Museum, measures almost $5\frac{3}{4}$ inches (146 mm.) in length;
two others were sent to the museum of the London
School of Hygiene and Tropical Medicine, London.

Atopos maximus is described in detail by Collinge
(Ref. 4). " Colour of the notum yellowish with
slatey-blue mottling, and an irregular yellowish-brown
band laterally, granulated, and minutely spotted
with black, notum extends over the head in a hood-
like manner; head white, facial region blue. Peri-
notum white; foot-sole (in alcohol) drab colour;
keel distinct, but not prominent."

Ulat kĕchar lotong is used as a poison with the
bristles of the marine worm, *ulat bulu laut,* mixed with
crystals (raphides) of decayed *rengut* fruit, and vegetable hairs scraped from the pod of a wild bean called
kachang rimau (Mucuma gigantea, D.C.—Leguminosæ). The dried slug, taken with the irritating
hairs and plant crystals, is said to cause blood-spitting
if swallowed by man. M. Phisalix makes no special
reference to poisonous slugs.

The Snail Kĕchar Lakum.—A large land-snail called
kĕchar lakum (Nanina humphreysiana—Stylommato-
phora), which is found on hills and may reach $2\frac{1}{4}$ inches
(57 mm.) in diameter, is employed as a poison. It is
crushed and used much in the same way as the millepedes. Uncertainty shadows the use of these molluscs;
they may form vehicles without being poisonous in
themselves. It is noteworthy that no reference is
given to them by M. Phisalix. Castellani and Chambers mention an unidentified poisonous snail in the
Solomon Islands and ascribe the harmfulness to a poison
gland in connection with their sharp-toothed lingual
ribbon (radula). Skeat refers to a Malay tradition
connected with a small air-breathing land-snail (? Aly-
cæus—Cyclophoridæ) found on limestone hills in

Perak, which is supposed to suck the blood of cattle through the medium of the grazing animal's shadow (*Selangor Journal*, 1892–97, Vol. III, No. 6, p. 91).

WORMS

The Bristle Worm Ulat Bulu Laut.—A polychætous free-swimming annelid (Chloia flava—Annelida), sometimes met with on sandy beaches, is the only marine worm used as a poison in Kelantan. It is stout and broad, from 4 to 5 inches in length, and nearly 2 inches in circumference, somewhat erroneously described as similar to the "sea-mouse" (Aphrodite aculeata) of British shores. The bristles are irritant, and are much dreaded by Malay fishermen on account of the serious wounds they cause by contact. To the naked eye the setæ look like small black prickles arranged in two rows along the whole length of the dorsal surface of the worm ; they support the lateral appendages (parapodia), which are also armed with two additional clusters of arrow-shaped bristles to each appendage. Under the microscope the bristles appear to be in little tufts of very fine brown pointed filaments. The bristles are said to be used as an internal poison when combined with other reputed gastro-intestinal irritants, especially the needle crystals of half-rotted *rengut* fruit, the sap of *jitong* (one of the *rĕngas* trees described in Chapter VIII), and pounded glass. Late in 1919 the Kelantan police sent a brown powder for examination ; it had been found on a bad character and was alleged by a *bomor* to contain the bristles of *ulat bulu laut*, the dried gall of a *buntal* fish, plant crystals of decayed *rengut*, and pounded glass.

REFERENCES

(1) ALDERWERELT VON ROSENBURGH, C. "Landsdrukkerig."
    1908. Batavia : Department of Agriculture, Netherlands
India.

(2) AUTENRIETH, W. "Laboratory Manual for the Detection of Poisons and Powerful Drugs." Authorised translation from sixth German edition by William H. Warren. 1928. London : Churchill.

(3) CASTELLANI and CHALMERS. "A Manual of Tropical Medicine." 1919. 3rd ed., p. 227. London : Baillière, Tindall and Cox.

(4) COLLINGE, W. E. "Report on the Non-Operculate Pulmonates." Fasciculi Malayensis : Zoology. 1903. Section 1, Part II, p. 213. Liverpool University Press.

(5) FLOWER, S. S. "Reptiles of the Malay Peninsula and Siam." *Proc. Zool. Soc.* (London). 1899.

(6) GRIFFIN, L. E. "Poisonous Snakes of the Philippine Islands." *Philippine Jour. Sci.* (Manila, P. I.). 1909. Vol. IV, No. 3, p. 203.

(7) HANITSCH, R. "Guide to Raffles' Museum." 1908. Singapore.

(8) LEFROY, H. MAXWELL. "Indian Insect Life." 1909. Calcutta : Thacker, Spink.

(9) LÜRING, Dr. H. L. E. "Über die medicinischen Kenntnisse der alten Ägypter berichtenden Papyri." 1888. Leipzig.

(10) LYDEKKER, R. "The Royal Natural History." 1923. Vol. VI. London : Warne.

(11) LYON and WADDELL. "Medical Jurisprudence for India." 1921. Calcutta : Thacker, Spink.

(12) PHISALIX, M. "Animaux Venimeux et Venins." 1922. T. ii. Paris : Masson.

(13) SKEAT and BLAGDEN. "Pagan Races of the Malay Peninsula." 1906. London : Macmillan.

(14) SMITH, SYDNEY. "Forensic Medicine." 1928. 2nd ed. London : Churchill.

(15) WILKINSON, J. R. "A Malay-English Dictionary." 1903. Singapore : Kelly & Walsh.

CHAPTER VIII

POISONS OBTAINED BY MALAYS FROM JUNGLE PLANTS

AKAR BATU PĚLIR KAMBING

Akar batu pělir kambing, or *Kambing-kambing*, is Sar-colobus globosus, Wall.—Asclepiadaceæ. The botany has been described by Ridley : " A long climber with a slender brown stem rather thicker than a crowquill covered with a brown thin bark. The leaves rather thin and fleshy, ovate to lanceolate, 3 inches long by 1½ wide with a broad rounded base, and a petiole ½ inch long, opposite. The flowers are in small clusters on short stalks ½ inch long. Each flower is ¼ inch across, pale purple in colour, with few rather broad lobes and a very short tube. The fruit is large and oval in outline with a strong keel on one side. It is 3 inches long and as much through, brown and rough with very small warts. When cut through it is seen to have a thick rind ½ inch through, white and pithy, and con-taining, as does the rest of the plant, a quantity of latex. This rind which when fresh is quite tasteless is the eatable part of the plant. The seeds are ovate, flat, thin discs, an inch long and ¾ inch across, and form a large mass overlapping each other. They are brown and possess a broad thin wing all round the seed itself " (Ref. 19). It is found in the Straits Settlements and Malay Peninsula, and extends as far north as India, being found near the sea-coast, in mangrove swamps, and along the banks of tidal rivers. The fruit resembles in shape and size the testicles of a goat, whence the Malay name.

Akar batu pělir kambing is used by Malays to poison

dogs, elephants and cattle ; the poison is contained in the seeds, which are called *pitis buah* by Kelantan Malays. They are so named from a fanciful resemblance to a coin of very small value used on the east coast : each seed is about the thickness of ordinary paper ; there are about 100 seeds in each fruit. As a poison for small animals the seeds from one half of a fresh green fruit are dried and powdered. This powder is mixed either with boiled rice or any other food that the animal is accustomed to eat ; it is employed by burglars to kill watch-dogs, and causes paralysis (*patah pinggang*) in them and other quadrupeds. For large animals, such as the elephant, bullock and water-buffalo, all the seeds from a fruit will be required. Although *pitis buah* will kill a dog outright, Malays add white arsenic and the juice of the lime fruit to the powdered seeds when they wish to make more certain of destroying the animal.

In September, 1920, I gave rather more than half the number of seeds of a Sarcolobus globosus fruit to a large healthy male pariah dog that weighed 28 lbs. The fruit had been gathered fresh three months before on a small island (*Pulau 'Chĕ Tahir*) in a tidal creek near Tumpat, the sea-port of Kelantan. The dried seeds were ground up, mixed with cooked rice, chopped meat, fish, and condensed milk. The dog ate the poison at 4.30 p.m. ; at 9 p.m. it was lying down and could not stand. It vomited and purged and died about fourteen hours after the administration. Shortly before death it was in tetanic convulsions ; the pupils were dilated.

The allied species of Sarcolobus, viz., S. Spanoghei, Miq., and S. virulentus, Griff., are recorded as poisons. The first of these two jungle climbing plants is called *wali kambing* in Java, where it is used for destroying tigers. Under the name of S. narcoticus, Greshoff gives an account of the poisoning of tigers by putting S. Spanoghei into the bait (Ref. 11, Vol. XXV, p. 138). He extracted a toxic substance from the bark, but did not ascertain its chemical nature. In his Indian Poison Reports, 1902, he remarks that S. narcoticus causes rigidity when the fruit is roasted, pounded, mixed with food and given to animals. Analyses of specimens of S. globosus sent to London from Kelantan have not been completed at the time of writing. Fresh coconut water is the antidote used by Malays to counteract this poison when accidents occur to man.

Like the poisonous yam *gadong*, the fruit can be used as food. The rind is often cooked and eaten as a vegetable ; but, like *gadong*, it is always carefully washed, generally in salt and water, before it is consumed. It is used to make a conserve in Malacca ; after being cut into pieces, soaked in salt and water for three days, and washed with fresh water for three days, it is put into boiling syrup. The Kelantan recipe is to remove and slice the rind ; the slices are hardened by soaking in lime water (aqua calcis ; *ayer kapur*) for two or three hours, washed in clean water and boiled for some time, and finally dropped into boiling syrup. This jungle climber, *akar batu pělir kambing*, must be distinguished from a small village shrub, called *pokok batu pělir kambing*, Rauwolfia perakensis (which see, p. 234).

AKAR KLAPAYANG

The seeds of *akar klapayang*, or *papayang ; truah* in Pahang (Hodgsonia capniocarpa, Ridl.—Cucurbitaceæ), are reputed to be poisonous. Akar Klapayang is a wild jungle creeper found along river banks and in durian gardens. The fruits are flat at each end and covered with a fine grey plush, 6 to 7 inches across, containing about eight seeds. The seeds have

been examined by B. J. Eaton, Director of Agriculture, F.M.S. They consist of a hard flat outer shell
of a dull drab colour, somewhat resembling a mango
fruit in shape, about 2½ inches long and 1⅞ inches wide.
The shell contains a soft oily kernel enclosed in a thin,
dry, mealy pericarp. He found that on extraction
with petroleum ether the kernels yielded 59·4 per
cent. of oil or fat, or 26 per cent. calculated on the
whole seed. The raw seed is bitter and probably
contains an alkaloid or some glucosidal substance
(Ref. 9). The seeds of *akar klapayang* resemble those
of the *payung* or *kĕpayang* tree and hence no doubt its
name, but the two should be carefully differentiated,
because each is of commercial value, but they are two
quite different plants. As shown above, *klapayang*
is a wild jungle climber belonging to the Natural
Order Cucurbitaceæ, while *kĕpayang* is often a cultivated village tree, Pangium edule Reinwdt.—Bixaceæ
(which see, p. 225). In the Malay Archipelago *akar
klapayang* is known in Dutch as *areuj kalajar badak*
(Sunda) *batang* (Celebes); *biloengkieng* in Sumatra,
and in Pahang it is said that " twenty seeds give a
bottle of oil, to get which the seeds are cut into pieces
and placed in the sun to dry for two days ; the pieces
are then put into a bag made of tree bark and pressed
by hand " (De Clercq).

BAMBOO

The very fine hairs—almost black specks—found
on the leaf-sheaths of the young sprouts of certain
bamboos, also the fine hair-like pieces of bamboo
seen when a dry bamboo cane is split or broken, are
prominent among Malay poisons. Most varieties of
bamboos produce hairs abundantly on the broad
sheath which covers the bud or growing point, but the
criminal favours those obtained from bamboos with

edible shoots, such as *buloh duri* in Pahang (Bambusa spinosa, Bl.—Gramineæ) and *buloh minyak* which is used for making baskets in the northern parts of the Peninsula (Oxytenanthera sinuata, Gamble—Gramineæ). Hairs from Dendrocalamus strictus, Nees and Ham. (*b. batu, b. bĕrang* and *b, tĕmpat*), from D. flagellaris, Munro (*b. bĕtong*), and from Bambusa vulgaris, Schrad., are chiefly used in the south.

The Hairs.—Bamboo hairs are known as *miang rĕbong* or *miyang buloh* in Malay (*miang* or *miyang*, fine vegetable hairs, also " itchy " ; *rebong*, the shoot of the bamboo ; *buloh*, bamboo). They are usually sepia-brown in colour, about 1 to 2 mm. in length, blunt at one end and sharply pointed at the other. The hairs are very irritating to the skin, especially when they come in contact with soft skin, *e.g.*, between the fingers. Under the microscope these slender hairs are seen as brown filaments, acuminate, like fine broken needles. Bamboo hairs are said to be frequently used with no other adjunct then Pounded Glass (which see). When administered in this way, a train of symptoms like that of a chronic pseudo-dysentery is set up which causes death from severe and prolonged mechanical irritation of the intestinal mucosa. Gilbert Brooke notes that the hairs are commonly mixed with black sand to render them less conspicuous and to sink them in the coffee or curry-stuffs to which they may be added. Ridley records that two valuable Siamese cats belonging to a European were poisoned in this way (Poisoning by Bamboo Hairs. *Jour. Trop. Med. and Hyg.* (Lond.), 1924, October 15th). In Kelantan bamboo hairs are sometimes mixed with the juice obtained from the fruits of *bĕrĕdin* (a poisonous palm tree described below), and the extract of a toad. This toad extract is made from the common brown toad, *katak puru*, by allowing the animal to decompose

in a bamboo cylinder containing a little water ; after
an interval of seven days this is smeared, or sprinkled,
over wearing apparel and the mixture is said to bring
about an incurable and painful skin disease like a
ringworm in appearance. The use of *miang rěbong* as
a fish poison is referred to under section Děpu Pělan-
dok. A combination of bamboo hairs with the needle
crystals of *rengut* and the fine hairs of *ulat bulu darat*
is mentioned under Moths. A case in which they
were mixed with oil is referred to under Kachang
Bulu Rimau.

BĚBUTA

The jungle tree *běbuta* or *buta-buta* (Excœcaria
agallocha, Linn.—Euphorbiaceæ) is so called from the
injuries it causes to the eyes ; *buta* means blindness.
The *běbuta* of Kelantan is a small bushy evergreen tree,
with bright green and rather thick leaves, found on the
sea-coast in tidal jungle growth or brackish backwaters.
Excœcaria agallocha is described botanically by Brandis : The bark is grey, smooth, shining, with numerous
round prominent lenticels, the wood very soft and
spongy. The flower is minute, fragrant, yellowish-
green, with catkin-like spikes (male), or pedicelled in
short racemes (female). The fruit is a very small
capsule, very variable in size, green going to black,
coriaceous, deeply trilobed. It ripens in January ;
seeds glabrous, smooth (Ref. 1). Excœcaria agallocha
occurs in India, where it is known as the " blinding
tree of Ceylon," and it is recognised as a native poison
under the name *uguru* in the Deccan. The " milky
mangrove," or " river poison tree " of Australia, seems
to be similar to *běbuta* from the description given by
Bailey and Gordon ; it is reputed to be injurious to
stock.

The milky latex obtained from the green bark is

used by Malays as an irritant poison ; it is so acrid when fresh that it blisters the skin and causes much swelling. When applied to the face, the features may be obliterated through swelling (compare with Rĕngas, p. 180) ; the eyes may be completely destroyed. In Kelantan *bĕbuta* is given internally as a homicidal poison by mixing the sap obtained from the trunk and the branches of the tree with the blood of the flying fox (*kĕluang* ; Pteropus edulis, Chiroptera) and is said to cause strangury, with hæmaturia and violent inflammation of the intestines. Excœcaria agallocha is well known in the Dutch East Indies under various names, *bomo, dari, pohun, kajoe mata bœta,* and others. The white sap given in milk causes vomiting of blood, purging with bloody stools and death (Greshoff : Indian Poison Reports). According to Bernhard-Smith the toxic principle of Excœcaria agallocha is oil of euphorbia (see " Poisonous Plants of all Countries " : The Manchineal Tree, p. 52. 1923 ; London). In the Malay States bĕbuta is sometimes used to prevent the theft of toddy by adding a few drops of the sap to the bamboo collecting cylinders, when the toddy thief suffers the agonies of a choleraic seizure.

A contributor to Smith's " Economic Dictionary " refers to the very singular use of Excœcaria agallocha in the treatment of leprosy in Fiji : " The body of the patient is first rubbed with green leaves ; he is then placed in a small room and bound hand and foot, when a small fire is made of pieces of wood of this tree from which rises a thick smoke ; the patient is suspended over this fire, and remains for some hours in the midst of the poisonous smoke and under the most agonising torture, often fainting. When thoroughly smoked, he is removed, and the slime is scraped from his body ; he is then scarified and left to await the result. The patient frequently dies under the ordeal."

It was well known years ago that crews of vessels suffered from the intensely acrid juice of *buta-buta* getting into their eyes when cutting firewood on shore. T. Powell describes Excœcaria agallocha under the native name of *toto* as one of the most virulent of the Samoan vegetable poisons used in the New Hebrides chiefly for poisoning spears and arrows. When describing the fate of some freebooters he writes as follows : " At a place called Mole near Eraker, the people, expecting a visit from these depredators, prepared for them in a way which they little suspected. They had, as is common in similar places, an enclosure of water on the beach which at low tide served both for drinking and bathing. They pounded a quantity of leaves of the *toto* previously dried in an oven ; and when they saw the canoe coming they threw these pounded leaves into the bathing-place. As soon as the canoe anchored, most of the crew, after native fashion, rushed to the fresh water to drink and to bathe. They were immediately thrown into convulsive agonies : those who only bathed became blind ; and those who drank died " (Ref. 17).

According to Ridley, a much smaller evergreen tree or shrub, Cerbera odollam, C. lactaria, Gærtn.— Apocynaceæ, is called *bĕbuta* in some places (Pahang and Selangor). The botany of C. odollam has also been described in detail by Brandis. It has a milky and very irritating sap, and is common in jungle about tidal creeks of low country near the sea (salt swamps) in various localities—India, Dutch East Indies, Madagascar, and the Pacific Islands. The flower is large, white, in clusters of corymbs ; the fruit is large and fleshy, somewhat of the shape of a mango, green or tinted with brown according to age, 2 to 4 inches long, usually having one large stone covered by a strong hard network of fibre. An incision into the rind causes

exudation of a white sap which produces itchiness on
contact with the skin. The leaves are dark green,
shiny, oblong and larger than those of Excœcaria
agallocha. Hullet says the Malay name is *bĕtak-
bĕtak*; in Java it is *bĕtah*, and *goro mata bœta* in the
Celebes, where it is used as a fish poison and said to be
deadly to rats. In other parts of the Dutch East
Indies, Cerbera odollam, Mamilt., is known as *bintaro*;
oil expressed from the seeds is used in native lamps
and in some places is said to be smeared on spears
and daggers to poison the blades. Greshoff records
that the sap of the pounded ripe fruit mixed with food
causes distension of the abdomen, diarrhœa and vomiting, dizziness, contraction of the tongue, convulsions
and death. In man the symptoms of cerbera poisoning
have been mistaken in Ceylon for those of arsenic—a
matter of some importance (Castellani). A glucoside
known as thevetin, a cardiac poison which also occurs in
C. thevetia (Thevetia neriifolia, Juss), has been found
in the milk-like juice of all parts of C. odollam. The
seeds are an irritant poison (Ref. 16).

THE BĔRĔDIN PALM

The old medical botanists held that " the majestic
tribe of palms, the nobles of the vegetable kingdom,
contained not a single noxious species," but among
palms that are known to be poisonous by Malays
are *bĕrĕdin, ibul, kabong, langkap* and *pinang*. Ridley
gives *dudok* and *tukus* as additional Malay names for
bĕrĕdin or *mĕrĕdin*, and refers to Caryota mitis, Lour.,
as the *brĕdin* of Province Wellesley. The botany of
C. mitis, Lour., a wild palm, never more than 25 feet
tall, has been described by Ridley. The palm forms
a tuft of about five stems, which succeed each other
until all have flowered, when the plant dies. The
flowers are purplish in long pendant branches of

racemes. The leaf is about 6 feet long, bipinnate with trapezoid leaflets, sheath covered with white mealy tomentum. The fruit, globular, flattened, ½ inch through, fleshy, purple. The palm is common in the Straits Settlements and Malay Straits, and is distributed in Burmah and Cochin-China.

The fresh juice of the fruit when applied directly to the skin is very irritating; blisters may form, as once happened to a small boy engaged in washing seeds of a tall species of Caryota in the Botanic Gardens, Singapore.

Bĕrĕdin fruit is put into wells with intent to cause annoyance. Bathing with well water treated in this way gives rise to an intense itching of the skin and may cause an acute inflammation of the eyes. Emollients, such as vaseline should be applied to the skin. The use of *bĕrĕdin* with a toad extract and bamboo hairs has been referred to above (see section BAMBOO). The hill or sago palm of northern India, or toddy palm of Ceylon, C. urens, which has similar properties, is not mentioned by Ridley as occurring in Malaya, but a single stemmed palm like it, C. æquatorialis, Ridl., occurs in the Perak hill forests.

Dr. Yvan, in his quaint little book, " Six Months Among the Malays " (1855), remarks, when referring to the dislike of Malays to strangers : " One day when the sailors came, according to custom, to fill their pitchers at the reservoir, on putting their feet and hands into the stream, they experienced a sensation both of heat and pain, and looking around to ascertain the cause of this change, discovered that this disagreeable feeling increased every time the skin came in contact with the berries of a green herb which was floating about in the reservoir ; some of this fruit they brought back with them to the vessel and I immediately recognised it to be that of Caryota onusta, a species

of palm described in the herbal of Father Blanco.
. . . Some of the men who had remained longest in
the water, suffered a great deal of pain which, however,
disappeared in a very short time and without any sort
of remedy ; the Malays make use of the saccharine
matter contained in this fruit as a sort of projectile
which, with the aid of a bamboo, they fling in the
faces of their enemies, thus forming a wound which
would require all the anodynes of M. Purdon to cure."
The wild tribes (Sakai) use the tomentum on the sheath
of *bĕrĕdin* as wadding for their blowpipes, and also
for tinder. The stem produces a kind of sago which
is occasionally used by Malays. Endeavours have been
made to obtain an analysis of *bĕrĕdin* fruit sent from
Kota Bharu to London, but no report has yet been
received. Mr. Ridley thinks that the poisonous property may be due to the presence of spicules of flint
(silex).

CHĔNGKIAN

A tropical species of the Spurge family, known in
Kelantan as *chĕngkian* or *chĕmkian*, is used by Malays
as a poison, but not with homicidal intent. *Chĕngkian*
is the well-known purging Croton Tiglium, Linn.—
Euphorbiaceæ, a small wild evergreen tree or shrub
found in the jungle or by the wayside, and widely
distributed in tropical Asia, America, and Africa.
Like the coral tree (Jatropha multifera—Euphorbiaceæ) it differs from other plants of this Natural
Order by having a flower with a corolla. The botany
is described in detail by Kirtikar and Basu (Ref. 15).
The *chĕngkian* fruit, about the size of the hazel nut,
a somewhat ovate and obtusely trigonous capsule,
¾ to 1 inch long, contains three seeds, each about
½ to ⅔ inch long, and flattened ovoid in shape, dark
reddish-brown when fresh, brownish-black or greyish-

brown when old. The seed consists of a thin, dark, brittle shell, containing a pale, yellowish-white albuminous kernel, enclosing a large leafy embryo ; inodorous ; taste at first mild, subsequently acrid and pungent ; in the fresh state the dark brittle shell is covered externally with a white membrane. The seeds of Croton Tiglium are readily attacked by moulds in moist climates ; they somewhat resemble a coffee bean in size and the smaller variety of castor-oil beans, but are without the beautiful marbled patterns of the latter.

Croton oil is not expressed from the seeds by Malays, but the fruits are used by them, sometimes vindictively, being given in water to those against whom they bear a grudge. In an example which occurred in Kelantan, a villager was celebrating the circumcision of his son and called two rival parties of bandsmen to play at the ceremony. Rivalry started and ended in a challenge to a display of efficiency. The losers, in their anger, boiled some *chĕngkian* fruit in water, some of which they succeeded in adding to the refreshments given to their rivals, with the result that the winning party had to cancel all their engagements for three days. *Chĕngkian* is sometimes put into wells ; the dried fruit of the shrub is so used, but seldom with a view to cause death. Greshoff records that the pounded fruits of Croton Tiglium are used as a poison, being put into drink and causing bloody stools and death, or when roasted and finely powdered and put into coffee, death may result in twenty-four hours. In one district, the sap of the leaves, mixed with slaked lime, is used to alter the appearance of the hair of stolen horses. The leaves are also one of the constituents of the Batak arrow poison. The ripe pounded fruits are used by natives of Java and Dayaks in Borneo to poison fish. The root is finely shredded, mixed with water, and drunk by Javanese women as an abortifacient (Greshoff : Indian Poison Reports). The root of the plant is also used in Kelantan as an abortifacient agent; it is boiled in water and the decoction is swallowed from time to time. The shrub is reported as being poisonous to cattle in Ceylon. The Abor arrow poison of the N.E. frontier of Assam is a paste believed to be made by pounding the soft parts of Croton Tiglium.

Ridley says that the seeds are ground up and sprinkled over food as a poison. They are used medicinally by the Kelantan *bomor ;* one is sufficient as a dose for an adult, but may excite violent vomiting and purging with severe griping pain and the passage of blood in the stools. Four croton seeds proved a fatal dose in the Punjab forty-three hours after the second dose (Ref. 3), and it has been said that forty croton seeds will kill a horse in seven hours (Landsberg). Thirty drops of the oil have killed a dog, and Pereira has described the case of a man who suffered severely from inhaling the dust from the seeds. According to an account of accidental poisoning by croton seeds published in the *Medical Times and Gazette,* twenty-four persons were poisoned in 1874 in the south of Ireland through eating some seeds of Croton Tiglium which had been washed ashore, supposedly, from a Dutch vessel that had foundered a few days before. The " nuts " were found by the country people and eaten accordingly ; the consequences may be guessed, but fortunately no deaths were known to have resulted.

Various glycerides, glycerin esters, acids, and especially the irritant crotonoleic acid, are contained in croton seeds ; they also contain croton-resin from which they derive their vesicant properties, and crotin a toxic albuminoid principle. Crotin is a vegetable toxalbumin which is chemically similar to

ricin, the toxalbumin of castor oil beans ; it also
resembles abrin, the toxalbumin of jequirity (Abrus
precatorius) seeds. They are all protein-like bodies,
perhaps resembling ferments in their action (Ref.
24), possessing the common property of clumping,
agglutinating and precipitating red blood corpuscles.
These poisonous toxalbumins are said to be especially
abundant in fresh seeds. Autenrieth, quoting from
R. Kobert, says : " Abrin and ricin agglutinate blood
corpuscles of all warm-blooded animals thus far
tested, but crotin does not manifest the same behaviour
with all kinds of blood." These substances may be
the source of delayed-action poisons, which are alleged
to be used by Malays and other races (see pp. 11, 264).
They are also able to engender antitoxins, the preparation and action of which have been studied by Ehrlich
and many other investigators. Much work has been
done to elucidate whether the protein is the actual
poison or whether some linked-on substance gives the
toxicity (Ref. 8). " The phytotoxins ricin and crotin
resemble snake venom and bacterial toxins in their
action, but, unlike the latter, may be absorbed to
some extent from the alimentary canal " (Ref. 23).
Elfstrand found that 34 mg. of crotin per kilo. body-
weight killed a rabbit by subcutaneous injection in
120 hours, and described the hæmolitic action on red
blood corpuscles and clumping effects in 1898 (Ref.
10).

Croton oil is freely soluble in ether and in chloroform ; it may be detected by extracting it from the
seeds or vomited matter by exhaustion with ether
slightly acidulated with tartaric acid, and then,
after evaporation, recognised by its vesicating action
on the skin. The oil turns brown, and nitrous fumes
are given off when it is warmed with nitric acid.
When croton oil is applied to the tongue a sensation

of burning and tingling occurs which is similar to that caused by aconite, but no anæsthesia is produced. Abrus precatorius, Linn.—Leguminosæ (*akar saga bětina* or *akar bělimbing*), is common at seaside places in Kelantan. I have no evidence that it is used by Malays for homicidal purposes or for poisoning cattle, as in India. *Jarak blanda* (Jatropha curcas, Linn.—Euphorbiaceæ), the " physic-nut plant " or " semina ricini majoris " of old pharmaceutical writers, which is allied to *chěngkian* and is common in Selangor, does not seem to be used as a poison in Kelantan, although its poisonous properties are known in India.

THE IBUL PALM

Buah ibul, the fruit of a very handsome, large, thornless jungle palm (*pohun ibul ;* Orania macrocladus, Mart.—Palmæ), is held by Kelantan Malays to be exceedingly poisonous. The *ibul* tree is not common in Kelantan, but it occurs in the Ulu Kěsial district on the high ground of Bukit Gadong ; it is more common in the forests of Malacca and in Java, but is also found in Singapore, Pahang, and the Dindings. The botany has been described by Hooker : " Trunk 40 feet, crown densely leafy, subhemispheric. Leaves 12 to 15 feet, pinnate-oblong in outline, leaflets $2\frac{1}{2}$ to 3 feet by 2 inches, white and scurfy beneath, petiole 5 feet, spathes and spadix scurfy. Spadix paniculately branched, nodding, branches slender ; flowers white. Fruit $1\frac{1}{4}$ to $1\frac{1}{2}$ inches in diameter, smooth, green. Seed globose " (Ref. 13). The *ibul* palm is also described botanically by Ridley, who says it woods to about 1,000 feet elevation (Ref. 20).

The *ibul* fruit when fresh is about the size of a walnut ; it is a hard, green, round and, except for a fibrous epicarp like the areca nut, solid nut. The thin, whitish, brittle shell of the dry nut encloses a very hard yellowish-white oily kernel which is very rich in fats. In Kelantan it is said that a single fruit is sufficient to kill an elephant; the poisonous nature of the fruit is said to be known to the jungle-folk of Selangor. The palm-cabbage (*umbut*) is also alleged to be poisonous, but Sir Hugh Clifford refers to the shoots as being edible when describing the manner in which some fugitives from justice cleared their way through the depths of a dense Malayan jungle : " Their line of march was marked by *bayas* and *ibul*, and other wild palms, which had been felled, that men might fill their empty stomachs with the edible shoots " (Ref. 5).

In August, 1919, a Kelantan Malay was charged with putting poison into a well. He was seen to throw wadding into a private well in Kota Bharu. The exhibit was of such small amount that it was hardly possible to say what it contained. The *bomor* I consulted thought it was wool from the cotton tree compounded with powdered datura seeds, the cabbage of the *ibul* palm, tobacco, and blood.

Constituents of Ibul Nuts.—Collections of *ibul* nuts from Ulu Kĕsial (Kelantan) were sent for investigation to Dr. J. A. Gunn (Professor of Pharmacology at Oxford) in 1914, and to Sir W. Willcox and W. G. Walsh in 1920. Dr. Gunn kindly reports that they contain such large quantities of fatty matter that if plentiful enough they might have a commercial value. He found that the alcoholic extract was innocuous in considerable doses, but that an acid aqueous extract was highly toxic ; but the toxicity was destroyed by heating this preparation. In rabbits the heart stopped very suddenly in diastole, both *in situ* and when isolated ; with fibrillation when quickly investigated. Unfortunately the outbreak of war prevented closer examination. Webster, Walsh and Willcox kindly report that no positive reaction for alkaloids was given with the general reagents on trial with an ether-shake-out in modified Stas method : much fat was present. An extract tried on the heart showed slowing of the beat by prolonged diastole and strengthened systole, thus resembling vagus action, but without the weakening. At the time of writing the investigation is not completed ; but it is regarded as probable that the active principle is of glucosidal nature, which is in accordance with Gunn's observation that heat destroyed the activity of the acid extract.

In October, 1913, pieces of a dried *ibul* nut were enclosed in bits of fish and given as an experiment to a lesser adjutant bird. This ungainly stork (Leptoptilus javanicus), accustomed to fend for itself, took a fancy to live in my compound, where it swallowed anything, but refused the *ibul* with some display of anger ; one small bit was apparently swallowed without ill effect. It also partook of some other (?) poisonous plants at my instance, but seemed hardy.

JELATANG

Jĕlatang gajah, the Malay nettle-tree (Laportea stimulans—Urticaceæ), also called *daun gatal* (" itchy leaf "), is known as *rumpai* in Pahang and other places. It is a fairly soft-wooded shrub, with large oval leaves, found along river-sides and in ravines. The " elephant " nettle-tree (*jĕlatang gajah*) is widely distributed, being found in Kelantan, Selangor, Perak, Penang and Pahang, and on Pulau Tioman ; it is a different species from the Indian plant (Laportea crenulata) which is known as the " fever " or " devil-nettle." The upper surface of the leaf of L. stimulans, and especially the petiole, is clothed with short, stinging hairs. Flowers green, fruit pink, eaten by birds. Another species, collected in Perak by Father

Scortechini, is named L. pustulosa, Ridleyi. The *jĕlatang gajah* plants are much dreaded by Malays; men have been known to lose their lives in Pahang on walking unwarily with bare bodies through these nettle-trees in wet weather. Susceptible people faint and are said to develop a rash resembling that of erysipelas, or are seized with frequent sneezing; all experience pain, which is always intensified by the application of water. Bailey and Gordon (1887) state that the acrid milky juice from the stem of an arum (Colocasia macrorrhiza, Schott.—Araceæ) gives instant relief from the pain caused by the sting of the nettle-trees. Forbes was relieved in Timor by the application of *chunam* (lime prepared for betel-chewing) to the stings of L. crenulata. The toxic principle is said to be formic acid.

There are several other kinds of *jĕlatang*, but none of them sting severely. *Jĕlatang rusa* (Cnesmone javanica, Miq.—Euphorbiaceæ) is described by Ridley as a climber of no great size, which is found in thickets and waste spots. It has a slender stem covered with stinging hairs; oblong cuspidate leaves covered with hairs, about 6 inches long, and 2 inches broad; the leaf stalk is from $\frac{1}{2}$ to $1\frac{1}{2}$ inches long. The inflorescence is a raceme about 2 inches long, axillary, the upper flowers male, the lower ones female. The flowers are small and green. The capsule is three-lobed, about $\frac{1}{2}$ inch long, covered with strong spiny hairs (Ref. 18). There is also Spærostylis malaccensis, Pax. (jelatang bulan, the "moon" nettle-tree), but neither it, nor *j. rusa*, the "sambar deer" and *j. badak* the "rhinoceros" are so poisonous as *jĕlatang gajah*, the "elephant" nettle-tree. The common little nettle, *jĕlatang ayam*, the "fowl" nettle (Fleurya interrupta, Gaud. Urticaceæ) and the "snake" nettle, *jĕlatang ular* (Tragia, spp.—Euphorbiaceæ) only sting feebly and not so badly as an English nettle.

Uses.—The leaves of *jĕlatang gajah* are sometimes strung on a cord and tied to the portal of a Malay house to scare evil spirits away, and in this connexion it is interesting to remember that the nettle was blessed by St. Patrick as useful both to man and beast. The *jĕlatang* is used, according to Vaughan Stevens, by the east coast negritos (Pangan) with the fresh juice of the upas tree (Antiaris toxicaria) for poisoning their darts. When used in Kelantan as a poison by criminals the flowers and leaves are said to be mixed in cakes with a view to causing death. In Java the green leaves of L. sinuata, Bl. are used by criminals to irritate cattle and buffaloes, and the fine hairs of a variant of L. stimulans are used to make horses " fiery " by rubbing the young stems between the hind legs (Greshoff).

JITONG (see also section RĔNGAS)

Jitong belongs to the genus Gluta of the poisonous Anacardiaceæ trees, and is better known as one of the *rĕngas* trees. The name *jitong* is generally applied to Gluta Benghas, Linn., a tall jungle tree with foliage and flowers like the horse-mango tree (*pokok machang;* Mangifera fœtida, Roxb.—Anacardiaceæ). The word *benghas* is an old miswriting for *rĕngas*. There are five species of the genus Gluta in the Malay Peninsula ; their sap yields a resinous product which is acrid and poisonous. The commonest is G. coarctata, a bush or tree which grows near tidal waters, and is easily recognised by the bright red colour of the young leaves and by the peculiar appearance of the fruit. The fruits, like those of the *jitong* tree, are fleshy, yellowish-brown in colour, warty, oval, but irregular, in shape ; they contain a black juice which is very

irritating to the skin. Another similar tree with a
red wood, G. virosa, Ridl., also has a bad reputation ;
it is known to Selangor Malays as *pohun kĕrbau jalang*,
or the " wild buffalo tree."

Cases of accidental poisoning by the fresh juice
of G. Benghas have occurred among native gardeners trimming the trees, and wood-cutters splitting
logs for domestic use, in the Botanic Gardens at
Singapore. Ridley met a European who had tasted
a fruit of G. coarctata and who suffered from violent
diarrhœa in consequence. Malays say that the pustular skin lesions caused by the black varnish of *jitong*
and *rĕngas* are almost as harmful as those caused by the
bristles of the hairy sea-worm *ulat bulu laut* (Chloia
flava). As a vindictive poison, the sap of the tree (*gĕtah
jitong*) is mixed with the setæ of the bristle-worm,
together with plant crystals from the decayed fruit of
rengut, and then smeared on the wearing apparel or
sleeping mat of the victim. Greshoff says that the juice
of *jitong* is used on the island of Siauw, in the Malay
Archipelago, as an arrow poison, and that man may be
killed by partaking of the finely powdered bark and
root in water.

KACHANG BULU RIMAU

In June, 1913, a Kelantan police exhibit consisted
of some rice cooked with a pickled vegetable called
maman (Gynandropsis pentaphylla, D.C.—Cappari-
daceæ) and a quantity of fine woolly hairs scraped
from the pod of an edible Mucuna bean called the
" tiger-hair bean " or *kachang bulu rimau*. An attempt
seems to have been made to poison the Tĕngku Woh,
a cousin of the late Sultan of Kelantan, or to incapaci-
tate her for a while pending a law suit. The Tĕngku
herself did not happen to eat any of the poisoned meal,
but three of her women who shared it were attacked

with vomiting, diarrhœa, and general prostration with violent itching of the skin in one case. They all recovered quickly with treatment by castor oil and a bismuth mixture. The Kota Bharu police sent another exhibit in February, 1920; it was a small glass bottle containing coconut oil and many vegetable hairs which they thought were those of *kachang bulu rimau*, but under the microscope these hairs were clearly recognised as bamboo hairs. A Malay had given the oil to a woman inside a dark house to rub over her body and so annoy her by causing great irritation of the skin. The light yellow hairs of *kachang bulu rimau* do not present any peculiar features under the microscope.

A wild inedible bean called the " tiger bean " by Malays (*kachang rimau;* Mucuna gigantea, D.C.— Leguminosæ) which is also well known in India for its urticating properties, is a much more serious poison if administered internally. Mucuna gigantea is a sea-shore species; generally the stem is slender and usually not more than about 50 feet long ; it is much smaller than the Indian variety, which may have a climbing stem of 250 feet long. The pod of *kachang rimau* is densely covered with adpressed, dark red and yellow hairs which suggest in colour and arrangement the skin of a tiger (*rimau*) when viewed as a whole. They are intensely irritating to the skin, and under the microscope can be recognised by having a series of short wide-based spines. Mucuna gigantea has been found to be a narcotic poison in Java, and it is said that when the hairs from the fruit of M. Blumei, Burk. are mixed with food, recovery is rare ; severe coughing with hæmorrhage and wasting occurs (Greshoff : Indian Poisons Reports, The Royal Colonial Institute, Amsterdam). Malay criminals combine the hairs of *kachang rimau* with the poisonous slug Ulat Kĕchar Lotong (which see, p. 147).

KĔLADI

Kĕladi is a general name given by Malays to a number of aroids ; some of the wild varieties are poisonous and are used by Malays with criminal intention. They are here considered under one heading for the sake of convenience. Among them are *kĕladi chandek* (Alocasia denudata, Eng.—Araceæ), *likir* or *lokie* (Amorphophallus Prainii, Hook. fil.—Araceæ), and the black and white varieties of Alocasia, called *birah hitam* and *birah puteh* in Kelantan. The acrid juice, which is characteristic of this family, is used as a poison, and generally in combination with the berries of the shrub *pokok batu pĕlir kambing* (which see, p. 234).

The juice of the swollen underground stems or corms of the *kĕladi* contains masses of fine needle crystals ; under the microscope they have an average length of four microns, and are colourless except in the case of *likir*, in which they are orange coloured in bulk. A note relative to them is given by Warden and Pedler and is quoted by Kirtikar and Basu under Colocasia antiquorum : " There appears to us no reason to doubt the fact that the whole of the physiological symptoms caused by Arums is due to needle-shaped crystals of oxalate of lime and that the symptoms are thus due to purely mechanical causes " (Ref. 15, p. 1344). The loss of practically the whole of the physiological activity on drying is explained by the writers in this way : In the process of drying or cooking the needles appear to arrange themselves more or less parallel to one another and the sharp points thus cover a smaller area. And so, instead of each crystal acting as a separate source of irritation and penetrating the tissues, the bundles act as a whole. None of the *kĕladi* mentioned above are used as food in Kelantan ; but the corms of other species, that are poisonous in the fresh state, are rendered harmless by washing before use as food by the Malay housewife.

The irritating effect of the fresh juice of this family on the skin is well known. In the sixteenth century the use of Arum maculatum, the only representative in England, is described by John Gerarde (1597) in his "Herball": "The most pure and white starch is made of the roots of the Cuckow-pint; most hurtful for the hands of the laundresse that hath the handling of it; for it choppeth, blistereth, and maketh the hands rough and rugged, and withall smarting." Dr. Parkins in "The English Physician" (1814) says: "The whole plant (Cuckoo-pint) is of a very sharp biting taste, pricking the tongue as nettles do the hands, and so abideth for a great while without alteration." A broken berry placed upon the tongue is sufficient to irritate it: a case is recorded in England in which three children ate some of the berries; their tongues became so swollen as to render swallowing difficult; convulsions followed and two died, but one recovered. Another patient who had eaten only a small piece of the corm, and who was promptly treated by lavage, passed into "a drowsy, stuporous condition a few hours later with paresis of the limbs and distension of the abdomen. Recovery, however, took place in twenty-four hours or so." These properties are well developed in the tropical varieties and are made use of by Malays, who also employ *kĕladi* as a contact poison.

An example of this occurs in a conspectus of contact poisons given to me by a Malay friend; it is quoted in its quaintness as written: "The following poisons when given to a man cause very severe itching sensation as if the man is getting mad:

(1) Ulat bulu hitam [which see, p. 139].

(2) Ulat bulu laut [which see, p. 148].

(3) Buah kachang rimau [which see, p. 170].

(4) Buah merdin [which see, p. 158].
(5) Pinang kotek bukit (insect) [which see, p. 144].
(6) Pohun jelatang gajah [which see, p. 166].
(7) Miang rebong [which see, p. 154].
(8) Keladi birah [which see, p. 171].

Each of the above things has to be dried first and then fry. After frying they have to be pounded until they turn into powders, but not to mix them with one another. They have to be kept separately. Directions :—(1) Take the eight different powders of same quantity and mix them together and put it in any food. It is said that the man who takes it will feel very severe itching inside his body and his throat and also he feels very hot. (2) If it is intended for rubbing over the skin, the *miang rebong* and the *keladi birah* are not to be dried, the fresh ones must be used. Take the juice of the *keladi birah* and mix it together with the *miang rebong* and then mix it with the six different powders of same quantity. It is said that if this mixture is rubbed over the body of a man, the man will also feel very severe itching. (This causes death sometimes after.)" This diabolical polypharmacy comes from Kelantan. The *bomor* prescribes *kĕladi* (Colocasia antiquorum) for disorders of menstruation (mĕroyan) : " Take mustard seed and garlic, bind then in a *kĕladi* leaf for a whole night ; next morning, very early before the flies awake, eat it in this way : sit over a hole facing the sunrise, and look for relief " (from the manuscript book of Malayan medicine, Pharmaceutical Society, see page 14).

LIKIR

The *likir* plant (Amorphophallus Prainii, Hook., fil.—Araceæ) is commonly found wild in Penang, Selangor, Perak, Sumatra and elsewhere. It has been described by Ridley : " Like all the genus the tuber throws up a single leaf at a time. The leaf stalk often attains a great size, nearly two inches through at the base and tapering upwards, it is smooth and green, mottled with white and brown, the leaf blade is much dissected, dark green in colour and is of large size. The flower spike appears after the fall of the leaf and is enclosed in a large funnel-shaped prim-rose-yellow spathe shorter than the spadix and re-curved above when fully developed ; the lower part of the tube inside is of a deep maroon colour. The male and female flowers are separated on the spadix which is terminated by a large primrose-yellow cone-shaped process. The whole inflorescence is about a foot high " (Ref. 18).

A *likir* bulb was sent from Kelantan to Singapore ; it flowered in the Botanic Gardens. Mr. Burkill identified it as A. Rex, a neighbouring species of A. Prainii. They are much alike, and it is improbable that a village Malay would distinguish them by different names. A. Rex (A. campanulatus, Bl.) is found in the Andaman Islands, Perak, Penang, Sumatra and Java. It is a larger plant, and more curious in its purplish brown sterile end to the swollen spadix, and has a longer style. The flowers of *likir* have an unpleasant smell : the expressed juice of the tuber is used by the negritos of Perak (Sĕmang) in the composition of their dart poison. They mix it with the fresh juice of the upas tree (Antiaris toxicaria), and it is said that a tenth part of *likir* juice in the mix-ture will make a poison strong enough to kill a rhino-cerous or a tiger ; but, according to Wray, *likir* only causes a local irritation which hinders wounded animals from escaping before the poison has had time to act. Ridley thinks that the addition is made to promote a flow of blood to the wounds and so cause the rapid absorption of the poison. *Likir* tubers are sometimes used as food by Malays, being sliced and washed with the same care bestowed on *Gadong* (which see).

THE LANGKAP PALM

Juice obtained from the fruit of the large *langkap* palm (Arenga Westerhouti, Griff.—Palmæ) is used by Malays to poison their enemies. The pulpy part of the fruit is boiled and crushed, and the juice, after straining, is administered in coffee. It is said to cause dyspnœa and restlessness. Madinier, quoted by Greshoff (Ref. 11, Vol. X, p. 153), says that the ripe *langkap* fruit is an irritant to the mucous membranes. It causes an acute swelling of the mouth and fauces when taken internally, and this probably is due to the mechanical irritation of needle crystals. In the Philippines it is used by the Tagelo for poisoning fish. Ridley, however, says that the pith of the *langkap* palm is eaten by Malays in curries. This palm tree is well distributed in the Malay Peninsula, and may be abundant in some places on dry wooded hills. It grows to a height of from 16 to 30 feet; the trunk attains 6 to 8 inches in diameter. The fruit is oblong, depressed at the top, 2 inches long and 2½ inches through, yellowish green and black in colour. The juice of *kabong* or *bĕrkat*, the sugar palm (Arenga saccharifera, Labill.—Palmæ), is said to be used as a poison in the same way as *langkap*. It is a large palm about 20 to 30 feet tall and 12 inches through or more, remarkable for its stout black fibres, which are known in England as "vegetable horsehair." According to Ridley the unripe fruits of *kabong* are made into sweetmeats. The ripe fruit is irritating.

MĔRBAU AYER

Although the seeds of *pokok mĕrbau ayer* (Afzelia retusa, or Intsia retusa, Kurzii—Leguminosæ) are not used for homicidal purposes, they deserve mention on account of their poisonous properties. During the floods of 1919, two hungry Kelantan boys were collecting drift wood from the swollen river. They found some seeds of *mĕrbau ayer* and *buah gĕtah*, the seeds of Hevea brasiliensis—Euphorbiaceæ (Para rubber) which had floated down from the rubber estates up country; they boiled and ate the seeds with *ubi kayu*, tapioca root : both little boys died the same night at their village, Kampong Laut, a fishing village on the bank of the Kelantan River a few miles from the sea-coast.

Afzelia retusa is a tidal swamp tree of no great size, much smaller and quite distinct from the large *mĕrbau* tree (Afzelia palembanica) which furnishes the well-known hard-wood timber and dark brown cabinet wood of the tropics. Ridley describes the botany of *mĕrbau ayer* as follows : " The commonest form of *mĕrbau ayer* is Afzelia retusa ; it is a small tree about 15 to 20 feet tall, with leaves 3 to 6 inches long, of two pairs of leaflets, 2 to 4 inches long, $1\frac{1}{2}$ inches wide. Panicles short, $2\frac{1}{2}$ inches long. Flowers have only one petal, pink or white. Pod, 5 to 6 inches long, 2 inches wide, with flat, round seeds an inch across. It grows by tidal rivers from the Ganges, Andamans, etc., all along to Polynesia, the seeds being sea-dispersed." The seeds of *mĕrbau ayer* are a famine food in eastern Malaysia : " the flat seeds are used by the poor, placed on hot coals or ashes until the black seed coat bursts ; then they are soaked for three to four days in salt water, cooked and eaten." Many of the seeds of Leguminosæ contain hydrocyanic acid, and it is curious how many tidal swamp fruits or seeds have poisonous properties. According to Ridley, the presence of poison in these seeds may serve as a protection against depredation by fishes. Afzelia bijuga (Intsia bijuga, O. Ktze), a much taller and less common

sea-coast tree also occurs in the Malay Peninsula ;
A. bijuga is very like A. retusa, and it is questionable
if they are really distinct species (Ridley).

Manihot utilissima, Pohl.—Euphorbiaceæ (*ubi kayu*,
Malay) has sweet and bitter races ; sweet " Cassava "
is wholesome as tapioca, but bitter " Cassava " is
poisonous owing to the presence of hydrocyanic acid
in the fresh, milky juice ; it cannot be eaten with safety
until the volatile acid is driven off by roasting, squeezing out the bitter juice and re-cooking the root. Bitter
" Cassava " is not found in the Malay Peninsula to
any extent ; it seems certain that the children were
poisoned by the seeds of *mĕrbau ayer* which had been
improperly cooked on the bank of the tidal river.

PĔDĔNDANG GAGAK

A bitter inedible gourd (*pĕdĕndang*, or *mĕn-timum
dĕndang* ; Trichosanthes Wallichii, Wight—Cucurbitaceæ) is used as a poison in Kelantan by pounding
the very bitter ripe fruit and mixing it with opium
(*chandu*) and the bile of the porcupine (*ĕmpĕdu landak*).
It is a strong jungle vine with deep crimson fruits
about the size of small hens' eggs that look so attractive
on the banks of Malayan rivers ; but these " apples
of Sodom " have been found poisonous by Greshoff,
while the fruit of T. palmata, an allied far eastern
variety, was reckoned poisonous by Roxburgh. Several
Trichosanthes are included under *pĕdĕndang gagak ;*
T. Wallichii is perhaps the most common. A person
with bloodshot eyes " like a ripe *pĕdĕndang* fruit "
is referred to in an old Malay romance, the 'Hikayat
Indĕra Mĕngindĕra. The name of the plant, *pĕdĕndang
gagak*, is intimately connected with the crow, which
is called *dĕndang* in Kedah, but more generally *gagak*
in the other Malay States. The Malay synonym
mĕn-timun actually means the " crow's cucumber,"

while the fruit of the plant is always referred to as *buah pĕdĕndang*, *i.e.*, " crow's fruit." The cherry-red fruit does not appear to be very deadly ; the long lived crow feeds upon it, but is said to be the only bird that will do so. Malays say the fruit is *mabok* (intoxicant), not *rachun* (poisonous). Greshoff, however, says that the fruit of a Trichosanthes or Thladiantha found along the sea-shore in Java when mixed with coffee or food, causes death in eight days after vomiting and purging.

RĔNGAS (see also section JITONG)

Gluta Benghas, the well-known Rĕngas tree of Malaya, is now accepted by botanists as Stagmaria verniciflua, Jack—Anacardiaceæ ; but the name *rĕngas* is given by Malays to several large jungle trees belonging to this Natural Order, such as Melanorrhœa Curtisii, Oliv., M. Wallichii, Hook. fil., and others of this genus, as well as those belonging to the genus Gluta, which have already been mentioned under section JITONG. The botany of the *rĕngas* trees has been described by A. M. Burn-Murdoch (late Conservator of Forests, F.M.S. and S.S.) (Ref. 4). M. Maingayi is one of the commonest of these tall, handsomely foliaged trees ; it occurs in the south of the Peninsula, in Sumatra, and is distributed widely, but not abundantly, all over the Federated Malay States. The stem is straight and without buttresses, the leaves large ; the flowers are white and the fruit red and rather large ; it is a small drupe with five red wings like a child's paper windmill. The bark is reddish-brown, moderately rough, coming off in scales ; but it frequently appears much lighter, a whitish grey, when the tree is growing in the open, in clearings, etc. Black markings are frequent owing to exudations of the black poisonous sap which is called *gĕtah rĕngas*.

The sap of M. Wallichii (*rĕngas manok*) is reported to be specially poisonous. All the Anacardiaceæ possess this resin in various proportions ; it gives the curious scent to the foliage and the flavour to the mango (Mangifera Indica, Linn.—Anacardiaceæ).

Poisonous Properties.—*Rĕngas* sap is exuded in small quantities ; it is thinly viscid, but clear when quite fresh, with an odour of crushed mango leaves. It becomes yellow in colour and, although still quite fresh, quickly turns dark red on further exposure, and finally coagulates to a black resin. The sap of all the *rĕngas* trees sets up an acute dermatitis when it touches the skin, causing much swelling, followed by a pustular eruption which sometimes ends in chronic ulceration. Fever and other constitutional disturbances may develop, according to the susceptibility of the patient, but death from accidental *rĕngas* poisoning seems to be rare. Carnegie Brown describes the action of the sap of M. Curtisii, Oliv., from Penang as follows : " If the healthy skin is rubbed lightly with the juice from a freshly cut twig, violent inflammation, with smarting and burning pain, follows within twenty-four hours, and results in a characteristic pustular eruption—an eruption of blebs filled with matter. If the injured surface be of any extent, fever and other constitutional disturbances follow the local injury. When a large extent of skin has been affected, as happens when a native with unprotected body struggles through broken branches, this fever is said to be so irritant and septic that it not infrequently ends fatally. I have not, however, seen a case of such gravity, but from the peculiarly severe symptoms produced by the sap on a small surface there can be little doubt that where a large extent of skin is involved, the consequences might be most serious " (Ref. 2).

Œdema of the skin is especially marked when

rĕngas sap touches the face. Thus Ridley remarks, when commenting on the sap of Gluta Benghas : " A Javanese coolie was weeding some seedlings when he accidentally broke one and, feeling a mosquito on his face, he put up his hand to brush it off. His face very quickly swelled to a great size, and he had to be sent to the hospital for treatment for some days." Mr. Skeat tells me that his Boyanese syce climbed a *rĕngas* tree to cut an overhanging branch in the garden, and, not knowing the nature of the tree, took no precautions : " when he got down his face was swollen till it became quite round like a football, his eyes disappearing into his head." A precaution sometimes taken by Malay and Chinese timber-cutters, especially when they know themselves to be susceptible to *rĕngas* poisoning, is the smearing of their bodies with oil, such as sesamum or jingili oil (*minyak bijan* or *m. lĕnga*). The clinical symptoms of *rĕngas* poisoning resemble those of " lacquer poisoning," which is described by Scheube as being common in Japan and caused by the lacquer tree (Rhus vernicifera, D.C— Anacardiaceæ). O. L. Levin, in a recent description of " mah jongg dermatitis," reports that the toxic substance in Japanese lacquer is an acid glucoside to which the name *urshiol* has been given and states that alkaline lotions are useful in treatment (*Jour. Amer. Med. Assoc.* (Chicago), 1924, February 9th, p. 465).

Dermatitis produced by Ningpo varnish has the same origin. Chinese workmen use " tea oil," an oil expressed from the seeds of Thea sasanqua, to relieve the irritation.

The Melanorrhœa species of *rĕngas* yield a rich red timber streaked with black resinous lines in their very handsome heart-wood ; this was formerly known as Bornean rosewood or as Singapore mahogany : the grain is straight and even, but the wood is rather brittle. It takes a very fine polish, but its economic value, both in making furniture and in construction work, is seriously impaired owing to the poisonous black resin it contains. The heart-wood resists the attacks of white ants. According to Ridley, " bad effects are said to be produced in many persons by use of the furniture made from it even long after the wood has been worked up." *Rĕngas* furniture may affect those who are susceptible when it begins to get old, worn out and dusty, by producing irritation of the mouth, nose and throat. The use of *rĕngas* as a lachrymatory gas was suggested ; but it was never used during the War. Captain George W. Templer, an ex-Army gas instructor who was familiar with *rĕngas* poisoning among coolies on his Kelantan rubber estates, told me that the eruption produced by *rĕngas* sap is similar to the intractable blisters caused by the oily liquid of " mustard gas."

Poisonous properties remain in *rĕngas* trees for a length of time. Carnegie Brown says that after years of seasoning when the wood is cut up it gives rise to painful and intractable eruptions on the hands of the workmen. Burn-Murdoch advises ringing the tree and leaving it until it is dead before felling, or felling it and leaving it to lie in the forest until the bark and white sap-wood has decayed. Evil spirits are supposed to lurk in these trees, and the *jampi-jampi* incantations of the *bomor* are frequently requisitioned by Malay wood-cutters before they will consent to fell a *rĕngas* tree or cut its branches. *Rĕngas manok* (Melanorrhœa Wallichii) is one of the jungle trees in which wild bees build their nests ; all the " bee-trees " are considered very unlucky, because evil spirits are said to haunt them.

Mr. James W. Agar, Manager of one of the Kelantan rubber estates, told me that on sawing up some *rĕngas* trees that had been lying on his estate for three or four years some of his sawyers " got covered with a swollen red rash with occasional sores." He continued : " I stopped them before it got serious and think the rash and sores were brought about by the sawdust falling on the sweating bodies." Ridley also observes : " that those affected seriously by the *rĕngas* are those who sweat most." A day or two after contact with the tree, pustules generally form on the front of the abdomen in natives, as well as on the arms, legs, thighs and face. Carnegie Brown writes : " The immediate treatment of the poison is generally successful. It should be to wrap the injured part in bandages with some dry alkaline powder, such as bicarbonate of soda, the object being to counteract the acid of the poison and to absorb the exuded secretion from the skin." The poisonous principle of *rĕngas* is probably an acid glucoside similar to that of Rhus vernicifera. This species of Anacardiaceæ yields a clear, amber-red, viscous or oily liquid which blisters the skin severely, but when mixed in proper proportions with water and laccase (the gum enzyme from the latex) and exposed to the air it soon forms the characteristic black non-toxic lacquer. Fresh *rĕngas* sap is stated to be highly dangerous on internal administration, acting as a violent irritant and causing vomiting and purging (Melanorrhœa Curtisii) (Ref. 2).

Greshoff says that the fresh sap of Gluta Benghas when mixed in food or coffee causes darkening of the skin, severe intestinal colic and death in one or two days (Indian Poison Reports, 1902).

Greshoff also, quoting from Upwich (*Gen. Tydschrift v. Nederl. Ind.*, XXXIV, p. 795), describes cases of poisoning by *rĕngas* (G. coarctata) in soldiers after crossing rivers into which the fruit had fallen ;

also cases at Banjarmassin, in Borneo, where, in 1862, two whole companies of a military expedition were affected with a painful and even dangerous eruption on the feet. The men had waded through rivers where the trees were growing ; the fruits falling into the water had exuded latex and so produced poisoning : for the same reason it is undesirable to shelter under a *rĕngas* tree during a tropical rain storm.

The binjai tree (Mangifera cœsia—Anacardiaceæ), discovered by Jack in 1830, is said to have similar poisonous properties to *rĕngas*, and it is perhaps worthy of note that the Kelantan *bomor* uses an infusion of the root of the *binjai* tree as an antidote to poisoning by *rĕngas*, and similarly that of *rĕngas* for poisoning by *binjai*. A Malay wood-cutter, however, covered with *rĕngas* pustules and admitted to the State Hospital, Kelantan, said he had applied an infusion of *binjai* bark to his skin with harmful results. He was soon cured in hospital by saline purgatives and the application of carbolic oil 1 in 40. *Rĕngas* fruits are sometimes maliciously thrown into wells by Malays. The criminal uses *rĕngas* sap with " toad venom " as an external application with *binjai* sap in addition (see section FROGS AND TOADS).

RENGUT

The *rengut* (Raphidophora giganteum, Schott, Araceæ) is a huge climbing jungle shrub ; the botany is described by Ridley : " Stem 40 to 60 feet long and over an inch through, green. Leaves 12 to 36 inches long, 6 to 8 wide, entire, oblong, very coriaceous, dark green, nerves very numerous, fine and close, apex blunt, base rounded, petiole 8 to 15 inches long, sheathing for its whole length. Peduncle an inch long, stout. Spathe 6 to 15 inches long, nearly 2 inches through, dull green, cylindric, cuspidate. Spadix yellowish-white,

10 inches long.   Flowers ⅛ inch across, very narrow, rhomboid, longer than broad.   Stamens white filaments, broad.   Stigma, linear depressed grey " (Ref. 20). *Rengut* has a spike of green flowers wrapped in a large spathe, arranged together like the corn-cob or head of maize.   The liquid contained in the spathe of flowers is very irritating to the skin ;   minute transparent crystals abound in the spadices, which are used, as referred to under section THE UPAS TREE, by the Pangan negritos as part of a poison for arrows and darts. The *rengut* plant is common in the jungle all over the Malay Peninsula.

Poisonous Properties.—When the fruit decays the softer tissues perish, liberating innumerable numbers of bast cells from the wall of the carpel of the flower ; these look like fine, sharply-pointed hairs, and under the microscope masses of needle-shaped crystals may be seen among them.   Malays call the fruit *buah rengut*, and it is known by them to be very irritant.   *Buah rengut* is a common ingredient in many Malay poisons : the chemical properties have not yet been determined ; but as so many plant crystals are composed of oxalate of calcium, some authors have asserted that the irritant action of these octrahedral crystals when administered internally may depend upon oxalic acid liberated by the action of the gastric juice.   The shape of *buah rengut* crystals would, however, disprove this supposition. When taken internally *rengut* is said to cause distension of the abdomen amounting to dropsy, followed by cough and emaciation, and terminating with intestinal hæmorrhage.   In 1912 a well at Tabal, a small fishing village on the sea-coast of Kelantan, was poisoned with *rengut* in combination with the pill-millepede and the bristle-bearing worm (*ulat bulu laut*).   These were weighted and sunk by means of a " thunderbolt-stone " (*batu lintar*) to which they were attached.

The people concerned experienced pain and distension of the stomach, but were not seriously ill. Magic powers are ascribed by Malays to the " celts," or " stone-age " implements commonly called " thunder-bolts."

Mixtures of Rengut.—A similar vehicle for the administration of *buah rengut* is prepared by crushing the pill-millepede in the same way and adding the galls of the honey-bear and horned toad-frog. Another combination is to take *buah rengut*, the bristles of the marine worm, and lime and make them up into a bolus with the gall of a frog. Or as a poison *buah rengut* may either be mixed into cooked rice, given in water, suspended in the bile of the globe-fish (*ikan buntal*), or, in combination with other things, put into wells, a procedure which is not an unusual method of adminis-tering other Malay poisons, such as datura, *bĕrĕdin*, *chĕngkian*, *rĕngas*, and *tuba*. Another poisonous pre-paration for consumption is made by combining *buah rengut* with the bristles of the " sea-worm " and the roasted substance of a jelly-fish (*gĕronggong laut*). These three ingredients are suspended in the mucus obtained by crushing the pill-millepede and the land-snail (Nanina hymphreysiana). The jelly-fish is the common small white " sea-nettle," which is itself able to inflict a very severe, and in some cases a dangerous, sting.

Malays are very chary about collecting even a single specimen of the *rengut* fruit ; even the negritos seldom gather the dry fruit, because the dust which is present may cause blindness. Malays say that wild monkeys pinch off the flowers to protect their young from being poisoned by the fruit, but in the Botanic Gardens at Singapore young monkeys have often been observed eating the pulvinus at the base of the leaf blade.

A preposterous Malay antidote for poisoning by

rengut, when compounded as a deadly poison (*rachun besar*), is to take bones of a whale, the solid casque of a rare hornbill (Rhinoplax vigil), a sea-porcupine's spine, stag's horn and rhinoceros horn, and rub them down together in hot water to make a draught. The following prescription, "beyond help from antidote," was given to me by the headman of the Kĕsial district in Kelantan, a district with an evil reputation in the art of poisoning : "Take *rengut* fruit, bristles of the ' hairy sea-worm,' hairs of the caterpillar (*ulat bulu darat*), juice of the millepedes (*pinang kotai* and *jĕlantor*), bile of toad and crow (*ĕmpĕdu katak puru* and *burong gagak*), and *miang rĕbong* (bamboo hairs), mix them, then add shreds of the dry *ibul* nut." The effect of this mixture is said to be a cough with spitting of blood, quickly followed by insensibility and death.

TANGIS SARANG BURONG

The *Tangis Sarang Burong* tree (Heynea trijuga, Roxb.—Meliaceæ) is not a very poisonous tree ; but the fruit is sometimes mixed with *chandu* (opium prepared for the pipe), or with *chandu* dross (*tengkoh*, opium prepared for resmoking), and with ripe areca-nut, and then used by thieves to stupefy people. *Chandu* dross, the *tengkoh* of the Chinese, is cheaper to buy than *chandu ;* it is a black, hard, dry stuff, which on the application of heat gives off the peculiar fumes of the opium pipe.

Heynea trijuga is one of the Indian medicinal plants described by Kirtikar and Basu ; the bark and leaves are said to possess tonic principles. Heynea trijuga is rare in the Malay States. Kirtikar and Basu describe it as a small, somewhat shrubby jungle tree, but attaining a large size when cultivated, with small whitish flowers : calyx campanulate, three to five cleft ; petals valved in bud ; fruit small, about ½ to

⅔ inch in diameter, red. Kelantan Malays say that the very pretty red fruit is a fatal poison to birds, hence the name *tangis* ("weeping") and *sarang burong* ("a bird's-nest"); but this is denied in Pahang, where the derivation of the word is taken as being due to the fruit, which, though so attractive in appearance, is useless as food. A dozen half-ripe fruits freshly gathered early in September from a large *tangis sarang burong* tree growing near the Sultan's palace, Kota Bharu, Kelantan, had no effect on a lesser adjutant bird which swallowed them.

A bitter stuff has been obtained from Heynea trijuga, but it is not a glucoside. Greshoff says that the bitter extract taken from the seeds of the allied H. sumatrana, Miq., was apparently not poisonous (Ref. 11, Vol. XXV, p. 40). Borsma, however, says that with 50 mg. of an extract obtained from the bark and branches he caused a marked intoxication with fatal effect in frogs.

THE UPAS CLIMBER

The Upas climber, Strychnos ovalifolia, Wall.— Loganaceæ, is *akar ipoh*, a jungle climbing plant, the *chettik* and upas tieuté of Java, the *ipoh gunong* of the Kedah negritos, the *blay hitam* of Vaughan Stevens, and Cerruti's *legop*. It is one of the poisonous plants used in making arrow and dart poisons by the jungle tribes of the Malay Peninsula, and has been botanically described by Ridley as follows: "A strong woody creeper attaining the length of 100 feet or less, and a diameter of 3 inches. The bark is smooth and black. The branches usually fairly stout, climbing by means of rather large woody hooks. Leaves, polished dark green, oblong acuminate, with the characteristic three parallel nerves as in other species, 3 inches long and about 1½ wide. The flowers are small and tubular,

with four lobes to the corolla, greenish white ; they
are arranged in short axillary panicles about an inch
long, in pairs. The fruit is a globular berry about 2
inches through, of a greenish grey colour. The rind,
about ⅛ inch thick, is woody but brittle, and encloses
a soft whitish pulp, in which are embedded numerous
oblong flattened seeds about ½ to 1 inch long, and ½ or
more wide, brown with silky coat. Every portion of
the plant has an intensely bitter taste, especially the
fruit and the pulp enclosing the seeds " (Ref. 18).

Mr. Ridley goes on to say that the Malayan species
of Strychnos are often troublesome to identify, as they
flower as a rule very irregularly, and, owing to the
height to which most species climb before flowering, the
flowers are very difficult to collect. The foliage, too,
is often very variable, according to the part of the tree
from which it is obtained. Strychnos Wallichiana,
Benth., is the *ipoh akar* of Borneo ; S. Maingayi,
Clarke, is the *akar lampong* of Malacca. The *upas*
climber is abundant over the greater part of the Malay
Peninsula.

The botany of *akar ipoh* is given at length because it
is important to distinguish it from *pokok ipoh*, the well-
known upas tree of Java. The Javanese word *upas*
means blood poison (especially the vegetable poison
used for darts), and confusion occurred when S. tieute
(*akar ipoh*), collected in 1809 by Leschenault in Java,
began to be known as upas tieuté. *Ipoh* is a Malay
word used for dart poisons in general, in the same way
as the word *tuba* is used for fish poisons (which see,
p. 236).

The active principle of Strychnos tieuté has been
shown by H. and G. Santesson to be the alkaloid
brucine (*Archiv. de Pharmacie*, 1893, p. 591). Brucine
is a derivative of strychnine ; it occurs in all the species
of Strychnos. It closely resembles strychnine in its

physiological action, and acts principally on the spinal cord, causing excessive reflex irritability, and in very large doses death from paralysis of the central nervous system ; but it is much less toxic, the relative toxicities of the two alkaloids being as 4 to 33 (Ref. 12). It also differs from strychnine in its more powerful curari-like action on the nerve terminations in voluntary muscle. Death is due to failure of respiration and stoppage of the heart. The poison contained in *akar ipoh* is somewhat akin to the curari or urari arrow poison of South America, which is an aqueous extract of various species of Strychnos indigenous to that country.

Dart Poison.—Poison prepared for blowpipe darts by the jungle tribes of the Malay Peninsula sometimes contains *akar ipoh* alone ; but is more often a mixture of *akar ipoh* and the fresh juice of *pokok ipoh*, the upas tree. The negritos of Perak (Sĕmang) poison both arrows and blowpipe darts with *akar ipoh*. The bark of the plant and its roots are shredded when fresh, and then boiled until the decoction thickens to a black paste with an intensely bitter taste. Ridley remarks that " intensely bitter as is the fruit and especially the pulp enclosing the seeds, both monkeys and civet cats eat it, the latter appearing especially fond of it."

Mr. Ridley's note is of interest because the immunity of monkeys to strychnine has been mentioned by other observers, and it may explain some of the jungle-craft of the wild tribes in choosing different poisons for different animals. In the *Pharmaceutical Journal* of March 28th, 1874, the following reference is made : " Plants which are poisonous to some animals are not so to others. Strychnia has no effect upon invertebrate animals and is said not to poison monkeys. Many of the poisons which destroy life of man and other carnivora are eaten with impunity by graminivorous animals. Thus, opium does not poison pigeons ;

tobacco and hemlock do not injure goats ; and stramonium, henbane and belladonna are eaten by rabbits " (E. M. Holmes). Seligmann, again, has shown that fowls, and to a less degree pheasants, possess a high degree of immunity to the poison of the upas tree (antiarin) when it is injected subcutaneously ; but pigeons, on the other hand, are killed by this poison with startling rapidity (Ref. 21).

The Malay jungle-folk have special markings on their blowpipe darts by means of which they differentiate their various poisons ; and among the savage Malays of Johore (*Bĕnua-Jakun*) there is an elaborate system of marking the poisoned darts, by means of which their different strengths can be recognised and their suitability for killing either large or small game kept in mind (Ref. 22, p. 331). The poison of the upas tree may be specially marked on the darts to distinguish it from the totally different poison obtained from *akar ipoh*, more especially when each is used by itself and not mixed with other things. Sometimes the wild *orang bukit* (hill-men) cut out the flesh round the wound before eating animals killed by darts tipped with poison (antiarin) obtained from the upas tree ; but it is uncertain whether they always do so in the case of the *akar ipoh* poison. It has been proved that the former (antiarin) taken internally by the mouth is harmless to human beings ; but the poison of the latter (brucine) may well be harmful. Some years ago a Sakai was accused of trying to poison a Malay with dart poison. Ridley gave the greater part of a slimy, black paste from a small box which formed the exhibit, to a spaniel dog without effect, but when applied to the tongue of a toad, the batrachian stretched out and expired. Toads are very sensitive to strychnine.

THE UPAS TREE

The celebrated deadly *upas* or *anchar* tree of Java,
which was at one time supposed to give off poisonous
fumes fatal to animal life, is the Malay *pokok ipoh* or
batang ipoh. It is Antiaris toxicaria, Bl.—Urticaceæ,
and has been botanically described by Ridley as follows : " A gigantic tree, attaining a height of over 100
feet and a diameter of 4 or more above the base where
it throws out large buttresses. The bark is grey, about
½ inch thick. Like nearly all of our largest trees,
it drops the lower branches as it grows, so that a large
specimen has a perfectly bare trunk for some 60 or
80 feet. The leaves vary very much in size and
hairiness, they are generally oblong-acuminate, inequi-
lateral, from 4 to 6 inches long, and 2 or 3 inches
broad, the leaf-stalk a quarter of an inch long, the
backs of the leaves as well as the buds are covered
with yellow hairs, and the upper surface of the leaf is
more or less hairy, especially in the case of young leaves,
though older ones are often glabrous above. The male
inflorescence is a small, fleshy green disc-shaped body
on a short peduncle ; and the flowers which are very
small are imbedded in it. The female flowers are small,
solitary, pear-shaped bodies with a pair of long, thread-
like styles. The fruit is a globular succulent drupe
about a third of an inch long, velvety and of a deep
claret colour, and bears the remains of the styles. It
contains a single, round seed " (Ref. 18).

Blume describes the fruit as of an elongate ellipsoid
form and as big as a plum ; but Ridley's specimens,
obtained from near the Batu caves at Kuala Lumpur,
Selangor, were much smaller and quite globular.
Kirtikar and Basu give a description of the upas tree of
India (Antiaris toxicaria, Leschen) : " A gigantic
ever-green tree, with soft, white, even-grained wood,

attaining a height of 250 feet, fruit, like a small fig, purple, scarlet or crimson ; piriform, velvety, fleshy, and ¾ inch in diameter " (Ref. 15, p. 1203). The botany of Antiaris toxicaria is quoted at length for the same reasons given under section THE UPAS CLIMBER. A. innoxia, a sister tree to A. toxicaria, is the " riti " or " sack-tree " of Ceylon and the Moluccas from which bark-cloth is made ; it has no medicinal or poisonous properties.

Few trees have been more amusing to the world than Arbor toxicaria, the *ipoh* or upas of Rumphius (" Herbarium Amboinense," ed., Amsterd. A.D., 1675). The fables connected with it were first recorded in 1783 by Foersch, a Dutch doctor in the service of the Dutch East India Company. Criminals condemned to die, he wrote, were offered the chance of life if they would go to the upas tree and collect some of the poison, and of those who accepted the offer " only two out of twenty returned alive." Those who were lucky enough to escape reported that " they found the ground under the trees covered with the bones of the dead." " Not a tree," he added, " nor blade of grass is to be found in the valley or surrounding mountains. Not a beast or bird, reptile or living thing, lives in the vicinity." A putrid steam was supposed to rise from the tree. The ridiculous tale told by Foersch about the upas tree of Java or poison tree of Macassar, originated in a misunderstanding. He was shown one or more of the volcanic valleys in Java which are deadly to pass over owing to an escape of carbonic acid gas and confused *upas*, a word used for poison generally in Java, and especially for fungi, with the tree Antiaris toxicaria. The mistake has been perpetuated by Darwin in his " Loves of the Plants " (Ref. 7, p. 143) :—

> Fierce in dread silence on the blasted heath,
> Fell Upas sits, the Hydra-Tree of death.

Charles Campbell very shortly refuted the " travellers' tales " of Foersch, and observed : " As to the tree itself I have sat under its shade, and seen birds alight upon its branches ; and as to the story of grass not growing beneath it, everyone who has been in a forest must know that grass is not found in such situations." These facts were corroborated many years later by Vaughan Stevens and Ridley, who, by personal experiments, also proved that the juice of the tree can be applied to the unbroken skin and can be taken internally by the mouth without producing poisonous effects in human beings.

Uses.—Hose records that the Punans of Borneo use it as a febrifuge in the form of a decoction, and also apply it to snake bites and festering wounds (Ref. 14, Vol. II, p. 208).

The milky sap of the upas tree was formerly used in warfare by Malays as an effective poison for arrows and blowpipe darts. When the siege of Malacca was commenced in July, 1511, Alfonso Dalbuquerque found that all his Portuguese soldiers who were wounded by poisoned darts died except one man, who was burned with a red-hot iron directly after he was pierced, so that ultimately his life was spared. Again, Danvers records that in the second assault on the city, which took place in August, 1511, a number of Portuguese were wounded, and the most fatal cases were those caused by poisoned darts expelled from blowpipes (Ref. 6, Vol. I, p. 228). Arrows and darts poisoned with the latex of Antiaris toxicaria are still used by the pagan tribes of Borneo and Sumatra in inter-tribal warfare. A correspondent writing (1915) from Sumatra to the *Journal of the Ceylon Agricultural Society* for October states that during the last inter-tribal war of the interior, men from the mountains came down to Kwala, a distance of 100 miles or more, to collect the juice of the tree for the poisoning of their blowpipe darts. Upas poison is essential to the jungle-folk of Malaya of the present day when hunting for their food supplies.

Dart Poison.—In a short paper entitled " The Poisonous Plants of the Malay Peninsula," Ridley has given a good deal of information about Malay arrow and dart poison and has compiled a bibliography for reference up to the year 1898 (Ref. 18). Very much more has been published by Skeat and Blagden in " Pagan Races of the Malay Peninsula " (Ref. 22). The composition of Malay arrow and dart poison is complex ; but the yellowish white sap of *pokok ipoh* (Antiaris toxicaria) is nearly always an important, if not the chief, ingredient. In the following lists those plants, etc., which are dealt with in this work are marked with an asterisk : the various wild tribes of the Malay Peninsula who use arrow and dart poison in every-day life specialise in it in different ways ; thus :—

(1) The negritos of the east coast (Pangan and Sĕmang), according to different authorities, use, in addition to the sap from the bark of the upas tree (A. toxicaria, Bl.), the bark and sap of the upas climber* and that of Strychnos pubescens, Clarke* ; the bark of Gnetum edule, Bl. (S. tieuté, Bl.) ; the bark and sap of Roucheria Griffithiana, Planch. ; the fruits of Pangium edule, Miq.,* and Epipremnum (Raphidophera) giganteum, Schott* ; the leaves of Laportea crenulata, Forst., * and Cnesmone Javanica, Bl.* ; the roots of Amorphophallus, sp.,* and Dioscorea, sp.* ; the seed capsules of Miquelia caudata, King; the bark of half a dozen unidentified plants or trees; the sap of two unknown jungle vines (*rotan*) ; and poison from the scorpion, centipede, and any kind of poisonous snake.

(2) The Bĕsisi tribe of Selangor, according to Skeat and Bellamy, use, in addition to the sap from the bark of the upas tree (A. toxicaria, Bl.), scrapings from the

root of the upas climber (S. tieuté, Bl.) and (?) S.
pubescens, Clarke ; roots of the pepper vine, Piper,
sp.* ; the fruit of Melanorrhœa Wallichii, Hook. fil.* ;
the sap of Excœcaria agallocha, Linn.,* and Gluta
renghas, Linn.* ; the roots (?) of Derris elliptica,
Benth.,* of Gnetum edule, Bl., of Lophopetalum
pallidum, Laws, and of Thevetia nerifolia, Juss.* ;
and in addition poison obtained from snakes, scorpions
and centipedes, as well as white arsenic.*

(3) The Mantra of Malacca use, in addition to the
sap obtained from the bark of the upas tree (A. toxicaria, Bl.), the bark (?) of Strychnos, sp. ; the sap of
Dæmonorps geniculatus, Martt., and of Alocasia singa-
porensis, Lindl.* ; the tubers of Dioscorea, sp. ; the
root of Derris elliptica, Benth. ; the root and bark of
Tabernæmontana malaccensis, Hook. fil. ; the bark of
Carapa malaccensis, Lam., and Lophopetalum pallidum, Laws ; the bark or roots of two unknown plants ;
the fruit of (?) a chilli ; the seeds of Citrus, sp. ; and
poisons derived from centipedes, snakes and scorpions,
as well as arsenic.

(4) The Bĕnua tribe of Johore use, in addition to
the sap obtained from the bark of the upas tree
(A. toxicaria, Bl.), the sap obtained from several
poisonous trees—Excœcaria agallocha, Linn., Cerbera
odollam, Linn.,* C. lactaria, Ham., and Erianthemum
malvaceæ, Clarke ; also various non-vegetable substances, such as centipede heads, millepedes,* the
stings of scorpions ; the poisonous spines of certain
fishes, such as Plotosus, sp.,* Clarius majur,* Trygon,
sp.,* and four other spinal salt-water fish or rays that
are unidentified, viz., *kitang, lĕpu, siong* and *tĕtuka ;*
the liver of Tetrodon, sp.* ; as well as snake poison,
including that of the cobra,* and the red variety of
arsenic.*   These particulars are taken from the tables
given in Skeat and Blagden's " Pagan Races," Vol. I,

p. 602 : it appears from them that many Malay poisons came into use from knowledge obtained from the wild tribes ; but the latter must have learnt the use of arsenic from their Malay overlords. Other plants, such as Coscinium fenestratum, Coleb., Menispermaceæ ; Medinilla, sp., Melastomaceæ (*asam lokan puteh*) ; and Aralidium pinnatifidum, Miq. (*selubat*), are also said to be put into arrow poisons by Malays.

Upas arrow and dart poison is generally a sticky stuff, something like black treacle in consistency and colour when freshly made. The basis is the inspissated sap of Antiaris toxicaria (*pokok ipoh*) with powerful adjuvants, such as Strychnos tieuté (*akar ipoh*), Dioscorea triphylla (*gadong*), and Derris elliptica (*tuba*) ; the other ingredients appear to resemble the correctives and vehicles which used to obtain in a model medical prescription. The employment of multifarious ingredients in the various arrow poisons suggests the habits of old-time medical practitioners, who used to prescribe a multitude of substances with a heroic disregard of compatibility, whether chemical, physical, or therapeutical, in the hope that some one of them would hit the mark.

Newbold (1839) describes the process of concocting a Bĕnua arrow poison : " The roots are carefully selected and cut at a particular age of the moon ; probably about the fall. The woody fibre is thrown away and nothing but the succulent bark used. This is put into a *kualli* (a sort of earthen pipkin) with as much soft water as will cover the mass, and kneaded well together. This done, more water is added, and the whole is submitted to a slow heat over a charcoal fire until half the water has evaporated. The decoction is next strained through a cotton cloth, and again submitted to slow ebullition until it attains the consistency of syrup. Red arsenic (*warangan*), which is rubbed down in the juice of the sour lime, the *limau asam* of the Malays, is then added, and the mixture poured into small bamboos, which are carefully closed up ready for use. Some of the tribes add a little opium, spices and saffron ; some the juice of the lancha, and the bones of the sunggat-fish burnt to ashes. A number of juggling incantations are performed, and spells gibbered over the seething cauldron by the *Poyangs* (magicians) by whom the fancied moment of the projection of the poisonous principle is as anxiously watched for as for that of the philosopher's stone or the elixir vitæ by the alchemists and philosophers of more enlightened races. When recently prepared the *ipoh* poisons are all of a dark liver-brown colour, of the consistency of syrup, and emit a strongly narcotic odour. The deleterious principle appears to be volatile, the efficacy of the poison is diminished by keeping " (Ref. 22, Vol. I, p. 332).

Kelantan negritos (*Orang Pangan*, inhabiting the Nĕnggiri district) use two kinds of dart poison, one stronger than the other. They use the sap of the upas tree (*gĕtah pokok ipoh*) by itself as a minor poison for small animals, etc. ; but when making the more poisonous preparation they add the young shoots of *gadong* and prepare it in the following way : The fresh juice is obtained by tapping the bark of *pokok ipoh* and collecting in bamboo cylinders ; it is then made viscid by partial boiling, the juice of the *gadong* shoots is added with a little water, and the whole boiled. It is next poured out on to a board and evaporated to dryness by heating over a fire. The inspissated juice is said to be now very poisonous to handle, and it is stated that even a little of it under the finger-nails may cause death. Hose, however, refers to the possibility of an acquired immunity by constant handling, especially among natives of Borneo (Punans), who use the poison of the

ipoh tree as a medicine (Ref. 14, Vol. II, p. 208).
L. Wray, jun., has also described the use of *gadong* as a
dart poison.

In the Malay Peninsula arrows are poisoned by
smearing layers of *ipoh* poison on the blade so as to form
a rather thick, hard cake ; it is also smeared on the
shaft of the arrow for about 2 or more inches. The
arrows are made from the stem of the *bertam* palm
(Eugeissoma tristis, Griff.) ; they are either wholly of
wood, spear-shaped, with a blade of 4 inches and length
of shaft of about 3 feet, or with a blade made of a
rough piece of barbed iron. It is said by Pahang
Malays that wounds caused by five arrows from a bow
at close quarters are sufficient to kill an elephant.
Ipoh poison is applied in the same way to darts used
with the blow-pipe ; these are about 10 inches in length
—*i.e.*, often the " breast to breast " measurement of the
maker—and made from the small palm Cyrtostachys
Lakka, Becc. Each dart is nicked near the point, and,
as they are only $\frac{1}{16}$ inch in diameter, the poisoned
part breaks off readily and remains embedded in the
flesh of the objective. The blowpipe is a narrow
bamboo tube about 6 feet long fitted with a small
mouth-piece to hold some pith (see section THE
BĔRĔDIN PALM). The method of shooting consists
in gripping the pipe close to the mouth with both
hands, swaying the weapon up and down until it
has been sighted, and then blowing fiercely. In
Kelantan it is said that an elephant shot in the morning
with two *ipoh gadong* darts will collapse before nightfall,
and that a monkey will fall dead almost immediately.

The poisonous effects of these darts on man can be
realised from an account of an accident in Perak given
by L. Wray, jun. : " While unloading and carrying the
baggage over the rocks, a poisoned blowpipe dart fell
out of a quiver and stuck in the upper part of one of the

men's feet. It was at once pulled out, and a Sĕmang squeezed the wound to get out as much blood as possible, then tied a tight ligature round his leg, and put lime juice into the wound. The man complained of great pain in the foot, cramps in the stomach, and vomited, but these symptoms soon passed off. The point only went into the foot about $\frac{1}{8}$ inch and the dart was instantly pulled out. The Sĕmangs said that, had it gone deep into the fleshy part of the body, it would have caused death."

Nature of Upas Tree Poison.—Although the powerful poison contained in the fresh sap of Antiaris toxicaria may be harmless when taken by the mouth, it is deadly when injected under the skin of human beings, causing violent intestinal paralysis : cases of accidental death have been recorded. The fresh sap has the odour of sour bread dough, the consistency of thin cream, and quickly decomposes. The active principle of Antiaris toxicaria is antiarin, a glucoside akin to strophanthin ; a large number of investigators have been interested in it. The physiology of antiarin has been studied by Hedbom, the chemistry by Killani ; while Seligmann, working with material obtained from the Kenyah district of Borneo (Ref. 21), has given a very excellent description of the symptoms of poisoning by antiarin. An extract from his paper is given in the *British Medical Journal*, Vol. I, p. 1129, for 1903. When experimenting on frogs, ·001 mg. of antiarin produced clonic spasms of the muscles, paralysis, and systolic arrest of the ventricles of the heart. Rapid fall of blood pressure and convulsions (clonic spasm) occurred, and paralysis was set up by the pure crystalline glucoside. With animals, gastro-intestinal symptoms, such as vomiting, salivation, and diarrhœa, were conspicuous, except in guinea-pigs. Dr. Seligmann remarks on the suddenness with which the poison acts on pigeons. He injected 3 mg. of *ipoh* into a pigeon weighing 290 grammes (about 10¼ ounces). After a few minutes, during which no special discomfort was observed—or at most the bird appeared a little weak on its legs—the respirations became deep, a single act of vomiting occurred by which the crop was partially emptied, and the bird pitched forward and became convulsed for about thirty seconds, at the end of which time it was dead. In the Dutch East Indies *ipoh* is found very fatal to monkeys, but not to fowls.

A native antidote for dart poison is the juice of the common " thin-skinned lime " (*limau nipis;* Citrus acida, Roxb.—Rutaceæ) which is squeezed into the wound ; but Kelantan Malays also pin their faith to a mouthful of dry earth eaten immediately on the receipt of the injury. The negritos of Kelantan (*Pangan*) rely upon the fruit of a jungle tree which smells very strongly of onions (*kulim;* Scorodocarpus borneensis, Beec.—Oleaceæ). The fruit of this tree is eaten, or if it is not available, an infusion is made of the bark. Human urine administered internally is also supposed by the Kelantan jungle-folk to be an antidote.

REFERENCES

(1) BRANDIS, D. " Indian Trees." 1921. London : Constable.
(2) BROWN, W. C. " A Note on Rengas Poisoning." *Jour. Straits Br. Roy. Asiat. Soc.* (Singapore). 1891. No. 24, p. 83.
(3) BURTON-BROWN, T. E. " Punjab Poisons," 1888. p. 163. Calcutta.
(4) BURN-MURDOCH, A. M. " Trees and Timbers of the Malay Peninsula." 1912. Selangor, F.M.S.
(5) CLIFFORD, Sir HUGH. " Studies in Brown Humanity." 1927. 2nd ed. London : Richards.
(6) DANVERS, F. C. " The Portuguese in India." 1894. Vol. I, p. 228. London : H. Allen.
(7) DARWIN, E. " Loves of the Plants." 1806. p. 143. London.
(8) DURHAM, H. E. " Einige Studien über Abrus-und Rizinus-Samen. 1913. *Archiv. für Hygiene,* Bd. 81. Munchen.

(9) EATON, B. J. " Kapayang Oil." *Agric. Bull.* F.M.S. (Selangor). 1913. No. 3, Vol. II, p. 67.

(10) ELFSTRAND. *Görbersdörfer Veröffentlichumgen.* I. 1898.

(11) GRESHOFF, M. *Mededeelingen uit s'Lands Planten.* 1893. Vols. X and XXV. Batavia.

(12) HENRY, T. A. "The Plant Alkaloids." 1924. 2nd ed., p. 194. London : Churchill.

(13) HOOKER, Sir W. J. "The Flora of British India." 1897. Ashford, Kent : L. Reeve.

(14) HOSE and McDOUGALL. " The Pagan Tribes of Borneo." 1912. London : Macmillan.

(15) KIRTIKAR and BASU. " Indian Medicinal Plants." 1918. Allahabad : Kegan Paul.

(16) MACMILLAN, H. F. " A Handbook of Tropical Gardening and Planting." 1925. Colombo : Cave.

(17) POWELL, T. " On the Nature and Mode of Use of the Vegetable Poisons employed by the Samoan Islanders." *Jour. Linn. Soc.* (London). 1877. Vol. XVI, " Botany." No. 89, p. 55.

(18) RIDLEY, H. N. " The Poisonous Plants of the Malay Peninsula." *Agric. Bull. S. and F.M.S.* 1898. No. 8, Vol. VII, p. 199. Singapore.

(19) RIDLEY, H. N. " Sarcolobus Globosus." *Agric. Bull. S. and F.M.S.* 1903. No. 7, Vol. II, p. 223. Singapore.

(20) RIDLEY, H. N. " The Flora of the Malay Pensinsula." 1925. Ashford, Kent : L. Reeve.

(21) SELIGMANN, C. G. " On the Physiological Action of the Kenyah Dart Poison, Ipoh and its Active Principle, Antiarin." *Jour. Physiol.* (London). 1903. No. 1. Vol. XXIX.

(22) SKEAT and BLAGDEN. " Pagan Races of the Malay Peninsula." 1906. London : Macmillan.

(23) SMITH, SYDNEY. " Forensic Medicine." 1928. 2nd ed. London : Churchill.

(24) STILLMARK. " Pharmak. Arbeiten, Dorpat. (Kobert)." 1889. III.

CHAPTER IX

OTHER POISONS OF VEGETABLE ORIGIN

CHĔRAKA

Chĕraka merah, an ornamental plant of evil reputation with small red flowers (Plumbago rosea, Linn.—Plumbaginaceæ), grows in Malay villages and gardens; it is the same plant as the Hindustani *lal chitra*. The botany of Plumbago rosea has been described in great detail by Kirtikar and Basu (Ref. 14). *Chĕraka merah* is an evergreen perennial shrub, 2 to 3 feet high, " very rarely annular " (Boissier)—perhaps only a cultivated variety of P. zeylanica (C. B. Clarke). The root of P. rosea is used by Malay women as an abortifacient: it is from $\frac{1}{4}$ to $\frac{1}{2}$ inch in thickness; when mature it is woody and solid, nodose, and contorted near the stem, with many rootlets, sometimes 2 feet long. When fresh it is darkish yellow in colour, becoming longitudinally striated when dry; on section, pale yellow, with a brown tinge in the central axis. In Kelantan it is used for the above illegal purpose in the form of a decoction compounded with the roots of four other village plants, which may be merely flavouring or corrective additions, as the root of P. rosea is well known to be acrid and vesicant.

These four agents are : (1) The root of henna or " tree-mignonette " (*inai ;* Lawsonia alba, Lam.—Lythraceæ), a shrub whose light green leaves are so often used for beautifying by young Hindu and Muhammadan girls by reddening their palms, finger and toe nails ; for this purpose a paste of the leaves pounded with a little boiled rice is applied. (2) The

root of *chĕmpaka hutan* (Gardenia Griffithii, Hook. fil.—
Rubiaceæ), a commonly cultivated plant much prized
by all Malays for its sweet-scented, orange-coloured,
and somewhat tulip-like flowers, that are so often
worn by women in the hair. (3) The root of *kĕnanga*
(Cananga odorata, Linn.—Anonaceæ), an evergreen tree
bearing bunches of sweet-scented, yellowish-green
flowers, the source of " ylang-ylang " perfume, which
are frequently used by Malay women to twist in the
coils of their hair. (4) The root of *kĕnĕrak* (Goniothalamus tapis, Miq.—Anonaceæ), a fair-sized village
tree with fragrant white flowers. The roots of these
five plants are all boiled together for a time, and the
decoction is swallowed, at intervals, until the desired
result is effected. It is so used only in the early
months of pregnancy.

Another method is to boil the root of *chĕraka merah*
with *puchok pinang*, the shoots of the areca palm, and
the root of a hedge-shrub (*akar guroh pĕriat;* Croton
caudatus, Griseb.—Euphorbiaceæ). This decoction is
given *ad libitum* by the mouth. To control the resulting hæmorrhage the following may be administered : a
decoction made from the roots of a pumpkin (*akar labu
ayer ;* Cucurbita pepo, Linn.—Cucurbitaceæ) and of
akar bayam merah (Amaranthus gangeticus, Linn.—
Amaranthaceæ). Another but different abortifacient
used in Pahang is *pĕriya laut*, a cultivated pumpkin
(Momordica Charantia, Linn.—Cucurbitaceæ), also
taken in the form of a decoction.

The active principle of P. rosea is " plumbagin," a
peculiar crystalline glucoside chiefly contained in the
root, but also found in the leaves and stem. When
given internally it acts as a narcotic irritant, producing
pain and tenderness in the stomach, with vomiting,
great thirst, and frequent purgation. The root has
vesicant properties, and is sometimes self - applied

externally by pregnant Malay women and worn daily
with a view to induce uterine contractions by counter-
irritation. Imported commercial naphthaline, powdered and made into a paste with turmeric (*tĕmu
kunyit ;* Curcuma longa, Linn.—Scitamineæ), is used
by Kelantan women in the same way and with the same
idea.

The direct application of plumbago rosea, as well as
P. zeylanica, to the vagina and uterus causes violent
local inflammation. In India the crushed root, in the
form of a paste, is used by natives as an abortifacient ;
it is applied either directly or smeared upon an " abortion-stick " made from a twig of one or other of
the two plants. This " abortion-stick " when introduced into the *os uteri* is liable to cause death from
either pelvic or general peritonitis ; it is not thus used
in Kelantan, and but rarely, if ever, in the other
Malay States. Violent massage to the abdomen is a
much more common expedient ; but the introduction
of foreign bodies into the pregnant uterus is known to be
practised by Malays in the State of Perak. *Chĕraka* is
not credited with use for homicidal intent.

DATURA

The Malay name for the datura plants is *kĕchubong ;*
these and some others of the nightshade family, such as
Atropa and Hyoscyamus, have long been known to
possess narcotic properties. Three so-called varieties
of the *kĕchubong* plant are commonly met with in the
Malay States : one is the " black " datura (*kĕchubong
hitam ;* Datura fastuosa, Linn.—Solanaceæ), with dark
purple stems and single purple or violet flowers, one
is a single, white-flowered plant (*kĕchubong puteh ;*
D. alba, Nees), and one has double violet flowers.
D. alba is the only species which is native to Asia ; it
is widely distributed all over Malaya, but the American

plant, D. stramonium, which is very common in India,
with D. metel, does not appear to occur in the Malay
States. The word *kĕchubong* is applied to other
plants having tubular flowers : *e.g.*, Randia macrophylla, Br.—Rubiaceæ, is *kĕchubong rimba ;* Gardenia
tentaculata, Hook. fil.—Rubiaceæ, is *kĕchubong paya,*
and from the slight resemblance of the prickly fruits,
Byttneria Maingayi, Mast.—Sterculiaceæ, is called
akar kĕchubong (Ref. 21). The word is also applied
to the amethyst, *batu kĕchubong,* the *kĕchubong* stone.
The *kĕchubong* plant is known as *tĕrong pungah* in
Kedah. The so-called " black " datura, D. fastuosa,
may only be a variety of D. alba ; the whole of D.
fastuosa is poisonous, hyoscine alone or with hyoscyamine being found in the fruits, leaves, branches
and roots (Ref. 11).

Botany.—Datura fastuosa is a quick-growing her-
baceous plant, about 4 to 6 feet high, with widely-
spreading branches, conspicuous trumpet-shaped
flowers (devil's trumpet flower of Ceylon), and globose,
thorny fruits about the size of a walnut (mad-apple
of Australia). Leaves : alternate, petiolate, broadly
ovate, often about 5 to 10 inches long and 4 inches
broad at the widest part, margin repandly toothed,
petiole $4\frac{1}{4}$ inches long, apex acute, base unequal,
glabrous or sparsely tomentose, upper surface dark
greyish-green, under surface paler, veins pellucid.
The fresh leaves exhale a somewhat offensive smell
when bruised, and have a slightly bitter taste. Flowers :
axillary, on peduncles about $\frac{1}{2}$ inch long, single,
erect. Calyx : tubular, five-angled, five-toothed, teeth
reaching about half the length of the corolla tube.
Corolla : tube over 7 inches long, infundibuliform,
purple, violet or white without, white within. Limb :
five-lobed, twisted when in bud, lobes oblong-ovate,
cuspidate. Stamens : inserted near the base of the

tube, included ; anthers linear with parallel cells opening by introrse slits. Ovary : two-celled, falsely four-celled by false septa ; style filiform, stigma bi-lamellate. Fruit : an oblong, globular capsule, 1½ inches in diameter, covered with numerous short, scattered, sharp, straight spines, dehiscing by valves. Fruit stalk recurving with maturity until the ripe fruit becomes pendant. Seeds : very numerous, closely packed.

Datura alba, the " white " datura, is the common datura of the Federated Malay States, but in certain districts the " black " datura is said to be the more common of the two plants ; soil and circumstance, however, may so modify the colour of the flower, or even double or treble the corolla, that no botanical distinc-tion can be made merely by reference to colour. Datura alba is a rather taller plant then D. fastuosa, with trumpet-shaped flowers, either pure white in colour or yellowish-white tipped with violet. The flower is smaller and more tubular, the teeth of the calyx being less than half the size and lanceolate-acuminate. The differences between the two plants, however, are so slight that they can scarcely be classed as specifically distinct. Both grow wild in any Malay village, and thrive especially on manured ground, so that it is not difficult for criminals to collect the seeds.

The Seeds.—The poisonous properties of the *kĕchubong* plants reside chiefly in the seeds. The Datura fastuosa seed is oblong, kidney-shaped, laterally compressed, with convoluted edges, the free convex edge being definitely double-ridged ; surface roughly mammillated with numerous small pitted depressions ; about ⅙ inch (4 mm.) long, one end smaller than the other, hilus towards the narrow end. Indefinite embryo with characteristic curvation ; for practical purposes, similar to the seeds of D. alba (described below), but flatter, smoother, and rather darker, fawn-coloured when ripe and after exposure. About eight D. fastuosa seeds weigh 1 grain (0·065 gramme), and about 120 seeds weigh 1 gramme (15·432 grains). The Datura alba seed is also reniform in shape, having one end smaller than the other. It has been compared, not altogether fancifully, to the shape of the human ear; but the margin, although thick, rounded and furrowed, is angular, making the seed appear wedge-shaped. In size the seed is about $\frac{1}{25}$ inch (1 mm.) thick, about $\frac{1}{4}$ inch (6·3500 mm.) in length, rather less in width; no marked odour; taste slightly bitter; light fawn-coloured when dry; surface somewhat shrivelled except on the two compressed sides; testa rough and tough, making it difficult to powder the seed unless previously roasted. By cutting parallel to the side of the seed so as to divide it into flat halves the plant embryo which is embedded in an oily white albumen may be seen by the naked eye to be curved, twisted and recurved, so as to resemble the head of a shepherd's crook. As pointed out by Burton-Brown, both ends point in almost the same direction (Ref. 3). This curvature is peculiar to the genus. Powdered datura seeds may be recognised by the cavernous appearance of their exosperm when seen under a low power of the microscope, but it is not possible to distinguish them from other fragments of solanaceous seeds by this means alone. Dried *kĕchubong* seeds are similar in shape to the blackish-brown seeds of D. stramonium and the brownish-yellow seeds of D. metel; hyoscyamus and belladonna seeds in the dry state are tiny, kidney-shaped, and light yellowish-brown in colour. Green *kĕchubong* seeds are more or less dirty white in colour in the unripe state.

Kĕchubong seeds bear a slight resemblance to those of the common red chilli (Capsicum spp., Linn.—

Solanaceæ), and at times have been mistaken for them. The resemblance is most marked in the unripe state, but a careful comparison of the two seeds shows many morphological points of difference.   In many instances the pale yellow colour and the pungent taste of the red pepper seed would be sufficient to distinguish it from the pale greenish-brown or dirty white colour and rather bitter taste of the datura seed when it is fresh, but when either is cooked with food, such as boiled rice, recognition by means of taste alone cannot be relied upon. The seed of capsicum is kidney-shaped, rather shorter and wider than that of datura and the convex border is single, sharper and not double-ridged ; pale yellow in colour ; not pitted when seen with a lens, and when a section is made as described above, or when the seed is simply compressed between two glass slides, the embryo plant appears curved like the figure 6, the two ends pointing in opposite directions (Ref. 3).   Red pepper seeds in powder may be recognised by means of the application of heat, the acrid fumes being at once detected by heating even a small portion.   A watery decoction of datura seeds when placed in the eye will cause dilatation of the pupil, but a watery decoction of capsicum seeds irritates the eye and does not dilate the pupil.

Datura dilates both pupils when introduced into the circulation at large, but when placed in the eye the action is local, being due to paralysis of the termination of the motor occuli nerve in the circular muscle of the iris.   In a medico-legal investigation when datura seeds cannot be recognised with certainty, this mydriatic reaction may be obtained by digesting the material (gastric and intestinal contents, and especially urine) for about half an hour in warm rectified spirit, filtering, and evaporating on an open water bath to dryness, then treating the residue with a little slightly acidulated distilled water and placing a few drops of this in the eye of a cat. At the same time a few drops of water, only very slightly and similarly acidulated, may be placed in the other eye as a control. The animal should be held up to a strong light and the two eyes compared after the lapse of about an hour. This physiological test is very reliable and delicate : in the human or cat's eye one drop of an atropine solution 1 : 130,000 will produce a characteristic myosis which is more extensive and more permanent than that caused in some stages of the action of cocaine, digitalis or coniin. The mydriatic reaction of datura can be obtained after some lapse of time from vomited matter or from earth upon which it has happened to fall. According to Ipsen, one seed in such circumstances is said to be sufficient after it has been cleaned, ground and extracted with very slightly acidulated water (Ref. 1). Atropine is remarkably resistant to putrefaction, and D. N. Chatterji has recently shown that although a putrid product in decomposed viscera is known to produce mydriasis, its presence is rare, and that the applicability of the mydriatic test to the detection of datura in decomposed viscera is of great value, especially when the history of the case is available (*The Analyst*, July, 1926 : Cambridge).

The existence of putrefaction bases ("ptomatropins") found in tinned beef, sausages, etc., which give rise to symptoms of poisoning similar to those produced by plants of the nightshade family, must be borne in mind. Poisoning by datura has been known since time immemorial. Witthaus says : " It seems probable that the poisoning of the army of Antony in Parthia, related by Plutarch, was caused by belladonna or by datura " (Ref. 27). Owing to the prolonged march provisions became very scarce and the Roman soldiers searched for any roots they could get as vegetables : " They chanced upon an herb that was mortal, first taking away all sense and understanding. He that had eaten of it remembered nothing in the world, and employed himself only in moving great stones from one place to another, which he did with as much earnestness and industry as if it had been a business of the greatest consequence " (Plutarch's " Life of Antony.")

Norman Chevers gives an interesting account of professional poisoners in Bengal, who in former days used to administer this drug to wayfarers with the idea of producing merely temporary insensibility : sometimes fatal overdoses were given either by design or by accident. Thus if a large quantity were put into food supplied to a party of travellers, the greedy man might pay for his gluttony with his life. Even to-day there is still a sect in Egypt which narcotises and robs country visitors to Cairo. The victims while delirious are taken to the hospitals by the police and wake up to find all their money gone. Professor Sydney Smith describes the usual method of procedure : " A countryman is walking or riding his donkey towards the town. He meets another wayfarer seated on the roadside and the latter offers the newcomer a handful of dates. The traveller eats them and lingers to talk for a certain time, then feels drowsy and sleeps. He awakes to find himself either in hospital or prison with the whole of his belongings gone, and without any knowledge of what happened after eating the dates." The Regius Professor continues : " When it is desired to obtain a rapid effect the seeds are added to coffee and, as a rule, the victim becomes unconscious in a few minutes " (Ref. 24, Appendix IV).

In the Far East the procedure was more subtle. During Mr. Ridley's time at Singapore, datura seeds were used as a dope at native public houses : " When a man came in to drink, the people of the house elicited which way he would take to go home, then if he did not spend all his money, at his last drink, they would whisk in a dose calculated to make him drop at a certain spot. Two men would go ahead and wait for him. When he collapsed, they would rob him of everything, clothes and all, roll him into a ditch and go away."

Among some clinical cases of datura poisoning in the Federated Malay States published by the writer in 1903 was one in which datura seeds were mixed with food by Pahang Malays : In April, 1896, a Malay was charged at Kuala Lipis, Pahang, with causing hurt by means of poison. He pleaded not guilty ; but, although the motive of his crime was never actually discovered, he was eventually convicted of having mixed *kĕchubong* seeds in a curry, thereby stupefying a Malay constable, the constable's wife, his niece, and a girl friend, as well as two men, who all partook of the same dish. The symptoms in each case were similar, namely, attacks of giddiness, passing into unconsciousness for a few hours, followed by complete recovery. This group of cases is of interest owing to the fact that one of my colleagues, the District Surgeon, Pahang, who appeared for the prosecution, was able to give evidence of a very practical kind. A sample of seeds in powder which had been found in the handkerchief of the accused was sent to the District Surgeon for identification. I am indebted to my colleague for the following notes of a personal experiment. He says : " I took pinch doses of the sample, which consisted of the bruised seeds, and had the following experience : I felt flushed, dry about the mouth and throat, and became hoarse. When I tried to walk, I staggered about like a drunken man and got very excited. I then took an emetic

of zinc, vomited, and slept for about five or six hours."
He was also observed in a delirious state, rolling on
the floor and uttering inarticulate cries like the mewing
of a kitten (Ref. 9).

Symptoms of Kĕchubong Poisoning.—The symptoms
of poisoning by datura are characteristic and are much
the same as those caused by hyoscyamus and belladonna ; they are due to the presence of the alkaloids
hyoscyamine and hyoscine (scopolamine) in the datura
plants. My medical colleague referred to above
experienced most of the usual symptoms of poisoning
by *kĕchubong* seeds, namely, dryness of mouth and
throat, hoarseness and difficulty in speaking, flushing
of the face, dilatation of the pupils and confusion of
vision. He was giddy, staggered as if intoxicated,
was restless and incoherent in speech. Vomiting is
uncommon in *kĕchubong* poisoning : if he had not
been sensible enough to take an emetic he might have
become more wildly excited before falling into a much
deeper sleep or even coma. On the other hand, he
might have gone to sleep and woken up and then
become delirious. Dried datura seeds are hard and
difficult of digestion. After an emetic has acted, an
energetic purgative should always be taken to remove
the seeds from the intestines.

In Singapore Ridley found a piece of *kĕchubong*
leaf in a tea-pot ; a decoction of the plant had been
poured into the pot without careful straining and all
the house servants had been poisoned out of spite
by those of a neighbouring house : " the men and
women were trying to climb up the walls or pulling on
an imaginary rope ; apparently they thought they were
in a well and could see high above ; the children were
running about the floor, naked, on all fours like
rabbits." In another case in the Federated Malay
States *kĕchubong* seeds were mixed in tea by Chinese ;

one of the victims, a Japanese woman, was semi-unconscious for a time, and kept picking at imaginary objects. Castellani says : " The people affected may be found searching their bedding most vigorously for some lost article." Again, the patient sometimes tries to thread imaginary threads and tries to pick them from the tips of his fingers, or he constantly gazes at his fingers and keeps passing his thumb over them in a most peculiar way ; so, too, with henbane. Holmes records that some monks ate henbane root by mistake at supper : " Those who partook of it were seized in the night with the most extraordinary hallucinations, so that the monastery seemed turned into a lunatic asylum. One monk rang the bell for matins at midnight, and of those who attended the summons some could not read, some read what was not in the book and others saw the letters running over the pages like so many ants " (Ref. 12). Laughter is not uncommon : " They always laugh and are very liberal, for they let people take such of their jewels as they choose, and only laugh or speak very little, and that not to the purpose. So that a robber has only to give this medicine (datura) in the food and the effect lasts twenty-four hours " (Garcia da Orta, 1563, Ref. 19). As seen in the case of the Singapore children, there is a tendency to discard the clothing and to go about naked.

Apart from the peculiarities of the delirium caused by datura, the most characteristic symptoms are the same as those caused by atropine—namely, the pupils are fully dilated and insensitive to light, diplopia and paralysis of accommodation are present, the conjunctivæ are red and injected and the skin hot and dry. The temperature is slightly raised and the respirations are increased ; death is uncommon, but would be due to respiratory paralysis. The pulse may be slow, but is generally rapid, up to 120 to 160 in the minute. The reflexes are exaggerated ; the saliva is inspissated. The vital centres in the medulla are depressed and paralysed. The inhibitory fibres of the vagus are paralysed. Symptoms of poisoning by datura seeds vary with the amount of the dose which is retained and the age of the victim ; they are more severe, as a rule, during childhood and old age, and generally follow about ten minutes after administration. The after effects, weakness, headache, dilatation of the pupils, thirst and difficulty in walking, may last for two days, but are seldom fatal when *kĕchubong* is used by Malays with the object of profligacy or plunder. There is a certain degree of impairment of memory before complete recovery ; the patient can speak, but appears not to understand ; he is timid and distrustful. A Malay expression *mabok kĕchubong* (lit. datura intoxication) is used of visionary dreamers. The bitter taste of the datura seeds may be complained of. When illness comes on soon after a meal, which perhaps has been shared by a group of people similarly affected, the peculiar delirium and dilated pupils serve to differentiate poisoning by datura from opium poisoning, apoplexy, acute mania, the delirium of fevers, epilepsy, heat-exhaustion and ptomaine poisoning.

Administration by the Mouth.—The favourite mode of administration by Malays is by the mouth, raw seeds of *kĕchubong hitam* (D. fastuosa) are preferred. About fifty dried seeds, weighing 8 grains (0·518 gramme) are crushed and put into tea or coffee, or mixed in rice and curry, whereby the bitter taste is masked. The professional Malay thief, like his Indian colleague, seems to know how to gauge the dose which will produce insensibility within a quarter of an hour without risk of killing the victim. Burton-Brown, however, records a case of premeditated murder in the Punjab : " A man visited a house while food was being cooked : he left suddenly, and the three persons who partook of the food were taken ill and one died. Datura seeds were found in the food, and also on the person of the man, who was sentenced to death. This case was important, as murder was evidently intended, and not robbery, the man having left before the unconsciousness occurred " (Ref. 3). The seeds are sometimes put into wells and water-jars by Malays to poison the drinking water.

Other Methods.—Ridley records poisoning by a decoction of leaves and flowers in Singapore. Greshoff says that in the Dutch East Indies, the excrement of small beetle-like insects (unidentified) fed on datura leaves is mixed with food or drink as a poison (Indian Poison Reports, 1902 : Amsterdam).

Application by Fumes.—The Malay one-storied house is invariably built on posts and raised some feet above the level of the ground ; so that, with a long bamboo tube or pipe, it is easy for a night thief to convey fumes of datura to the sleeping-room above by roasting the seeds on the ground below. If necessary, he may have previously poisoned the watch-dogs. He then cuts through the thin wall of the house, which is generally of plaited split bamboo, and removes even heavy boxes, without disturbing his victims in their stupor. In the process of burning or fuming, the narcotic agents contained in datura seeds must be diffused and drawn into the lungs, thus causing the drowsiness which passes into stupor.

When used to produce lethargy by means of the fumes *kĕchubong* seeds are sometimes burnt with the well-known incense called eagle-wood or lign-aloes (*gĕharu :* Aquilaria malaccensis, Lam.—Thymelaceæ, and other varieties). This much-prized product, which is used for scenting joss-sticks, burns with a strong perfume. It is supposed to be under the care of *hantu* or evil spirits, while the tree itself is believed to cause illness or death to those who cut it down wrongfully. Skeat says : " When the tree has been felled you must be exceedingly careful to see that nobody passes between the end of the fallen trunk and the stump ; whoever does so will surely be killed by the ' eagle-wood ' spirit, who is supposed to be extremely powerful and dangerous " (" Malay Magic "). Another incense, a clear, almost transparent, resin known as the cat's-eye resin, obtained from the *chĕngal* tree (Balanocarpus maximus, King— Dipterocarpaceæ), and a similar resin obtained from *kayu lĕban* (Vitex pubescens, Vahl.—Verbenaceæ) are burnt also with *kĕchubong* seeds in the same way. The *lĕban* tree is one of the haunted " bee-trees " of Malaya. A few years ago two cases of poisoning by datura fumes were reported from the Temerloh district in Pahang in which these two resins were used.

In Bombay fumes from datura seeds are used to increase the intoxicating power of liquor. Dymock says : " Liquor is made more intoxicating by placing some of the seeds upon red-hot charcoal, and inverting an earthen vessel over them ; when this is full of the smoke it is removed, filled with liquor and tied down " (Ref. 7). In the Federated Malay States, 1916, it was alleged that toddy adulterated with datura, and causing death, was being sold in the coast districts of Selangor. Toddy is extracted by Malays from various palms, chiefly the coco-nut, by tapping and bruising the flower while it is still in its bud sheath. The sweet juice soon becomes turbid and alcoholic owing to fermentation by yeasts. The allegations were serious, because the sale of toddy in the Federated Malay States is under Government control, and large numbers of Tamils buy it, their customary alcoholic drink, on the various rubber estates. Analyses carried out in the Institute for Medical Research, F.M.S., failed to reveal the presence of datura.

In Kelantan, when collecting *kĕchubong* for nefarious purposes, sometimes a candle is lit in mid-day underneath the plant, and the seeds are separated from their capsules with a *pĕrangan* or split stick which has become scorched and charred by roasting fish over a fire.

Fatal Dose.—It is difficult to give even an approximate opinion as to the number of seeds required to cause death, because " the alkaloidal content varies within wide limits, and no doubt the amount of mastication is a very important factor in liberating the alkaloid " (Ref. 24). A hundred datura seeds weighing about 1 gramme woulu cause severe symptoms of poisoning, but death is rare and recovery the rule, although a far greater number of seeds may have been swallowed and not retained. In India 125 seeds have caused death (Ref. 26).

In 1903, after determining the activity of alkaloidal extracts of parts of the plant (D. fastuosa), I collected a number of seeds of both varieties in Selangor and Perak and submitted them to Professor Wyndham Dunstan at the Imperial Institute, London. He found that seeds of D. fastuosa, var. typica, from these States contained 0·39 per cent of alkaloid, almost entirely hyoscine (scopolamine), while those of D. fastuosa, var. alba, only furnished 0·21 per cent. of alkaloid, chiefly hyoscine with a little hyoscyamine. Some people are more susceptible to hyoscine than others ; but $\frac{1}{2}$ grain (0·03 gramme) is a fatal dose. Serious but non-fatal symptoms of poisoning have been caused by $\frac{1}{25}$ grain (0·0025 gramme) of hydrobromate of hyoscine (Ref. 25). The official medicinal dose of hyoscine as hydrobromide in the British Pharmacopœia of 1914, is $\frac{1}{200}$ to $\frac{1}{100}$ grain (0·3 to 0·6 mg.).

In an important trial for murder held in London (Rex v. Crippen, 1910) the accused was sentenced to death for poisoning his wife by means of hyoscine. Portions of her body had been buried from four to eight months and were found to contain an alkaloid. This alkaloid proved to be mydriatic (by the physiological test on a cat's eyes) ; positive to Vitali's test, *i.e.*, a purple-violet colour when treated with nitric acid and potash successively ; non-crystalline under the microscope, and the gummy residue gave round spheres with hydrobromic acid. Hyoscine gives these spheres, while atropine and hyoscyamine both give needle-shaped crystals. This was the first trial for poisoning by hyoscine to be held in England. Sir William Willcox estimated the amount of alkaloid present in the putrid organs : stomach, $\frac{1}{30}$ grain ; one kidney, $\frac{1}{40}$ grain ; intestines, $\frac{1}{7}$ grain ; and liver, $\frac{1}{12}$ grain—total found, $\frac{2}{7}$ grain.

Mixtures of Kĕchubong.—A Malay proverb runs : *kĕchubong bĕrhulam ganja* : " datura eaten with Indian hemp ; poison added to poison ; worse and worse."

Datura and Cannabis Indica. — The products of the hemp-plant are all dangerous drugs. Cannabis indica, var. sativa, Linn.—Urticaceæ) is the " hashish " of evil fame used by the Moors, Arabs (*kinap*), Egyptians, Turks and other natives in the Near East, as an aphrodisiac and intoxicant liquor. *Ganja* corresponds pretty closely with " hashish " ; it is smuggled into Kelantan from Bombay, Bengal and the Central Provinces of India, in the form of the dry, resinous flowering shoots of the female plant before fertilisation, collected from plants grown at an altitude of 6,000 to 8,000 feet. The poisonous principle is developed only before fertilisation of the flowers ; no resin is produced except in plants grown between the altitudes mentioned above. A decoction made of *ganja* is used by Indian fakirs as a comforting narcotic, and it is sometimes mixed with tobacco for smoking in a pipe like the more expensive *charas*, a resinous powder that exudes from the leaves and flower stalks of the green plant. *Charas* is collected in skin bags, hence the name (from *char*, a skin). Datura flowers are sometimes mixed with *ganja* in preparing *majun*, a narcotic sweetmeat made with clarified butter, sugar and *bhang*, the mature leaf and smaller stalks from plants grown on the lower hills of the Punjab. The narcotic principle in the leaf is only developed after the plants are fertilised and the fruits matured. *Bhang* has 20 per cent. of the narcotic principle and *ganja* only 10, while *charas* has 40 per cent. Burton-Brown records a case of poisoning with *majun* in which datura seeds had been mixed : " Both men became insensible, and were conveyed to the hospital, where they were found to be in a state of complete coma with dilated pupils and stertorous breathing ; no pulse could be felt at the wrist, and both soon died. Datura seeds were found in the stomach of each of them " (Ref. 3). The mature leaves of Cannabis indica (*bhang*) are deep green in colour and in commerce are generally broken, then forming a dry, coarse powder ; the smell and taste is peculiar and characteristic. *Bhang* is used as an infusion at religious festivals in India ; it tends to become a decoction and then the toxic effects become apparent. Over-indulgence in Indian hemp is recognised as a common cause of insanity among the male population of India. Apart from taste and smell, both *ganja* and *bhang* can be defined under the microscope ; the leaf is thickly covered with acuminate, claw-shaped hairs. According to Burton-Brown : " The smallest fragment of these leaves may be detected by microscopical examination of the hairs with which the leaves are covered. These hairs arise from a short base which is at right angles to the surface of the leaf, but the greater part of the hair is again bent at right angles, in such a way as to lie parallel to the surface of the leaf, and have its point directed to the apex of the leaf. These hairs are unicellular, and all lie parallel to one another and close together. The hairs are thicker and stronger on the upper surface of the leaf and on the veins of the lower surface " (Ref. 3). The poisonous principles found in Indian hemp seem to be produced only in plants grown in warm climates ; an oleo-resin *cannabinol* has been isolated, but probably the plant contains a number of active principles.

Physiological experiments made by feeding a dog or cat on Indian hemp show narcosis with swaying of the head from side to side. *Kĕchubong* seeds combined with *ganja* and *chandu* (opium) and made up with slime from the cat-fish *ikan kĕli*, sap from the sago palm and juice from the horse-radish or " drumsticks " tree of Ceylon (*mĕrunggai* ; Moringa pterygosperma, Gærtn.—Moringaceæ) occur in a combination used by the Kelantan poisoner.

Datura and Opium.—Opium, the sun-dried latex of the unripe fruit of the opium poppy, is imported, and when prepared for smoking is known throughout Malaya as *chandu* (dry extract of opium). Datura seeds are combined with opium and the fresh green shoots of a wild yam called *gadong* (which see) and the inner green bark of a shrub with honey flowers (*pohun nĕrapih* ; Glycosmis citrifolia—Rutaceæ). A mixture of *kĕchubong* such as this is said to cause a form of insanity with hallucinations of sight followed by death in a few months' time. This form of insanity is said to be a sequel to a preliminary delirium. *Chandu* does not appear to be very commonly used by Malay

criminals when compared to its use in India, and this
perhaps may be explained by the fact that opium is
a Government monopoly in the Federated Malay States,
and expensive to buy. The use, however, of *chandu*
in various mixtures is mentioned under the following
sections : *Pědĕndang gagak*, *Pinang* (areca-nut), *Tangis
sarang burong*, Cyanide of Potassium, Mercury and
Arsenic. When swallowed by Chinese bent on suicide,
chandu is sometimes mixed with the lime fruit (Citrus
acida, Roxb.—Rutaceæ), the acid of which is supposed
by them to increase the toxic properties of opium.

Datura and Cyanide of Potassium.—A particularly
deadly poison made with dried *kĕchubong* seeds,
potas (potassium cyanide), opium, snake bile and the
roasted gall of a toad, is described under section
CYANIDE OF POTASSIUM.

Use as a Medicine.—The root, flowers and especially
the leaves, of *kĕchubong hitam* and *k. puteh* are used
by the *bomor* as medicines (see p. 124). The leaves,
as well as a tincture made of the seeds of D. fastuosa,
Linn., var. alba, Nees, are official preparations of the
British Pharmacopœia of 1914.

DĚPU PĚLANDOK

Dĕpu pĕlandok is a moderate-sized shrub growing
in sandy places by village waysides. It is peculiar
to the north-east coast of the Malay Peninsula from
Pahang northwards, and is a plant belonging to the
Nat. Ord. Thymelæaceæ, identified botanically by
Burkill as Wikstrœmia Ridleyi from a specimen sent
to him from Kelantan. Height about 4 or 5 feet ;
leaves glabrous, dark green, oblong-lanceolate, sub-
opposite, 2 to $3\frac{1}{2}$ inches long ; flowers few, perianth
greenish-yellow. Fruit scarlet when ripe, ovoid, $\frac{1}{4}$
to $\frac{1}{3}$ inch long. Both the root and the berries are said
to be toxic : the latter are sometimes mixed with food

and given as a poison in Kelantan. Wikstrœmia Ridleyi is closely allied to Wikstrœmia indica, C. A. Mey, found in China, Mauritius, and the Philippine Islands.

Use as a Medicine.—The medicinal properties are similar to those of Daphne Mezereon. The leaves are used by the *bomor* as a medicine : they possess powerful purgative properties, and one or two of them constitute a full medicinal dose ; they are ground up, mixed with a little boiled rice and turmeric, and given by the mouth. The bark is given in a composite drink for small-pox ; it is also used in the treatment of boils when pounded and mixed with boiled rice and turmeric as a poultice. The bark is also used for poisoning river fish in Kelantan ; it is ground up, mixed with fine bamboo hairs and decayed copra (the dried kernel of the coco-nut), and then thrown into the water to stupefy fishes. Greshoff also records that two or three of its allies are poisonous to fish in Java (Ref. 10, Vol. X, p. 121), and says that the fruits cause headache, spitting of blood, diarrhœa and death when administered as a poison to man (Indian Poison Reports).

GADONG

Gadong belongs to the Yam family, and affords the large tuberous, acrid roots which are called *isi gadong* in Malay. It is Dioscorea triphylla, Lam.—Dioscoreaceæ, with the synonyms D. dæmona, Roxb., generally used by English botanists, and D. hirsuta, Blume, by Dutch and German botanists : it is a twining plant found wild in the jungle, but generally cultivated. Leaves trifoliate ; leaflets 3 to 7 inches long by 2 to 4 inches wide. *Gadong* is well known by Malays to possess narcotic properties and to cause vomiting ; the juice is very acrid like that of the *kĕladi* tubers (see

section KĔLADI), and may cause violent inflammation
of the eyes : as a Kelantan poison *gadong* is sometimes used in combination with *kĕladi* as an internal
poison, but more frequently with datura (see section
DATURA).

A case attributed to *gadong* occurred in August,
1913, when a fairly well-to-do Malay carpenter and his
son were poisoned. It occurred during the fasting
month, when no meal is allowed between sunrise and
sunset. These two persons happened to be living alone
in Kota Bharu because the man's wife was ill and away
at the seaside ; in her absence a sister-in-law prepared
their evening meals and sent them to the house. The
two returned home about 10 p.m., and found a sweetmeat (a conserve made with banana) that had been
brought at dusk by a strange girl, who came and went
in a hurry telling a neighbour that the sister-in-law had
sent it. The carpenter ate most of it and gave a small
portion to his son, who enjoyed it, but noticed a peculiar
earthy taste. They lay down to sleep together and
quickly became stupefied ; they found they had lost
the power of moving their legs, their throats got
parched and their heads giddy. About 4 a.m. thieves
broke the door open and plundered the house : their
victims, although awake, were unable to rise and
protect their property. The son managed to strike a
match, but stumbled and fell on attempting to get up ;
the thieves escaped, but the man was able to recognise
one of them. I saw the patients about 11.30 a.m. the
next day ; both had dilated pupils, inactive to light.
The man was lying on a mat ; he was still dazed, but
in a peculiarly cheerful frame of mind. He had
diarrhœa and distension of the abdomen. Both of
them still complained of being thirsty, of pain at the
angles of the jaws, and of inability to rise—evidently
not a case of simple datura poisoning. The boy's

grandmother was looking after them and giving them the charmed water which has been described in a former chapter, with successful result (see p. 56).

Another combination of *gadong* with datura seeds is to mix them together in the form of a dry powder with the tissues of the half-rotted *rengut* fruit, the fine hairs of the bamboo, and crumbled pieces of an edible fungus (*kulat taun*). A dry powder of this description was exhibited by the police, and a conviction obtained, at the Pahang Assizes in Kuantan, July, 1901. In this instance the poison was used by Kedah Malays on Chinese shopkeepers. Poisonous fungi do not appear to be used by Malay criminals for lethal purposes. The young shoots of *gadong* are used by Malays to poison fish, and are combined with upas poison by the jungle-folk of the Peninsula in the manufacture of dart poison as described under section THE UPAS TREE.

Dioscorine, the active principle of *gadong* (D. triphylla), belongs to the pyrrole group of alkaloids. It was isolated by Boorsma and afterwards investigated by Schutte and by Gorter. It is bitter and poisonous ; it produces paralysis of the central nervous system, and in general behaves like picrotoxin (Ref. 11). Malays use *gadong* as a food, but take great precautions to prepare it in such a way that it is rendered wholesome. The yam must be mature, not wet or newly dug up. It is sun-dried and then peeled and sliced into thin pieces, which are washed for three days in a running stream, or it is sliced and steeped in salt and water for five days, the water being constantly changed before the yam is fit for food. The slices are sometimes shredded and made into cakes. When not previously steeped in water, *gadong* causes headache, cramp in the stomach, dizziness, vomiting, paralysis and eventually death if much be eaten (Greshoff).

KĔNĔRAK

Kĕnĕrak (Goniothalamus tapis, Miq.—Anonaceæ), or an allied species, is used when combined with *chĕraka* as an abortifacient by Malays (see p. 203). A closely allied plant, Oxymitra macrophylla, Baill.—Anonaceæ, is recorded by Greshoff as an abortifacient and A. squamosa, Linn. is listed as a poison : " dried and pounded fine before the fruit is in season, the root is poisonous." He found indications of an alkaloid or alkaloids in the bark of two species of Goniothalamus and extracted from Unona dasmychala, Bl.—Anonaceæ, an alkaloid of which 12 mg. did not kill a large toad. An amorphous alkaloid extracted from A. murticata, Linn., however caused tetanic convulsions when injected into a toad to the extent of 3 mg., and an injection of 8 mg. from A. reticulata, Linn., caused lameness of the hind feet ; 5 mg. from Alphonsea ventriculosa, Hook. fil. and Thoms.—Anonaceæ, caused the death of a toad, and 5 mg. of the alkaloid extracted from Alphonsea ceramensis, Scheff.—Anonaceæ, caused cramps and death in toads (Ref. 10, Vol, XXV, pp. 11 and 15). The well-known species Anona reticulata, the " bullock's heart " or true custard-apple of the West Indies, is known to Malays as *nonah kapri*, and is used as an astringent in the form of the powdered bark.

KĔPAYANG

The poisonous component of the large cultivated *kĕpayang* tree (Pangium edule, Reindw.—Bixaceæ) is hydrocyanic acid, which is contained in large quantities in the fruits, but like Manihot, they are edible when properly cooked. The seeds of the young fruit, however, are too toxic for consumption. The *kĕpayang* or *payung* tree is a quick-growing, spreading tree with huge heart-shaped leaves, rather large axillary, greenish-white flowers, and big, ovoid, reddish-brown fruits. In size the fruit roughly resembles a small-sized unpeeled coco-nut, and may be from 7 to 12 inches in length and 3 to 4 inches or more in width. Each fruit contains some twenty to thirty seeds, which are nearly 2 inches in length, roughly triangular, grooved, woody, and embedded in an oily pulp. Pangium edule grows abundantly in Selangor, Pahang and Perak, and in the Malay Archipelago generally, but is not common in Kelantan. A good specimen, however, thrives well at Kuala Bala on the Kuala Pergau estate in Ulu Kelantan ; this sporadic example is probably a relic of former virgin jungle. Sir Hugh Clifford, when describing the Pahang disturbances of 1894, remarks : " At spots where the *kĕpayang* fruit grew plentifully the refugees had camped for over a week, and many new graves marked their resting-place, for the *kĕpayang* bears an ill name " (Ref. 6). This is exemplified in the Malay proverbial saying : *laksana buah kĕpayang, di-makan mabok, di-buang sayang* (" like the fruit of the *kĕpayang*, which intoxicates you if you eat it and which you have not the heart to throw away ; pretty but harmful ").

The poisonous properties of *kĕpayang* are well known to Malays ; they are said to resemble those of Gadong (which see). The seeds are the most toxic part of the tree, but apparently only when they are quite fresh and in the raw state. In November, 1913, the kernel of an old dry *kĕpayang* seed obtained from Pahang was given to a half-tame lesser adjutant bird (Leptoptilus javanicus) in Kota Bharu, Kelantan, without any effect, and three others were given in rice to four domestic fowls without result. The fresh seeds are said to be very poisonous to poultry and the fresh leaves fatal to goats in twenty-four hours. When dry the seeds are often cooked and eaten by Malays.   They are known as *kluak* in the Singapore market, and are sold in Java (*kluwek*).   Oil expressed from raw seeds is added to cakes by Malay criminals to cause death, but oil expressed from sun-dried seeds is often used as an article of food in the uplands of Pahang and in the " up-country " villages of Kelantan, although it is said to cause diarrhœa.   Blume states that it is useful as an anthelmintic.   The bark of the tree is a fish poison, and according to Vaughan Stevens the fresh seeds are used in making dart poison by the Pangan jungle tribe.   In the Dutch East Indies the raw seeds are put into food as a poison and cause vomiting, distension of the abdomen and contraction of the tongue.   Draughts of water are given as an antidote.

The toxic properties of Pangium edule have been investigated by Greshoff ;   they are contained in a cyanogenetic glucoside, which on hydrolysis by certain enzymes or other substances (Ref. 10, Vols. XXV and VII, also in Nuttige Indische Planten., No. 4).   Other genera of the same Nat. Ord., Bixaceæ, have oily seeds, and three of these are used medicinally in the treatment of leprosy, viz., Taraktogenos (syn. Hydnocarpus), Kurzii of Burmah and Assam, from which the true chalmoogra oil is obtained, and H. Wightiana and H. anthelmintica, both with very similar physical and chemical properties.   The crushed seeds of H. anthelmintica (2 parts), after sieving, with Cannabis indica (1 part) form the " Tai Foong Chee " treatment of leprosy used by Dr. E. A. O. Travers with signal success at the Leper Asylum, Selangor.   H. inebrians, Vahl., is used as a substitute in southern India and Gynocardia odorata, Roxb., in northern India, although its oil is entirely different from those of the Hydnocarpus series.   Taken incautiously, serious results seem to follow on the swallowing of oils from many plants of these genera : H. venenata, Gærtn., gets its name in consequence. As another instance to the point, it may be cited that a species of Hydnocarpus, probably H. Wightiana, Bl., caused poisoning in Germany towards the close of 1910 ; the oil, imported from Bombay, had been used in the manufacture of margarine. These oils contain physiologically active substances called chalmoogric and hydnocarpic acids, which cause irritation of the mucous membrane of the stomach, with consequent nausea and vomiting, owing to their peculiar chemical properties.

PAPAYA

Three varieties of Carica papaya, Linn.—Papayaceæ, the papaw fruit tree or " tree-melon," are cultivated and freely grown in villages and gardens throughout Malaya. The tree (*pohun bĕtek*) was introduced from South America, and fruits all through the year. In Brazil, the black or olive-coloured, rather pungent cress-like tasting seeds are used as a vermifuge ; and according to Peckholt the milky juice of the unripe fruit is given with excellent results in small doses against round worms (Ref. 20). The juice is slightly caustic and irritating to the skin, but is used as a cosmetic in Brazil for removing freckles and making the skin smooth and delicate. The latex (*gĕtah*) of the papaw (*buah bĕtek*, or *b. papaya ; buah kĕtela* in Penang), is said by Malays to be an abortient agent, and the unripe fruit is considered to be dangerous in pregnancy ; the seeds are also believed by Malays and Indians to be an abortifacient, if eaten in the early months of pregnancy. *Gĕtah bĕtek* is said to cause intestinal inflammation. It is used in Kelantan as a poison mixed with the juice of the immature capsules of the horse-radish tree (Moringa pterygosperma, Gærtn.—Moringaceæ) and the white of a lizard's egg. When taken internally in this way, the combination is said to cause great abdominal pain and the presence of blood in the urine.

The use of the horse-radish tree (*měrunggai*) as a poison is also referred to under section DATURA; the powdered bark of Moringa combined with pepper-corns is used as an abortifacient in Bengal, sometimes with fatal results, but this has not been met with in Kelantan. Greshoff obtained the alkaloid carpaïne from the fruit and seeds, but more especially from the leaves of C. papaya (Ref. 10). Merck and others have studied it, and the alkaloid has more recently (1910) been investigated by Barger: it crystallises in monoclinic prisms and has an intensely bitter taste. According to Plugge it depresses the action of the heart and adversely affects the respiration (Ref. 11). The action on the heart is said to resemble that of digitalis. The digestive properties of Carica papaya are due to " papain," a proteolitic ferment contained in the milk-like juice of the tree and its unripe fruit. The juice and even the fresh leaves of the *papaya* tree are said to render the toughest beef tender in the space of two hours. It acts in acid, alkaline and neutral media, and will digest fibrin even to 200 times its weight, or casein ten times its weight in an hour (Martindale). Papain is a whitish amorphous powder in its refined pharmaceutical state, but is more active when in the crude form of brownish gummy granules. Crude papain contains a lipase of considerable activity which has been investigated by M. Sandberg and E. Brand (*Jour. Biol. Chem.*, 1925, 64, 59–70).

PEPPER

Lada hitam, or black pepper (Piper nigrum, Linn.— Piperaceæ), is sometimes used by Malay women as an abortifacient. For this purpose it is made into pills with honey and the so-called " black " variety of

ginger root (*halia bara ;* Zingiber officinale, Roxb.—
Scitamineæ) ; these are swallowed before meals.
Piper nigrum contains an alkaloid called " piperine "
which was isolated in 1819 by Oersted from the fruit :
it exerts an action similar to quinine, but is much
less active and rather uncertain in effect (Ref. 11).
In very large doses it is probably an irritant poison.
The pepper vine is extensively grown in Sumatra,
Ceylon and southern India for its fruits (the undicor-
ticated berries or peppercorns) which are round and
green when young and red when ripe. On being sun-
dried they become black and shrivelled, forming the
black pepper of commerce when ground into powder.
White pepper is prepared from ripe peppercorns by
soaking them in water to aid the removal of the dark
outer covers of the pericarp. Ground pepper is mixed
with quicklime by Malay gang-robbers in order to
blind or discomfort their pursuers.

PINANG (Areca-nut)

The feathered-leaved *pokok pinang* or betel-nut
tree, straight-stemmed, slender and graceful, has been
poetically described as " an arrow dropped from
heaven." The *pinang* palm (Areca catechu, Linn.—
Palmæ) originally indigenous to the Sunda Islands,
is largely cultivated in Malaya. Betel-nuts form a
Kelantan export of considerable value. The areca
fruit or betel-nut is usually about the size and shape
of a small hen's egg ; it is covered with a very woolly
husk which is green in the unripe state, and yellow
or orange-yellow when the contained brown, conical
nut (seed) is ripe. Garcia da Orta, who found the
pinang tree in Malacca in 1563, comments on the
unripe fruit as follows : " When this *areca* is green
it is stupefying and intoxicating, for those who eat it
feel tipsy, and they eat it to deaden any great pain

they have " (Ref. 19). The green fruit in the unripe
state is said to be used as a poison in Kelantan in combination with opium (*chandu*). A Malay criminal
may also attempt to poison his victim during the process of betel-chewing, by smearing poisonous bile on
the *gambir* (see p. 134). The practice of betel-chewing
is well described by Marsden (Ref. 15) : " All the preparation consists in spreading on the *sireh* (betel-vine)
leaf, a small quantity of the *chunam* (prepared lime
used in the betel quid), and folding it up with a slice
of the *pinang* nut. Some mix with these gambier,
which is a substance prepared from the leaves of a
tree of that name, by boiling their juices to a consis-
tence, and made up into little balls or squares, as before
spoken of : tobacco is likewise added, which is shred
fine for the purpose, and carried between the lip and
upper row of teeth. From the mastication of the
first three, there proceeds a juice which tinges the
saliva of a bright red, and which the leaf and nut,
without the *chunam*, will not yield. This hue being
communicated to the mouth and lips is esteemed ornamental, and an agreeable flavour is imparted to the
breath. Along with the betel, and generally in the
chunam, is the mode of conveying philtres, or love
charms. The practice of administering poison in
this manner is not followed in latter times ; but that
the idea is not so far eradicated, as entirely to prevent
suspicion, appears from this circumstance : that the
guest, though taking a leaf from the betel service
of his entertainer, not infrequently applies to it his
own *chunam* and never omits to pass the former
between his thumb and forefinger, in order to wipe
off any extraneous matter. This mistrustful procedure
is so common as not to give offence."

Early in 1921 the Kelantan police sent an exhibit
that had been found in the possession of a bad character

for examination. It consisted of a small paper packet containing a fine dull brown powder which on microscopical examination appeared to contain fragments of datura seeds and chopped bristles of the hairy sea-worm (*ulat bulu laut*). A two-ounce medicine bottle containing some bad-smelling water accompanied the paper packet ; this was said to be *ayer jĕrok pinang*, or water taken from a big pickle-jar full of unripe *pinang* nuts. In addition to the stupefying effects of datura, the preparation was said to cause loss of voice.

The betel-nut found a place in the materia medica of the ancient Chinese (*Pin lang*) for its therapeutic properties. It is used not only as a masticatory and dentrifrice, but as a vermifuge, especially for expelling tape-worms from dogs and cats. For this purpose 60 grains of powdered areca nut may be given by the mouth or the chief active principle, arecoline, in the form of the crystalline soluble hydrobromide in doses of about one-thirteenth of a grain (0·004 to 0·006 gramme). As an anthelmintic, arecoline resembles pelletierine, one of the alkaloids of pomegranate root bark.

Several alkaloids have been isolated from areca or betel-nuts ; the seeds were first examined by Bombelon in 1886 and in 1888 by Jalns who obtained choline, a fairly widespread plant alkaloid, and the following, all of which are closely related : guvacine, arecaine, arecaidine and arecoline. Arecaine is now known to be identical with arecaidine, and two others have been added ; arecolidine (Emde, 1915) and guvacoline (K. Hess, 1918). Arecoline, a colourless, oily, strongly alkaline liquid, is the only alkaloid of the group which is highly toxic. According to Meir, arecoline belongs to the nicotine-pilocarpine group, and acts on the central and peripheral parts of the nervous system, producing paralysis, which may be preceded by convulsions (Ref. 11). It is like pilocarpine in its action, but is closely related to muscarine which again is closely related to choline. Arecoline acts on the heart in a similar way to fungus-muscarine, the alkaloid of the toadstool " fly agaric " (Amanita muscaria). Complete stasis of the heart occurs in diastole. The lethal dose of arecoline for a rabbit is 10 mg., but small dogs have survived doses of 50 to 75 mg. of the base (Ref. 1). Many pharmacologists consider that the action of fungus-muscarine on the heart is that of a direct muscle poison which causes paralysis. Arecoline contracts the pupil more strongly than pilocarpine and in this respect again strongly resembles muscarine. Introduced into a cat's eye it may cause the pupil to disappear almost completely (R. Kobert, quoted by Autenrieth). The employment of " fly agaric," so called from its use as a fly poison, by the peasants of Siberia as an intoxicating beverage is of interest when compared with the observations of Garcia da Orta given above (see G. Kennan, " Tent Life in Siberia," new ed., 1910, p. 198). Malay women use the young green shoots (*puchok pinang*) of the *pinang* palm as an abortifacient in early pregnancy. Choline is one of the constituents of ergot and uterine contraction has been noted in poisoning by muscarine. Large doses of areca nut cause vomiting and diarrhœa. The sialogogue action of the drug is exemplified in the process of betelchewing, but as the juice is not swallowed no harm results. In the Dutch East Indies the root of *pohun pinang hitam* (Areca catechu, Linn., var., nigra) is used as a poison ; it is shredded, steeped in water, pounded and the juice, after straining, is put into food or drink. This causes giddiness and sleep, also raving, the poison affecting the brain severely. After an emetic, molasses in coco-nut water is promptly given as an antidote (Greshoff—Indian Poison Reports).

PINE-APPLE

Nanas, the pine-apple (Ananas sativa, Linn.—Bromeliaceæ), is used in its unripe state by Malay women as an abortifacient ; a young green pine-apple about half-grown is either eaten raw or the fruit is sucked *ad libitum* so as to absorb the juice. Sometimes salt is added. Pine-apple juice contains a free acid unequally distributed and " bromelin," an unstable proteolytic ferment, which has long been used as an aid to digestion, somewhat resembling papain in this respect. Bromelin has the power of digesting proteids, and this is manifested in fluids of all reactions, acid, alkaline, and neutral ; in this respect the ferment resembles trypsin rather than pepsin ; it acts, however, like pancreatin, most strongly in neutral or alkaline media. In India the fresh juice is supposed by natives to be poisonous if injected hypodermically.

POKOK BATU PĚLIR KAMBING

Pokok batu pělir kambing is a Kelantan village plant quite distinct from the better known jungle climber of almost the same name (*akar batu pělir kambing*), which has already been described as Sarcolobus globosus, Wall.—Asclepiadaceæ. The poisonous village plant now referred to is Rauwolfia perakensis, King and Gamble—Apocynaceæ ; it was identified by Mr. Burkill from a specimen sent to him in 1913 from Kelantan. Rauwolfia perakensis is a small shrub with small yellowish-white flowers and small red berries, which from their peculiar shape give the Malay name for this plant—that of a goat's testicle. *Pokok batu pělir kambing* is not widely distributed, but is found in Perak and Pahang.

Although Malay children sometimes poison themselves unwittingly by eating the berries, the plant
itself does not appear to be very poisonous ; Greshoff
however, lists R. serpentina as an East Indian poison :
" The roots are pounded, and the juice then used in
food causes abdominal pain." In Kelantan the effect
of the fresh ripe berries of R. perakensis is said to
be very serious when combined with poisonous aroids,
such, for example, as *kĕladi chandek* and *likir*, which
are mentioned under section KĔLADI. This mixture
when given in food is said to cause very great swelling
of the throat and fauces, so that the tongue cannot
be protruded ; this is followed by unconsciousness.
It is prepared by taking the fresh ripe berries and
grinding them carefully (so as to avoid irritation of
the compounder's skin) with the juice of the tubers.

The genus Rauwolfia contains several known poisonous plants, of which R. serpentina, Benth.—
Apocynaceæ, is perhaps the most familiar. It contains an alkaloid allied to brucine, which acts on the
heart ; this shrub is known to be poisonous to cattle
in Ceylon. Rauwolfia sinensis, Hemsl., R. verti-
cillata, Baill., and R. vomitoria, Afzel., all belong
to the same Natural Order (Apocynaceæ) and are
poisonous. This N.O. also contains Acocanthera and
Strophanthus (which have glucosides as active principles, and are used by natives of Africa as arrow
poisons) and many other poisonous plants, among
which is the sweet-scented or " true " oleander with
white or pink flowers (*bunga anis ; b. Jipun :* Nerium
odorum, Linn.). This plant is very common in India
and has been introduced into Kelantan by the Chinese.
The " bastard " or yellow oleander (Thevetia neriifolia) is also naturalised in Malaya and cultivated
in gardens for its flowers. The trees thrive well, but
the poisonous properties of their roots do not seem

to be known to Kelantan Malays. Neriodorin and thevetin, the glucosides of the oleanders, are powerful cardiac poisons; they resemble digitalis, but also approximate strychnine.

TUBA

The Malay word *tuba* is used generically by natives in Malaya for several poisonous plants which are chiefly used by them for catching fish. Among those found in the Malay Peninsula, Derris elliptica is the most important.

Derris elliptica, Benth.—Leguminosæ, is described botanically by the Director of the Royal Botanic Gardens, Kew (1922) as follows: " Large climbing shrub, the younger parts rusty-pubescent. Leaves, impari-pinnate, 6 inches to 1 foot long; leaflets in four to five pairs, oblong to obovate-lanceolate, shortly and abruptly acuminate, 3 to 6 inches long, chartaceous, glabrous above, more or less pubescent beneath; petiolules $\frac{1}{5}$ inch long. Panicles axillary, elongated, narrow, rusty-pubescent; pedicels bracteoled, $\frac{2}{3}$ to 1 inch long. Flowers rather large. Calyx broad, nearly $\frac{1}{6}$ inch deep, rusty-pubescent. Corolla $\frac{2}{3}$ inch long, pink with adpressed tawny silky pubescence. Ovary tawny-villous. Pod oblong, compressed, rather acute, about 3 inches long by 1 inch broad, one to four seeded, glabrescent, narrowly winged along the upper suture. Hab. Chittagong to Java. Fl. March. Fr. Aug."

Derris elliptica is indigenous in the Malay Peninsula; the bark and wood of the roots are highly toxic, but the stems only slightly so, while the leaves possess no poisonous properties. Thus whilst dilution of the whole root pounded with water killed tadpoles at 1 : 160,000 in seven and a half hours, similar preparations of leaves and stems were not lethal at

1 : 1,000 ; in such comparative trials it is important
that the amount of fluid should be the same in each
case (Ref. 8). The root varies in size from about 1
inch in diameter to ¼ inch or less ; when newly dug
up it is darkish-brown in colour and tough, but cuts
easily and has a pleasant " clean " smell somewhat
remindful of liquorice-root, and a sweet taste. A
white creamy fluid (*gĕtah akar tuba*) comes out on pressure, especially from the wood ; on drying it turns
lemon-yellow. When dry the root yields a slight
cloud of powder on fracture. The following report
on dried *tuba* root (Derris elliptica) by Mr. Boodle
was kindly supplied by Sir David Prain, Director
of the Royal Botanic Gardens, Kew (1922). Authentic
samples from Singapore were used in drawing up the
description :—

" **Tuba Root** (Derris elliptica).—Roots long, tapering
very gradually, mostly with very few branches except
in the lower region. Surface of roots dark-brown
(or sometimes pinkish-brown), longitudinally wrinkled,
and often showing somewhat numerous, slightly
raised lenticles, which are round or transversely oval
or linear, and may occur in horizontal rows of two
or three.

" The following data refers to roots 4 or 5 mm. in
diameter measured dry, becoming 6 to 7 mm. on
boiling :—

" A clean-cut transverse surface of the dry root
usually shows a more or less distinct yellowish colour,
and, when examined with a lens, the yellow colour is
seen to occur especially in the immediate neighbourhood of the pores (wood-vessels). The bark (chiefly
phloem) is pale brown or pinkish, and thin in the dry
root, but is about 1 mm. thick after boiling. On
mounting a dry section of the root in a drop of water,
the latter becomes milky. This is due to a secretion,

which is present in parenchyma-cells of the wood and bast, often occupying large tracts of this tissue in the wood. The secretion as occurring in the cells appears white by reflected light and dark-grey, brownish or yellowish by transmitted light. It is soluble in spirit.

" A transverse section of the root, examined under the microscope, shows at the periphery several layers of low, rather thin-walled cork-cells, of which the outermost have brown or orange contents. In the bast (phlöem) numerous groups of fibres occur. The arrangement of these groups may be partially tangential, partly irregular, while their shape varies, being round or oval, more or less rectangular (tangentially elongated) or decidedly irregular. Some groups may contain thirty to forty fibres, others have various smaller numbers, while isolated fibres are not uncommon. The groups of fibres are accompanied by solitary crystals of calcium oxalate placed in small cells arranged in vertical series (' chambered crystal-parenchyma '). The individual fibres are mostly 10 to 21 μ in diameter, the larger measurements belonging to fibres having a flattened form ; the lumen is usually small. The primary walls of the fibres are lignified and sometimes yellowish, while the thickening-layer or later-formed part of the wall consists of cellulose, and occasionally contracts away from the primary wall. The wood (xylem) includes a large proportion of parenchymatous tissue, and therefore the medullary rays are not very conspicuous in a transverse section. Starch is present in some of the parenchymatous tissue (of the wood-parenchyma and of the medullary rays).

" Numerous groups of fibres occur in the wood-parenchyma, and are precisely similar to those found in the bast. The wood-vessels occur singly and in rows or groups of two, three or more, the isolated vessels being usually elliptical, and the largest of them reaching nearly 0·2 mm. in diameter. Some of the parenchymatous tissue of the wood is lignified, especially in patches enclosing one or more groups of vessels. Pith is not present in the specimens examined."

D. elliptica grows readily in the Straits Settlements ; the roots are put on the market in two grades. There is a good local demand for them done up in bundles for sale by weight in native shops. It would seem that they are frequently adulterated by the substitution of other roots. The Director of the Botanic Gardens, Singapore, prosecuted a Chinese in 1918 for causing damage to a ficus tree in the garden ; the accused pleaded in court that he was taking the aerial roots as a medicine. A fortnight later he came back with an accomplice and a cart and carried away a further quantity for the adulteration of *tuba* roots. The detection of spurious *tuba* roots is of considerable economic importance ; it will be seen later that only two kinds (D. elliptica and D. uliginosa) have been proved to be useful for insecticidal purposes. Three samples of commercial " coarse roots " and " fine roots," which were supplied as " good specimens " of D. elliptica, were sent to Kew Gardens for verification, where considerable adulteration was detected.

D. elliptica, though indigenous, is frequently cultivated, especially in Borneo, where it is planted in patches on the *padi* fields (Ref. 13). It strikes readily from cuttings, which soon grow into a tangle of straggling stems. In Perak it flowers in February and March, and the fruit ripens in May and June (Ref. 28). The juice of the root is used by Malays and Dayaks in temporarily poisoning jungle streams, because fish are quickly stupefied when it is put into water and are easily caught when they rise to the surface. L. Wray, jun., mentions some nearly allied leguminous genera, such as Pongania, Milletia and Tephrosia, as being used as a means of catching fish in the East Indies. Tephrosia toxicaria, Persoon, and T. piscatoria, Persoon, are used in Java and Sumatra; while Lonchocarpus and Piscidia erythrina, Linn., or Jamaica dogwood (all belonging to the Leguminosæ), are used in the same way in other parts of the world. Mention may here be made of *jĕring* (Pithecolobium lobatum, Benth.—Leguminosæ), which has caused poisoning in Sarawak. The evil-smelling pods of the *jĕring* tree are often eaten by Malays and are innocuous to monkeys, but may cause intestinal and urinary disturbance. D. elliptica and other species of an allied genus, Leguminosæ, are extensively used by Chinese gardeners in Malaya as an insecticide. It is said that the rhinoceros and the porcupine can feed on the roots of *tuba* with impunity. In man an increased secretion of saliva is caused by D. elliptica, which gradually lessens until a feeling of numbness about the tongue and soft palate occurs; ultimately speech is affected.

Varied Uses of the word " Tuba."—As the word is used loosely by natives for several plants, it is expedient to refer here to some of the plants called *tuba*. It may be noted that S. F. Blake (Ref. 17) considers that the genus Leguelia of Aublet has botanical priority over the name Derris, Benth., but Derris seems to be generally accepted at the present time. In Kelantan, among Malay names are: *tuba jĕmu* (probably D. elliptica) and *tuba katak puru* (" toad " *t.*); in Pahang, *tuba jĕnĕrak, tuba kapur* (" lime " *t.*), and *tuba sĕluang*, a kind of reed with less powerful properties. Ridley lists *tuba-tuba* (Kedah) as Derris Maingayana, Hook. fil., which is probably the same as *tuba gajah* (" elephant " *t.*), or *tuba panjang* (" long " *t.*), of Sarawak, with thick root. Ridley and Curtis give *akar tulang bukit* as D. thyrsiflora, Benth., and D. uliginosa, Benth., as *akar kĕtuil* (Ref. 21). In Borneo there are *tuba bĕnar*,

t. rabut (with pointed leaf), *t. tĕdau* (Dayak, *rowie*), the
bark of the *pĕrakol* tree, also *t. China* and *buah tuba*
(the fruit of a tree). There is also a yam with a white
flower called *t. ubi*, as yet unidentified botanically, but
apparently closely allied to Dioscorea birmanica, Prain
and Burkill. Dayaks use the long root-like stems of
D. uliginosa, Benth., or an allied plant, which is common in flooded zones of riverside jungle land in Borneo.
D. uliginosa occurs in India and in the Fiji Islands.

The word *tuba* also appears among Kelantan Malays
in the expression *tuba tikus* (more commonly pronounced *tĕba tikus*) for white arsenic, which is frequently used to poison rats and is equivalent to the
English word rat's-bane (*tikus*, a rat). The stick-
insect (Phasmidæ) is called *tuba gajah* (*gajah*, an elephant) on the east coast, because it is believed to poison
any elephant that eats one by accident. Mr. W. W.
Skeat told me that he was riding on an elephant when
he was told about this by the mahout. " There were
many stick-insects about, which were swept into the
howdah as we pushed through the tangled jungle
growth about the jungle path ; so collecting a couple
of these creatures, I gave them to the mahout, who
placed them at my direction in the midst of a sheaf
of wild ginger plants and gave them to the elephant.
The elephant seized the wild ginger plants eagerly
and began to eat them, but finding the stick-insects
presently, at once threw them away."

**Methods in which Tuba is used by Natives for
Fishing.**—The method in which tuba is used by Malays
in sea fishing is described by Wray : " It (the root) is
pounded or ground fine and mixed with stiff clay and
crushed refuse, shrimps or small fish, and the mixture
is then made into balls and dried. These balls are
thrown into the sea, like ground bait, and fish eating
them become poisoned, rise to the surface, and are

caught by the watching fishermen. This way of using it is probably not very harmful, though the same cannot be said of its use in fresh waters."

River fishing with *tuba* is now prohibited in the Federated Malay States ; but it used to be done to a very large extent in the following way : The effective part of the plant, *i.e.*, the sap, is obtained by pounding the roots with clubs to a pulp under water, to which lime is sometimes added to make the resulting milky watery fluid sink and spread when poured into the river. Two or three bucketfuls of the milk-like extract when thrown into a river or pool will stupefy the fish and bring them to the surface. Sometimes a stretch is dammed for the express purpose of spearing, clubbing, netting and trapping them. The roots may also be bruised with lime and tobacco in dug-out canoes half full of water, which, when the pounded roots have been thoroughly soaked, are upset into deep places between rocks, or baled out within an enclosure. About 5 or 6 cwt. of the roots may be used. The prepared root is thrown into the water about a couple of miles above an improvised fence of stakes. In about twenty minutes, as the *tuba* comes down, the fish are struck with panic and rush wildly down-stream to the fence, where they are speared or clubbed. In staking the stream to make the barrier, space may be allowed between the stakes to let small-sized fish pass and so escape, as they are liable to be killed outright by *tuba*.

The exciting sport of tuba-fishing has been described by G. Maxwell (Ref. 16), Hose and McDougall (Ref. 13), and is mentioned in Dr. W. H. Furness's sketch " Folk-Lore in Borneo." The sport goes on for several hours : fish of all kinds, except small fry which escape by keeping on the surface, and cat-fish which hide in the mud, are affected by *tuba* : at first the big ones make desperate efforts to get away by leaping over the down-stream barricade ; but they gradually become stupe-fied, and turn on their backs on the surface of the water, until they gradually cease to breathe, if the dose of poison should be a large one. When Malays are tuba-fishing mention of fish by name is tabooed by the *bomor* —everybody takes care not to do so : it is thought better to refer to them as leaves whirling down the stream. The fish that are stupefied have no ill effects when used as a cooked food by man, because the amount of *tuba* required to stupefy them is infinitesimal, but they are said to go bad more quickly than usual.

It has been found by experiment that fish first become very lively, then for a while they were more responsive to a poke with a stick than the controls before final stupefication, with occasional spasms : the respiration becomes slow ; thus a gudgeon with respira-tions 106 per minute slowed down to sixty-nine after five minutes, forty-six after forty-five minutes, and in ninety-nine minutes they had ceased. Exposure to the poison for a while may be followed by death although the fish is transferred to fresh water. In frogs to which the poison is given by injection, the heart is found gorged at apparent death, though a beat may be elicited by stimulation ; there is also some slight response of nerve and muscle to direct stimulation, but the spinal cord is paralysed (Ref. 8). Argyll Campbell, experimenting in Singapore with an extract of *tuba* prepared in the same way as Malay fishermen use it, found that fish of about 50 grammes weight (1¾ oz.) were killed by solutions as weak as 1 in 100,000 : the fresh-water fish Ophiocephalus gacha, Buch., Ham. (murrel), were used in these experiments. It seemed highly probable that death was due to asphyxia, from the post-mortem examina-tions of these small fishes (Ref. 4).

The white sap of *tuba* (D. elliptica) has been shown to be an emulsion with no tendency towards coagulation, and little, if any, loss of toxic action on boiling for a short period. Campbell says that the watery extract is faintly acid in reaction, and that it is not antiseptic.

Other Uses of Tuba.—The sap of derris combined with that of the upas tree is used in Borneo as one of the ingredients of the Kayan dart and arrow poison for hunting. A similar use of the sap by the pagan races of the Malay Peninsula was reported by Newbold in 1839, and is mentioned under section THE UPAS TREE. As a Malay poison *tuba* is sometimes put into wells with criminal intent ; but death as a result of its use so administered to human beings seems to be rare among Malays, probably because it would be necessary to employ large quantities of the root ; moreover, a strong enough emulsion would be detected by its milky appearance. It is said, however, in Kelantan that many Malay girls have lost their lives by uterine hæmorrhage through drinking an infusion as an abortifacient. In pregnant women abortion would appear to be due to the asphyxia produced by the poison and uterine hæmorrhage to dilatation of the blood vessels (A. Campbell). Brooke says that the root of *tuba* itself is used to procure abortion by insertion and retention in the vagina, which causes metritis. He also remarks : " Decoctions have been occasionally used criminally and for suicide, but as large quantities are required, it is seldom used." (Ref. 2). In Singapore, one of Mr. Ridley's staff had two wives who hated each other. One, a Malay from Ceylon, stole some *tuba* roots from the Botanic Gardens, made a decoction from them, and persuaded the other to take it as a medicine for indigestion. The victim drank a mouthful, but found it too nasty to persevere with. The would-be murderess fled. " The other wife was never well from that day, wasted away and died within a year." Greshoff records that drinking the poison produces general malaise, headache, dizziness, vomiting, copious and painful diarrhœa, collapse and death (Indian Poison Reports, 1902, second edition, No. 202. Royal Colonial Institute, Amsterdam). The poison is sometimes administered in sago-toddy. It is said that Javanese girls and Dayak girls employ *tuba* as a means to commit suicide. Acute cases of poisoning are characterised by fixation of the jaws. In Sarawak native methods of treatment consist in the administration of sugar and immersion of the patient in cold water. In the island of Siauw (Celebes Sea), besides catching and killing fish, the roots of *tuba* are also used to kill small birds in the rice fields to protect the crops. The sap mixed with water is put in small bamboos for birds to drink from.

So long ago as 1848 Oxley found that a decoction made of the roots of derris was effective in destroying an insect infesting the leaves of the nutmeg tree in the Straits Settlements. The watery extract used by Chinese market gardeners from early times, for killing insects, to which reference has already been made, is very effective, especially for spraying cultivated spices. Ridley praises this custom in his book on Spices, and says : " The decoction is poisonous to human beings, but only when taken in large quantities, and the risk from it in the case of our spice plants is infinitesimal " (Ref. 23).

The application of D. elliptica as an insecticide which has so long been in vogue among Straits Chinese gardeners is now used extensively in England and is found to be very potent. Its value in this respect has been investigated by McIndoo, Sievers and Abbot (Ref. 17). These American scientists found that derris acted both by contact and as a stomach poison, but that it had no value as a fumigant. Six species of derris were tested, but only two of them (D. elliptica and D. uliginosa) were considered useful for insecticidal purposes. It kills some insects easily and others with difficulty, but it usually acts slowly and seems to kill by motor paralysis. It proved to be efficient against most of the aphides in the form of a spray. The green apple aphis (Aphis pomi, De Greer) is destroyed at the rate of 1 lb. of derris to 200 gallons of water under field conditions. Dr. H. E. Durham found (1903) that the most sensitive animals are perhaps the Daphnid crustacea. Tadpoles and water-snails are also easily killed. Caterpillars are easily poisoned ; especially sensitive is the gooseberry saw-fly (Nematus ribesii), but Durham found that it had no effect as a contact poison on the black bean aphis (A. rumicis) and the woolly aphis of the apple (E. lanigera). Trial on frogs' hearts showed that the vagus was paralysed, so that stimulation of the nerve failed to cause the normal vagus inhibition (Ref. 8).

Campbell found that an extract from 30 grains (2 grammes) of the root was sufficient to kill a large monkey in about forty minutes. He observed that it usually stimulates the respiratory centre before depressing it and that it acts as a vaso-dilator. " The poison acts upon the respiratory nervous centre in the medulla and not on the vagal endings in the lungs, because the same results are obtained if the vagi are cut. Also if the poison is injected into the carotid artery, the respiration is affected in a few seconds." He found that post-mortem examinations only showed venous congestion of the organs.

In 1902 Durham (Ref. 8) commenced a series of experiments with *tuba* as a larvicide in the Federated Malay States. In England he found that Culex larvæ

(Theobaldia annularis) were killed in 1 in 40,000 suspension of the dried powdered crude root of D. elliptica. A solution of 1 in 10,000 killed the larvæ in twenty-nine hours and the pupæ in twenty-four hours to three or four days. Another experiment with the larvæ of Culex pipiens showed that the larvæ died in less than sixteen hours (pupæ in less than twenty-four hours) with solutions of 1 in 1,000, 1 in 2,000 and 1 in 5,000 of the whole root ; with 1 in 10,000 the larvæ were killed in twenty hours and the pupæ in twenty-four hours. A solution of 1 in 1,000 of the extract is enough to make the water cloudy. Durham notes that the drug dried in Malaya loses much moisture when air-dried in England ; using wetter or fresh root undried would make the effective proportion of the root to water much higher ; at the same time crushing the root up with water is likely to extract more of the juice when not so dry.

Derris elliptica is being cultivated on a larger scale than formerly in the Federated Malay States, and now forms an ingredient of cattle dips in Europe. There seems no reason why it should not become a profitable addition to the industries of British Malaya. The valuable property of *tuba* as a larvicide may prove to be a practical asset in malaria and filaria campaigns ; but it must be remembered that fish will also succumb. In an exhaustive report on a large number of plants tested for insecticidal properties McIndoo and Sievers (1924) confirm their previous work on D. elliptica and D. uliginosa and find that out of 260 species catalogued only derris and three other plants can be regarded as satisfactorily efficient. Recently at the Rothamsted Experimental Station, Harpenden, Herts, the active principle of derris has been found in two plants from British Guiana, known as White and Black Haiari, both species of Lonchocarpus and used as fish poisons (F. Tattersfield).

The possibility of a purified preparation from D. elliptica being valuable as a therapeutic agent was mooted many years ago; during the War the writer suggested that as a drug the active principle might prove to be a definite poison to the protozoa causing malaria; but it was considered inadvisable to experiment with it clinically without previous standardisation which was not practicable at that time.

The Chemistry of Derrid.—In 1890, Greshoff described the active principle of *tuba* (Derris elliptica) and named it " derrid," a nitrogen-free, non-glucosidal resin containing no sulphur; he found it was chiefly contained in the bark of the root, and gives the yield from a whole root as 2·5 to 3 per cent. ; a brown mahogany-coloured body called " derris-red," possibly derived from the tannin of the plant was also found, but no white crystalline product was isolated. L. Wray, jun., who extracted the resin independently (1892), called it " tubaine," being unaware of Greshoff's discovery. Wray found that one part of his " tubaine " in 350,000 parts of water quickly proved fatal to fish, and that water containing a millionth part of " tubaine " killed fish in fifteen to thirty minutes, according to species (Ref. 28). Greshoff found that a much smaller quantity of his " derrid " would kill fish: " A solution containing only one five-millionth part stupefied goldfish and killed them within half an hour " (*Pharmaceut. Jour. and Trans.*, 1890, 3, XXI, p. 559. London). Van Sillevoldt (1899) next investigated the chemistry of Greshoff's active principle, but did not refer to the crystalline product which had separated out during Wray's experiments. In 1903 Power investigated the poisonous properties of D. uliginosa as regards fish, and van Hasselt reported on D. elliptica in 1911. The work of H. E. Durham given below is privately communicated.

Durham found that the very active constituent is in two forms, crystalline and resinoid ; both of these are highly toxic, but the resin is more active : dilutions of one part in four or five millions of water will kill tadpoles within twenty-four hours, but in dilutions four or five times such strength only three or four hours elapse before death. Gudgeon exposed for four hours in two-million-fold dilution of the crystals did not recover in fresh water ; one in a million of the resin, freed as much as possible from crystalline matter, killed a roach in four hours. The crystals are beautiful white, non-nitrogenous, crystalline bodies consisting of carbon, hydrogen and oxygen, with a definite melting point at $164\frac{1}{2}°$ C., soluble in petrol-ether and chloroform, benzine, toluene, etc., but in water only to the extent of about one in six millions. The pure crystalline form is not very soluble in cold alcohol, and thus it can be separated from the more soluble resinoid part of crude " derrid." The crystals (colourless, long laminæ, with sometimes small hexagonal plates, suggesting that they belong to the rhombic system) are altered and reddened by exposure to even diffused light, but keep well in the dark ; they are also altered by too long heating with alcohol or other water-containing liquids. The resinoid form melts at about 61° C. ; it is rather more soluble in water than the pure crystalline form. Thus a saturated solution made by exposing the crystals to water for a week or two and then filtered will kill tadpoles when diluted four-fold but not ten-fold, whilst a similar solution made from the resinous residue (which is probably not entirely freed from the crystalline substance) will kill at ten-fold but not at twenty-fold dilution. The active matter is best extracted from the root by means of petroleum ether or hot paraffin (burning oil), from which on cooling it separates out as impure and resinous canary-coloured masses. From these masses the crystalline body may be purified by extraction and re-crystallisation from alcohol. A characteristic colour reaction is given by both the crystal and the resinoid " derrid," according to Durham : " treated with a drop of strong nitric acid without heating on a glazed porcelain plate both become red, and then a drop of ammonia causes an evanescent deep rich peacock blue-green (signal green) coloration, fading to chocolate and yellow. Caustic potash after nitric acid gives a similar reaction, less lasting, passing to purple then yellow." This is a distinctive reaction which might prove useful in criminal cases, as it is very sensitive (Ref. 8). The chemistry of the main constituent of Derris elliptica, namely, the colourless crystalline derivative, was investigated by Ishikawa in 1917, who named it " tubo-toxin," but it is now sometimes known as rotenone (S. Takei. Uber Rotenon. *Ber. der Deut. Chem. Ges.*, 1928, No. 5, p. 1003). According to Campbell, it should be easy enough to detect the presence of *tuba* poison in the stomach contents by simply testing the effects, after boiling and filtering, of some of the fluid upon small fish, seeing that they are killed by very weak solutions of the poison. He also showed that *tuba* acts as a stomach poison towards monkeys (Ref. 4).

REFERENCES

(1) AUTENRIETH, W. " Laboratory Manual for the Detection of Poisons and Powerful Drugs." Authorised translation from sixth German edition by William H. Warren. 1928. London : Churchill.

(2) BROOKE, G. E. " Medico-Tropical Practice." 1920. 2nd ed. London : Baillière, Tindall & Cox.

(3) BURTON-BROWN, T. E. "Punjab Poisons," 1888, p. 128. Calcutta.

(4) CAMPBELL, J. A. "An Experimental Investigation Concerning the Effects of Tuba (Derris Elliptica) Fish-Poison." *Jour. Straits Br. Roy. Asiat. Soc.* (Singapore). 1916. No. 73, p. 129.

(5) CHEVERS, NORMAN. "A Manual of Medical Jurisprudence for India." 1870. Calcutta : Thacker, Spink.

(6) CLIFFORD, Sir HUGH. "Studies in Brown Humanity." 1927. 2nd ed. London : Richards.

(7) DYMOCK, W. "The Vegetable Materia Medica of Western India," 1885, p. 627. Bombay.

(8) DURHAM, H. E. Private communication.

(9) GIMLETTE, J. D. "Datura Poisoning in the Federated Malay States." *Brit. Med. Jour.* (London). 1903. Vol. I, p. 1137.

(10) GRESHOFF, M. *Meded. uit s'Lands Planten.* 1893. Vols. X and XXV. Batavia.

(11) HENRY, T. A. "The Plant Alkaloids." 1924. 2nd ed. London : Churchill.

(12) HOLMES, E. M. "Vegetable Poisons and their Antidotes." *Pharmaceut. Jour. and Trans.* (London), June 20th, 1874, p. 1014.

(13) HOSE and McDOUGALL. "The Pagan Tribes of Borneo." 1912. London : Macmillan.

(14) KIRTIKAR and BASU. "Indian Medicinal Plants." 1918. Allahabad : Trübner.

(15) MARSDEN, W. "The History of Sumatra." 1811. 3rd ed. London.

(16) MAXWELL, Sir GEORGE. "In Malay Forests." 1925, p. 246. London : Blackwood.

(17) McINDOO, SIEVERS and ABBOTT. "Derris as an Insecticide." *Jour. Agric. Res.* (Washington). 1919. Vol. VII, No. 5, pp. 177–200.

(18) NEWBOLD, T. "Political and Statistical Account of the British Settlements in the Straits of Malacca." 1839. London.

(19) ORTA, GARCIA DA. "Colloquies on the Simples and Drugs of India." 1563. Translation by C. R. Markham. 1913. London : Sotheran.

(20) PECKHOLT, T. "Carica Papaya and Papayotin." *Pharmaceut. Jour. and Trans.* (London). 1879. 3, X, p. 346.

(21) RIDLEY, H. N. "List of Malay Plant Names." *Jour. Straits Br. Roy. Asiat. Soc.* (Singapore). 1897. No. 30.

(22) RIDLEY, H. N. "The Flora of the Malay Peninsula." 1925. Ashford, Kent : L. Reeve.

(23) RIDLEY, H. N. "Spices." 1910. London : Macmillan.

(24) SMITH, SYDNEY. "Forensic Medicine." 1928. 2nd ed. London : Churchill.

(25) TAYLOR and SMITH. "The Principles and Practice of Medical Jurisprudence." 1928. Vol. II, p. 748. London : Churchill.

(26) WINDSOR, Captain F. N. "Indian Toxicology." 1906. Calcutta : Thacker, Spink.

(27) WITTHAUS, R. A. "A Manual of Toxicology." 1911. 2nd ed. New York : W. Wood.

(28) WRAY, L., jun. "The Malayan Fish Poison called Aker Tuba, Derris Elliptica." *Pharmaceut. Jour. and Trans.* (London). July 23rd, 1892. No. 1152, p. 61.

CHAPTER X

ARSENIC

ARSENIC is one of the commonest agents used by the homicide and by the suicide or taken by accident : it is an important factor in many widely used preparations—for instance, those for combating pests on fruit trees, weeds, etc., in the West, and white ants, flies, etc., in the East, and in the treatment of disease ; from such sources it may cause calamity through crime or carelessness. The white arsenic of commerce, arsenious acid, was formerly sold without restriction in the market-place at Kota Bharu, Kelantan, under the name *tuba tikus* (*tikus*, a rat), the Kelantan name for rat's-bane. White arsenic is also known as *warangan puteh* (*puteh*, white) ; it used to be exposed for sale in the market-place at Indian stalls, or it could be bought at any Chinese " drug-shop " in the form of vitreous masses, curiously shaped and stratified, which had evidently been chipped from the flues of some factory.

These lumps of arsenic probably came from Burmah by way of Singapore, or from the open-cast tin mines of Siam, where Chinese miners used to smelt their ore locally in small, primitive, earthen blast furnaces. Arsenpyrite is abundant in limestone formations which frequently yield deposits of tin ore. A specimen of *tuba tikus* bought in the Kota Bharu bazaar for a few cents in 1905 was analysed by Mr. P. Burgess, Government Analyst, Straits Settlements ; it was found by him to be pure arsenious oxide, or white arsenic. Anybody could purchase any quantity of *tuba tikus* for use either as a medicine, for damascening the blade of a kris, or for killing rats. Legislation controlling the sale of certain dangerous drugs, including arsenic, was decreed by the late Sultan, on the advice of his British adviser, in 1913 : consequently it has become impossible to buy *tuba tikus* in the open market of late years. The poisonous dose is very small. At a murder trial in Hereford (*Rex v. Armstrong*, April, 1922) the fact became public that sixty-six lethal doses of white arsenic (3½ grains to a dose) could be bought in England for the sum of one penny. At this rate enough to poison 3,000 people could be bought for one Straits dollar, *i.e.*, at 2*s.* 4*d.* per lb.

Arsenic Used by Malays for Assassination.—White arsenic is reputed to be one of the chief poisons employed by Malays for killing or attempting to kill. But it appears to be much less used in Malaya than in India, where it is commonly used out of revenge with murderous intent, also for poisoning cattle in order to procure the hides. In Egypt also it is much used to poison neighbours and their cattle. A common device for cattle-poisoning is to scoop out the central pith of an ear of maize (corn-cob), fill the resulting space with arsenic and close it with dough.

The alleged Kelantan practice of poisoning the Malay kris with arsenic to make assassination doubly sure has been referred to on page 4. It cannot have been universal among Malays. William Marsden, writing so long ago as 1811 about the Sumatran kris, says : " The abominable custom of poisoning them, though much talked of, is rarely practised, I believe, in modern times. They (Malays) are frequently seen rubbing the blades with lime-juice, which has been considered as a precaution against danger of this kind, but it is rather for the purpose of removing common stains, or of improving the damasked appearance." In Kelantan according to the late Dato' Lela 'diraja of Kota Bharu, when the blade of the kris was to be poisoned it was smeared with a mixture of white arsenic and the juice of the small chilli. Compare this with pp. 4, 134, and section CYANIDE OF POTASSIUM. The wearing of the kris in public was prohibited in Kelantan by an Order in Council of 1909. The typical execution kris wound, a thrust from above downwards penetrating the heart, is no longer seen.

Other Uses of Arsenic.—As a medicine arsenic is valued by Malays as an external application in the treatment of Yaws (*puru*), being used either by itself in the form of a powder, or as an ingredient in a vegetable paste made either by grinding down the root of a wild red vine (Leea rubra) or the root of a shrub called *chĕkor manis* (Sauropus albicans) with a little water. When using white arsenic the *bomor* endeavours to prevent the pain which it causes by burning it in a slow fire until it is blackened ; he then pulverises it in a mortar and makes it up either with coco-nut oil or with the juice of the common " thin-skinned lime." The yellow sulphide of arsenic (orpiment : the *bĕrangan kuning* of Java) and the red sulphide (realgar : *bĕrangan* or *warangan merah*) are also used as local applications ; but they cause pain, and the use in days gone by was mainly in connection with finishing the blade of a kris, which, when damascened, veined and watered, is called the *pamur* on the kris.

The process of *pamur* is described by Newbold (1839) as follows : " Place on the blade a mixture of boiled rice, sulphur, and salt, beat together, first taking the precaution of covering the edges of the weapon with a thin coat of virgin wax. After this has remained on seven days the damask will have risen to the surface. Take the composition off, and immerse the blade in the water of a young coco-nut, or the juice of a pine-apple, for seven days longer, and brush it well with the juice of a sour lemon. After the rust has been cleared away, rub it with arsenic (*warangan*) dissolved in lime-juice, wash it well with spring-water, dry and anoint with coco-nut oil." The process has been described elsewhere as due to the action of acids on a blade forged by beating steel and iron together when in a state of half fusion.

For use as a Malay poison *tuba tikus* is pounded in a mortar with the pips of the lime fruit ; except for its grittiness, as it is colourless, free from smell, and practically speaking, tasteless, it can hardly be detected when mixed with cooked rice and curry into which a poisonous dose can be so easily dropped.

A fixed oil has been expressed from the pips of West Indian limes ; in the crude state it is reddish-brown in colour with a distinctly bitter flavour and free acidity (as oleic acid) 2·8 per cent. (*The Analyst*, May, 1926 : Cambridge).

The strength and violence of arsenic as a poison has been recognised from very early times ; the earliest record of it is said to date back to a period about 400 B.C., and it is curious that the plan of procuring *tuba tikus* (*tikus*, a rat) for homicidal purposes on the plea of " killing rats " should have been in vogue from the fourteenth century down to the present day.

In Chaucer's " Canterbury Tales " we read :

> And forth he gooth, no lenger would he tarie,
> Into the toun, un-to a pothecarie,
> And preyed him, that he him wolde selle
> Some poyson, that he mighte his rattes quelle ;

This cursed man hath in his hond y-hent
This poyson in a box, and sith he ran
And borwed (of) him large botels three ;
And in the two his poyson poured he ;

The quotation above is taken from the Pardoneres Tale (Ref. 10). " Three rioters in a tavern agreed to hunt down Death and kill him. As they went their way they met an old man, who told them that he had just left him sitting under a tree in the lane close by. Off posted the three rioters, but when they came to the tree they found a great treasure, which they agreed to divide equally. They cast lots which was to carry it home, and the lot fell on the youngest, who was sent to the village to buy food and wine. While he was gone the two who were left agreed to kill him, and so increase their share ; but the third bought poison to put into their wine, in order to kill his two *confrères*. On his return with his stores, the two set upon him and slew him, then sat down to drink and be merry together ; but, the wine being poisoned, all the three rioters found Death under the tree as the old man had said " (Ref. 2).

As a medicine, arsenic is mentioned by Chaucer in " The Canon's Yeoman's Tale " (Ref. 10). As a poison, D'Avenant, the playwright and poet laureate (1672) makes the younger Pallatine tell his mistress Lucy to put arsenic into broth : " An ounce of ars'nic to mix in thy aunt's caudles." [1]

White arsenic is only slightly soluble in water, about ½ grain dissolves in 1 ounce of cold water, and 6 to 12 grains in the same amount of boiling water. The solubility is increased in the presence of alkalies or acids, and this is probably why the Malay poisoner combines *tuba tikus* with the pips of the sour lime

---

[1] " Dramatists of the Reformation," D'Avenant, *The Wits*, Act I, Scene 2, 1872, Vol. II, p. 172. London.

(Citrus acida). When white arsenic in powder is added to liquid food or water it floats and forms a scum which cannot well be got rid of by stirring ; contact with greasy matter may delay the action of the drug. As a poison used for homicidal purposes the absolute number of cases far exceeds those of any other poison (Ref. 12).

Deaths from poisoning by arsenic occurred in Kelantan in 1910, in 1914, and in 1919. They were examples of acute poisoning which is the only form at all common in the East. In 1910 a Tamil traveller put up for the night in an eating-house kept by a fellow-countryman. He found an old mortar and used it in the dusk for preparing his curry stuff. The pestle and mortar had unfortunately been used for pounding up *tuba tikus* for killing rats ; it was forgotten that arsenic remained in the mortar, and death from misadventure resulted. Symptoms of poisoning commenced in the early morning following the heavy evening meal, with nausea and stomach-ache ; death supervened about seven hours afterwards. There was no definite algide stage, but violent vomiting occurred, with burning pain in the throat and stomach, cramp, diarrhœa with dark motions, collapse, suppression of urine, and the passage of much mucus from the bowel with straining. Asiatic cholera was epidemic in Kota Bharu at the time, so the case was instructive : the clinical picture resembled that of Asiatic cholera, and might also have been very difficult to diagnose during life from ptomaine poisoning in the absence of chemical and bacteriological analysis. Dr. Burton-Brown records a similar fatality in India : two native cavalrymen and two other natives showed signs of poisoning by arsenic shortly after their evening meal ; arsenious acid was found in the crevice of a stone used to prepare curry powder for the dinner. He also records another case in which a hollow glass pestle was found filled with arsenious acid : the poison could easily be mixed with curry powder by inverting the pestle and removing the finger over the opening at the top (Ref. 4).

In 1914 a Chinese coolie, under arrest for theft, managed to commit suicide by swallowing a quantity of powdered *tuba tikus* in a single dose. He died within eight hours after violent vomiting and purging. The body was brought to the State hospital from a distance, and on examination the poison was recognised without difficulty by the touch and naked eye as a gritty white powder in the stomach and intestines, which were otherwise empty, but acutely inflamed. Arsenic is seldom used as a means of suicide by Chinese in Malaya on account of the violent vomiting it causes if taken in one or possibly two lethal doses ; opium finds greater favour for the purpose. In 1919 a Tamil woman employed as a coolie by the Kelantan railway department, lost her life from acute arsenical poisoning by mistaking " white-ant-killer " for the lime which is used in the Far East for betel-chewing.

In India arsenic, as mentioned above, is in common use for murder. Burton-Brown, writing with the ripe experience of many cases, sums up the effects among natives of India as follows : " The smallest fatal dose is from 2 to 3 grains. The earliest appearance of symptoms (otherwise than the taste) recorded was three minutes. The longest interval between taking the poison and the occurrence of symptoms was ten hours ; in this case, however, the action was delayed by much food having been taken previously. The usual interval is from half an hour to an hour. The earliest period of death on record took place two hours after the poison had been swallowed. Deaths have occurred as late as two or three weeks after the poison has been taken.

The average period, however, of the fatal termination is eighteen hours, but more than half the cases terminate within six hours of the time at which the poison was swallowed " (Ref. 4).

This terse summary of the acute poisoning common in India may be augmented by remembering that it is the absorption of two grains (0·13 gramme) into the system that is fatal, and that a dose of two ounces (56·699 grammes) has been recovered from. In one case death occurred from shock twenty minutes after a large dose. Much depends on the condition of the stomach as to the presence or absence of food, but it does not necessarily follow that where arsenic is found mixed with food in the stomach it was taken with the food. Arsenic administered in solution on an empty stomach is likely to be far more rapid in its action than if the dose is in coarse fragments which may be got rid of by vomiting. Finely powdered arsenic adheres to the gastric mucous membrane. The absence of arsenic from the stomach probably means that none has been taken during the last six hours of life. The presence of arsenic in large quantities in the intestines and the contents means that a large dose must have been taken within forty-eight hours of death.

Symptoms of Acute Poisoning.—The irritant action of arsenic is generally first felt, in acute cases, in the stomach causing burning pain ; there is nausea, then vomiting, retching, dryness and itching in the mouth and throat, intense thirst, followed by severe diarrhœa, either choleraic or dysenteric in character. The vomiting and purging give no relief. A feeling of faintness and an expression of great anxiety are striking features, but the symptoms are very variable in their nature and occurrence. With the usual symptoms of gastro-intestinal catarrh caused by irritation, are headache, dizziness, small and irregular pulse, coldness of the extremities, hoarseness, cramps, collapse and convulsions. Death may be preceded by coma, but usually the mental condition is unimpaired until a few hours before death (Ref. 12). Sleep may delay the appearance of the symptoms; the urine may be scanty and usually contains blood and casts. Death is generally due to collapse and heart failure, because arsenic is a most powerful tissue poison and the toxic effects are especially found in the structure of the heart, kidneys and liver. Fatty degeneration is set up in the cardiac muscles, in the kidneys, in the gastro-intestinal epithelium and in the liver especially. The kidneys are quickly affected, *i.e.*, within twenty-four hours, and as the poison is chiefly eliminated from the body by the kidneys, the urine should be analysed as soon as poisoning is suspected. Arsenic may be present in the urine from six to ten hours after a poisonous dose has been absorbed and may be found from four to ten days after a single dose. The poison takes about twenty-four hours to pass through the body and may be observed in the stools and vomit. When absorbed from the stomach and intestines it is obliged to pass through the liver before it can enter the general circulation, and in consequence, the largest amount of arsenic is usually found in this organ after death from acute arsenical poisoning. Continued small doses are cumulative and act slowly on the peripheral nerves, not causing symptoms of arsenical neuritis until the lapse of ten or fourteen days, but multiple neuritis has followed a single large dose (Ref. 12). The central nervous system and spinal cord are affected; the skin, hair and nails suffer, and finally, the poison may, with time, be stored in the bones as calcium arsenate (Ref. 1).

White arsenic is absorbed by the living hair and firmly held there even long after it has disappeared from the liver and long bones. It may be detected in the ·hair years after death in protracted cases of poisoning and the arsenic-content is usually high. The absence of arsenic in the hair when the poison is present in the liver and kidneys indicates acute arsenical poisoning. When the poison is present in the hair but not in the internal organs, the supposition is that arsenic was administered many years ago (Ref. 1).

The total amount of arsenic found by analysis in the various organs after death indicates that a much larger quantity was given in a number of large doses extending over a period of probably not less than three days or a week before death. It would certainly indicate that the terminal poisonous dose was given shortly, *e.g.*, twenty-four hours before death. The presence in large quantities in the liver (2 to 3 grains) and in the kidneys, as well as the presence of arsenic in the skin and bones also point to the fact that arsenic has been taken during the period preceding forty-eight hours before death. Massive doses are given by poisoners in the East, but when repeated doses are given symptoms of chronic arsenical poisoning may be added to the acute symptoms, viz., conjunctivitis, laryngitis, skin affections, diffuse or localised pigmentation, sore tongue, etc., and signs of multiple neuritis. Medical practitioners—in Malaya especially—will remember that an appreciable amount of arsenic was found in the hair of Chinese pigtails and in the nails of Chinese who were the victims of beri-beri, when, for the moment, beri-beri was suggested to be due to arsenical neuritis, similar to that which occurred in epidemic form among drinkers of cheap beer and porter in England about the same time (*Brit. Med. Jour.,* December 1st, 1900).

At a recent trial (*Rex v. Pace*, 1928), the accused was acquitted of poisoning her husband, a Gloucestershire sheep farmer. Evidence was given as to the large amount of arsenic found in the remains five days after death: stomach, ·01393 grain and stomach contents, ·000997 grain; intestines, 1·703 grains and intestinal contents, 3·041 grains; liver, 3·62 grains; kidneys, 1·018 grains; heart, ·024 grain; brain, ·0017 grain; a piece of skin, ·0003 grain; a piece of rib, ·0009 grain—total found 9·42 grains. In this case the source of the poisoning was in sheep-dip. An analysis of the solution recommended by the makers resulted in a 0·2 per cent. solution only. Arsenic is not absorbed through the healthy unbroken skin, but it may be absorbed through rashes, abrasions or wounds: when absorbed through a wound more immediate and violent symptoms of gastritis are produced than when the poison is administered by the mouth; such symptoms precede signs of inflammation in the poisoned wound (Lauder Brunton).

Arsenic usually retards decomposition of the stomach and intestines; maggots will be absent from the alimentary canal. When a large amount has been absorbed before death, arsenic may be found many months afterwards in the internal organs which then show yellow post-mortem stains from the conversion of white arsenic into the sulphide of arsenic. Subendocardial hæmorrhages should be looked for especially in the left ventricle. At exhumations it is well to remember that arsenic can be found in the soil at the bottom of the grave which has been wetted by juices that have soaked out of the corpse, and if found, an additional control sample of uncontaminated soil taken in the neighbourhood of the grave must be analysed. The grave clothes (*kain kafan*) must also be examined. White arsenic sublimes on heating, and it is said that candles with poisoned wicks were used to poison Leopold I. of Austria in 1670. Death lamps, in which oil impregnated with arsenic and other substances is burnt, are in use in certain parts of the East (Ref. 11). It has been suggested that the " time-poisons " used by the notorious women poisoners, La Spara and Tofania may have been preparations of arsenic in solution (see pp. 12, 163). Malay poisoners are said to use arsenic in combination with datura, opium and metallic mercury (which see, p. 266). A combination of this sort is referred to as a deadly poison (*rachun bĕsar*). The opium contained in it would modify the symptoms and render the arsenic more deadly.

CYANIDE OF POTASSIUM

Before the sale of powerful poisons was controlled by Government in 1913, cyanide of potassium was freely bought and sold in Kota Bharu, Kelantan, without restriction. It used to be sold to Chinese photographers and Malay and Indian goldsmiths under the name of *potas* or *ubat bĕrchĕlup mas* (medicine for dyeing gold) from native dispensaries.

Methods of Poisoning by Cyanide of Potassium.—An abominable example of premeditated murder occurs in the use of potassium cyanide with honey by Malay criminals. Reference to this practice has already been made (see p. 4) ; the late Dato' Lela 'diraja of Kota Bharu, Kelantan, told me that the procedure was as follows : " The poison and honey are smeared on the under surface of a knife, which is then used for dividing a water-melon. The criminal, eating and sharing the melon with his victim, is careful to take the part of the fruit remote from the poisoned side of the blade as his own share of the meal." Any long-bladed knife that is used in the larder is sharpened to a fine edge ; one side of the blade is then smeared every day with cyanide of potassium dissolved in honey for three days prior to the day on which the murder is to be committed. On the appointed day the water-melon is cut longitudinally into halves and the rind of one half trimmed in the usual way, except that the poisoned surface of the knife is held inwards, *i.e.*, towards the fruit ; this half of the fruit is next cut into blocks of conventional size for eating ; but, in cutting, the poisoned side of the blade is held towards the part of the fruit which is offered to the victim, the trimmed rind serving as a convenient dish or container. The poisoner then proceeds to prepare his half of the water-melon, but is careful to keep the poisoned side of the blade away from the fruit, *i.e.*, towards the rind, thus ensuring his own safety. Water-melons are common throughout the Malay States ; about 5 grains (0·25 to 0·35 gramme) constitute a fatal dose of commercial potassium cyanide, but half this quantity has caused death.

When a large poisonous dose of potassium cyanide is given, death occurs with startling rapidity ; a few breaths are drawn and all is over. The pupils are widely dilated. Erosion of the buccal mucous membrane may be found. When the cyanide is given in a smaller dose, but sufficient to cause death, dizziness, headache, uneasiness, dimness of vision, oppression, pains in the chest and palpitation, precede violent convulsions and insensibility, until finally respiration ceases. The heart continues to beat until the very end (Ref. 1). Cyanide of potassium is recognised by Malays as a deadly poison under the name of *potas* ; sometimes it is said to be mixed with opium and datura for internal administration ; for instance, powdered seeds of the " black " datura, cyanide of potassium and opium prepared for the pipe are mixed with the bile of the tree-snake (Dryophis prasinus) and of the common toad (Bufo melanostictus). The Kelantan antidote for poisoning by *potas* is one that is hardly likely to be at hand in an emergency. It is to take the helmet of the solid-billed hornbill, the tusk of an elephant, the bones of the dugong, and rub them down with the root of the white-flowered variety of the shoe flower (Hibiscus rosa-sinensis, Linn.—Malvaceæ). (See also p. 56).

Other Uses.—Cyanide of potassium is used in plating and gilding brass and silver in Kota Bharu. In days gone by it was used with nitric acid by Kelantan coiners when making counterfeit coin from brass, copper and zinc.

MERCURY

The sale of the very poisonous salts of mercury, such as the perchloride, is now restricted in Kelantan, and, although it is occasionally prescribed by Chinese quacks in over-doses, corrosive sublimate does not appear to be used as a homicidal poison by Malays. Mercuric sulphide (cinnabar) may be bought as vermillion, but the only way in which mercury appears to be used as a poison by Malays is in its metallic form in combination with dry datura seeds, opium prepared for smoking, and white arsenic. These are carefully ground in a mortar. Metallic mercury (*raksa*, quicksilver) in a finely divided state is readily absorbed from the skin and mucous membranes and produces toxic symptoms such as mercurial stomatitis, purging and vomiting of stringy mucus and blood, anuria and collapse.

POUNDED GLASS

Malay poisoners are said seldom to employ crushed glass alone, but to use it always in combination with well-known vegetable irritants such as bamboo hairs. Glass is not likely to cause many symptoms if given alone, except perhaps when in the form of fine splinters, then possibly a splinter might perforate and cause death from peritonitis, but in all probability pounded glass is quickly enveloped in an excess of mucus caused by mechanical irritation of the stomach and intestines. The more finely powdered, the less likely it is to cause harm. Much depends on the condition of the stomach as to the presence or absence of food. Professional jugglers, who take care to chew the glass well before they swallow it, do not appear to suffer any ill effects. Experiments conducted in 1918 by Simmons and von Glahn on animals that were given measured quantities of broken Petri dishes and test tubes, graded by means of seives, from " large broken to fine powdered " suffered no ill effects, and the microscopical examination of the alimentary canal and viscera showed no lesions after the animals had been killed (Ref. 8). The administration of powdered glass caused gastro-enteritis in a case reported from India. Intense burning pain in the stomach with persistent vomiting of blood in small quantities, but without nausea or pain in the throat, came on eight hours after a breakfast in which it had been concealed (Ref. 5). In another case it was found in a dish of rice and curry, and on one occasion it was administered in a " cocktail " served with crushed ice. Used in this way in India and the West Indies as a poison, it is generally a failure. The fatal dose is not known. According to Peterson and Haines : " There is no doubt that a tea-spoonful of pounded glass would in most cases be capable of producing serious effects, especially if the particles were of considerable size and presented numerous sharp angles ; but the same quantity if finely pulverised might usually be taken with little or no effect " (Ref. 7). In a suspected case, if specks of glass cannot be observed by the naked eye in the vomit and stools, the dejecta should be treated with hydrochloric acid and chlorate of potassium by which means the organic matter passes into solution and the glass is left (Ref. 11).

Diamond dust has been said to be more effective, but this form of poisoning is not likely to be met with in Malaya and is mainly of academic interest. Garcia da Orta, writing so long ago as 1563 on the simples and drugs of India, says : " So that they who say that diamonds are poisonous deceive, for it is not a thing written by authentic doctors " (Ref. 6).

Methods Employed by Malays with Pounded Glass as a Poison.—Pounded glass, or *sĕrbok kacha*, is generally mixed, as stated above, with the short, fine hairs of certain kinds of bamboo : these hairs are known as *miang rĕbong* (see section BAMBOO). The combination is mixed with some kind of food such as boiled rice. In 1913 a Malay girl came to the State hospital, Kelantan, with a dirty scrap of newspaper containing bamboo hairs and pounded glass. She required a second opinion, because another Kelantan woman, a fellow wife, had recommended it as a reliable medicine for a cold in the head. Sometimes the scrapings from the dried bark of a jungle vine called *rotan sĕga* (Calamus cæsius, Bl.—Palmæ) are combined with crushed glass instead of the fine bamboo hairs ; the combination is said to cause blood-spitting. Tiny scraps of this smooth rattan bark can be recognised under the microscope with a low power as oblong or square, sharply cut, siliceous cells with small fragments showing stomata (Ref. 3).

SAND AND QUICKLIME

A blinding powder, that is to say, a powder used by thieves to disconcert their pursuers, obtained in 1913

from the Ulu Kĕsial district in Kelantan, was found by
Dr. Dent, Government Analyst, Straits Settlements,
to consist of pounded glass and sand containing
grains of alluvial tin ore (*bijeh*). Another blinding
powder used by Malays for the same purpose is composed of quicklime and ground pepper.

REFERENCES

(1) AUTENRIETH, W. "Laboratory Manual for the Detection of
Poisons and Powerful Drugs." Authorised translation
from sixth German edition by William H. Warren. 1928.
London : Churchill.

(2) BREWER, E. C. "Dictionary of Phrase and Fable." 1923.
New ed., p. 821. London : Cassell.

(3) BROOKE, G. E. "Medico-Tropical Practice." 1920. 2nd ed.
London : Baillière, Tindall & Cox.

(4) BURTON-BROWN, T. E. "Punjab Poisons." 1888. p. 88.
Calcutta.

(5) MODI, J. P. "Medical Jurisprudence and Toxicology for
India." 1920, p. 490. Calcutta.

(6) ORTA, GARCIA DA. "Colloquies on the Simples and Drugs of
India." 1563. Translation by C. R. Markham. 1913.
London : Sotheran.

(7) PETERSON, HAINES and WEBSTER (Editors). "Legal Medicine
and Toxicology by many Specialists." 1923. 2nd ed.,
Vol. II, p. 862. Philadelphia : Saunders.

(8) SIMMONS and VON GLAHN. *Jour. Amer. Med. Assoc.* (Chicago).
1918. Vol. II, p. 2127.

(9) SIMPSON, A. P. "Native Poisons of India." *Pharmaceut.
Jour. and Trans.* (London). 1871. 3, II., p. 602.

(10) SKEAT, W. W. "The Works of Chaucer—Canterbury Tales"
(text), 1900, pp. 315–316. Also "The Canon's Yeoman's
Tale" (text), p. 534. Oxford University Press.

(11) SMITH, SYDNEY. "Forensic Medicine." 1928. 2nd ed.
London : Churchill.

(12) WILLCOX, Sir WILLIAM H. "Acute Arsenical Poisoning."
Brit. Med. Jour. (London). July 22nd, 1922. No. 3212,
p. 118.

APPENDIX I

SPELLS AND CHARMS TRANSCRIBED INTO ROMANISED MALAY.

A Formula to cast out Forest Spirits and Demons, or any Disease. (Page 45.)

Al-salam 'alaikum, hai maseh di-rimba pĕnghulu di-hutan,
Yang tanggong sahat bumi,
Putĕra di-sini yang mĕmĕgang da'erah bumi hutan sini,
Aku tahu asal-mu ;
Nama-mu yang asal-mu-lah yang bĕrnama Sang Ranjuna,
Jadi charang dewana, jadi gunong Sang Bima,
Jadi (?) pĕlana sari maha puteh, jadi laut ;
Dĕngarkan oleh-mu pĕrkataan-ku, aku tahu asal kĕjadian-mu,
Mu jadi dari-pada chahaya yang kĕlam, aku jadi dari-pada chahaya
    yang chĕrah,
Mu jadi dari-pada tanah yang halus,
Aku jadi dari-pada tanah yang kasar, aku jadi tĕrlĕbeh dahulu dari-
    pada-mu,
Hai sakalian Aja-aja di-gunong sini,
Aja-aja di-sini, di-luwok sini,
Dĕngar-dĕngar kata-ku, kalau mu tidak dĕngar aku, dĕrhaka-lah
    mu ka-pada pĕrbakala Dewa,
Yang sĕdia, Dewa yang lĕnyap,
Dewa yang ghaib pada pandangan, dan pada pĕnguchapan, tamat.

A Charm for Small-pox. (Page 46.)

Hai orang baik aku tahu asal-mu,
Kĕjadian-mu dudok dalam nĕraka jĕhĕnam tiada bĕrsifat ;
Maka kamu kĕluar dalam nĕraka jĕhĕnam, kamu singgah ka-pada
    anak Adam, baharu-lah kamu bĕrsifat ;
Aku tahu asal-mu tujoh bĕradek,
Kamu jadi dari-pada dadeh yang hitam, kĕluar dari-pada roma yang
    hitam, kamu kĕluar dari-pada kulit yang hitam,
Kamu kĕluar dari-pada daging yang hitam, kamu kĕluar dari-pada
    urat yang hitam, kamu kĕluar dari-pada lĕndir yang hitam,
    kamu kĕluar dari-pada tulang yang hitam.
Bukan aku yang ĕmpunya tawar, Dewa Bĕntara Narada yang
    ĕmpunya tawar ;
Bukan aku yang ĕmpunya tawar ; Dewa Sang Samba yang ĕmpunya
    tawar ;
Bukan aku yang ĕmpunya tawar, hampas nĕraka jĕhĕnam yang
    ĕmpunya tawar ; aku tahu sakalian yang bisa,

Aku padam sakalian yang nyala,
Jikalau bisa minta tawar, jikalau nyala minta padam,
Sidi guru sidi-lah aku ka-pada guru-ku, tamat.

Exorcism of the Pĕlĕsit. (Page 47.)

Hai pĕlĕsit aku tahu-kan asal-mu,
Kĕluar dari-pada Sak Uri, Tembuni Kĕtuban Bata,
Mu keluar dari-pada darah sambang.
Kĕmang nama-mu,
Jikalau mu lenggok ka-langit muntah darah,
Tundok ka-bumi muntahkan tahi ;
Dĕmi Allah dĕmi Rasul'llah,
Bĕrkat la-ilaha ila'llah ; Muhammad rasul'llah.

An Alternative Exorcism for Pĕlĕsit. (Page 48.)

Hai Segerban di-langit, Segerban di-bumi,
Kĕmbang di-langit, kĕmbang di-bumi,
Umbang Lela nama bapa-mu,
Nagaram nama-mu, Sĕmoran nama hamba-mu,
Mu pindah-lah dĕngan kuasa Allah,
Bĕrkat kata la-ilaha ila'llah ; Muhammad rasul'llah.

Smoked over a Fire to Drive Out an Evil Spirit. (Page 49.)
Pĕngasoh—16–2–1923.

Sa-orang pĕrĕmpuan bĕr-umor lĕbeh kurang 19 tahun, nama-nya Meh Mas anak Meh Lumat, Kampong Pasir Penambang dalam bandar Kota Bharu tĕlah bĕranak sulong. Budak itu laki-laki.

Pada pagi Isnin 26 December, 1922 tĕlah merasa sakit handak bĕranak. Bila sampei pukul 11 tĕngah hari, hathir-lah bidan. Waktu budak mĕnemba handak kĕluar, iya-nya tidak mahu mĕngemat (meneran) sĕpaya chĕpat kĕluar budak dan tidak mahu dudok mĕlĕntang tĕtapi di-pĕgang orang, orang. Didalam pukul 11½ kĕluar-lah budak itu dĕngan chomel-nya dan ibu-nya tiada sĕdarkan diri sa-kĕjap. Bila dapat bĕrnyawa dan bĕrkata-kata, kĕluar-lah perkata-an di-mulut-nya dĕngan ta'tĕntu, biji butir, tiada hiraukan anak, handak di-susu tidak di-bri. Pada hal iya nampak sĕgar dan sĕgala yang mĕngiriggi kanak-kanak dĕri dalam pĕrut sĕmua-nya tĕrbit bĕrseh skali. Uleh sĕbab itu nyata-lah pada bomor, bomor dan bidan, bidan tĕlah masok hantu yang di-gĕlar-kan Maryam (Iya-lah sĕlalu mĕngĕna diatas orang bharu bĕranak). Maka jampi-lah masing-masing bĕrbuweh mulut-mulut ambuweh babeh-nya (kĕrana hantu ini, kata Meh Penjami itu), kĕmdian di-ambil ampat lada hitam di-bri kapada ampat laki-laki yang kuat, kĕmdian lada itu di-tĕkam bĕrsunggoh-sunggoh hati diatas bunga kuku pĕrĕmpuan, itu (ibu jari kaki dan tangan). Bila di-tĕkan bĕrjĕrit-lah pĕrĕmpuan itu makin bĕrjĕrit sa-makin kuat tĕkan-nya (bĕrtambah heiran lagi diatas ke-kĕras-an hantu polong chĕlaka itu bĕgitu sakit tiada mahu kĕluar juga nanti-lah kamu mĕrasa malam ini ! !).

Didalam hal itu habis-lah siyang masok pula malas thalatha. Maka bĕrkata sa-orang dĕripada yang hathir yang tĕlah biasa kalau orang bĕranak sĕpĕrti ini di-ambil tĕmpurong nyior sĕpĕrti yang di-shur itu, tĕtapi pĕrĕmpuan itu bĕgitu juga dan tiada mahu bĕrdiyan. Bila bĕgitu di-kata pula kĕna rabun (pĕrasap api) tĕtapi jauh-jauh tiada bĕrguna, kalau yang kĕras bĕgini. Uleh sĕbab itu, di-buat satu greh tinggi-nya satu hasta lĕbih kurang, di-lĕtak pĕrĕmpuan itu ka-atas-nya, kĕmdian di-buat bara dĕripada tĕm-purong sa-banyak yang tĕrsĕbut di-buloh dalam suatu bĕkas dan di-taroh ka-dalam-nya bĕnda-bĕnda yang busok-busok dan panas sĕpĕrti bĕlĕrang busok-busok, lada kĕring, lada hitam dan lain-nya, di-taroh ka-bawah greh sama bĕtul dĕngan muka si-pĕrĕm-puam tadi dan pĕrĕmpuan itu di-tiyarankan sĕpaya muka-nya mĕngadap api. Maka bila asap-asap panas busok dan kĕras bara tĕmpurong itu bĕrgĕlumpur-lah pĕrĕmpuan itu, lalu di-pĕgang dĕngan kuat dan di-tindeh, yang dĕmikian tiada-lah dapat lagi iya bĕrgĕlumpur, bila bĕgitu bĕrtambah karut lagi pĕrchakapan-nya.

Maka bĕrkata pĕnghalau hantu itu, Tengo' kĕras-nya, jangan lĕpas sampai dia kĕluar. Dalam hal bĕgitu, datang sa-orang To' Guru-lah pada orang disitu, lalu di-tĕgah. Maka kata-nya ini bukan bahagian To' Guru dan bĕbrapa orang lain tĕlah mĕnĕgah di-kata Kamu tiada mĕngĕrti. Bila siyang hari dapat muka pĕrĕmpuan itu mĕlĕtup dan sĕdikit di-dada. Bila di-tengo', bharu tĕrkejut masing-masing apa-tah lagi ibu-nya dan laki-nya hal pĕrbuatan itu di-suka-i-nya. Apa handak di-kata lagi, bĕrtambah-tambah-lah lĕteh pĕrĕmpuan itu. Dalam waktu lohor hari Rabu ka-esokkan-nya kĕmbali-lah ka-rahmatu'llah dan anak tujoh hari bĕlakang mĕngiring-lah ibu-nya. Ini-lah mĕnjadi suatu tĕladan jangan kamu sĕlalu ikut pĕrkata-an yang tiada di-tĕrima uleh akal.

An Incantation for Snake-bite, Stings of Scorpions, Stings of Centipedes and other Poisons. (Page 52.)

Al-salam 'alaikum,
Ong tawar maha tawar
Aku hĕndak tawar di-daging,
Aku hĕndak tawar di-urat, hĕndak tawar di-lĕndir,
Hĕndak tawar di-tulang ;
Tawar datang dari-pada Allah, tawar datang dari-pada Muhammad ;
Tawar datang dari-pada Baginda rasul'llah, tamat.

The Hundred and Ninety Charm for any Kind of Poison (Page 53.)

Ong tawar maha tawar, tawar sa-ratus sĕmbilan puloh,
Bukan aku ĕmpunya tawar, Dato' Mĕngkadom puteh yang ĕmpunya tawar,

Turun tawar dari-pada gurda yang puteh,
Turun tawar dari-pada gajah yang puteh,
Turun tawar dari-pada batu yang puteh, turun tawar dari-pada
    darah yang puteh,
Turun tawar dari-pada tulang yang puteh, turun tawar dari-pada
    hati yang puteh ;
Ayer laut aku tawar,
Lagi 'kau aku tawar,
Jika bisa minta tawar,
Jika nyala minta padam.

An Alternative Charm for any Kind of Poison. (Page 53.)

Ong tawar maha tawar,
Tawar sa-ratus sĕmbilan puloh,
Bukan aku punya kĕhĕndak punya tawar sakalian bisa.
Kĕluar dari-pada biji yang hijau ;
Yang bisa aku hĕndak minta tawar rachun di-dalam badan manusia,
Jika ĕngkau tiada tawar aku sumpah dĕngan kata Nabi Isa yang
    ĕmpunya tawar ;
Insha'llah.

A Spell to neutralise the Effect of Jack-a-Lantern or the Will-o'-the-Wisp. (Page 55.)

Al-salam 'alaikum,
Hai Jin ibni Jan,
Iblis anak Sĕrdan Pĕraun ;
Aku ini-lah Iblis anak Sĕrdan Pĕraun, aku-lah Dato' ;
Panchong maha buta,
Panchong tiada bĕrtanya,
Bunoh tiada bĕr-dosa ;
Aku-lah raja sakalian yang bĕrnyawa, Hak.

A Charm for neutralising Poison. (Page 61.)

Upas-pun t'ada bisa,
Rachun-pun t'ada bisa,
Ular berang pun t'ada bisa,
Ipoh Brunai pun t'ada bisa,
Ah ! sakalian yang bisa t'ada bisa,
Bĕrkat aku memakai do'a guliga kĕsakatian.

The Bullet Charm. (Page 69.)

Al-salam 'alaikum,
Nabi Jankia nama bapa-mu,
Nabi Rabbana nama ibu-mu,
Sang Mabok nama obat-mu,
Naga Umbang nama pĕluru-mu,
Jala patah nama suara-mu
Aku-lah anak-mu Radin Aria Misan Sĕkar dari dunia ini.

The Sacrificial Prayer of the To' Bomor Pĕtĕri.

(Page 79.)

A-uzu-billah-himinashshaitani-arrajim,
Bismillahi-arrahmani-arrahim,
Hamba di-angkat-kan khĕdĕmat (kendĕri) ini,
Nasi kunyit, dadar, bĕrteh, dĕngan ayer sa-titek,
Sireh pinang sa-piyak,
Mĕnyampaikan ibu dari bumi,
Bapa di-langit,
Nenek asal guru yang mula,
Nenek tĕrsĕnang di-tanah chuchi,
Guru tĕrsandar di-tiang dua,
Di-kokboh (kubor) kĕramat,
Di-Makkah, Mĕdinah, Baitollah.
Guru ĕmpat, malim kĕtiga,
Kĕchil dosa bĕsar di-ampun,
Bĕsar hĕndak minta' atas sifat nama . . .
Jikalau tajam hĕndak minta' tumpul,
Jikalau bĕrat hĕndak minta' rengan,
Jikalau sakit hĕndak minta' baik,
Jikalau panas hĕndak minta' sĕjok.
Di-dalam sifar dua puloh, di-dalam alam dua-bĕlas,
Di-anggota tujoh, muktabat ĕmpat,
Tanah, Ayer, Api, Angin, ĕmpat nasir, ('anasir).
Sĕrta hĕndak minta' di-panjangkan langkah,
Di-lanjutkan umor,
Di-murahkan rizki.
Tanggong-lah guru rahsia hamba,
Hamba mĕnjadi tabib,
Sa-orang mĕnjadi bomor,
Sĕrta di-unjong khĕdĕmat (kĕndĕri) ini.
Ka-pada Shaikh ĕmpat,
Auliya tujoh,
Shaikh mĕnaalok di-dalam ĕmpat tapang,
Tujoh jĕrong, lapan desa,
Di-sinar naik, di-sinar rundok,
Di-hulu bumi, di-hilir bĕsawan,
Di-bawah langit tĕrukop,
Di-atas bumi tĕrhampar,
Yang mĕmĕgang sakat,
Mĕmĕgang daerah,
Mĕrentah tĕlok di-dalam kampong dusun ini.
Maalom tĕrsĕmbah kĕramat tujoh !
Kĕramat kĕtumboh-tumbohan !
Kĕramat kĕjadian !
Kĕramat kĕsaktian !
Minta' di-tĕrima ambil nasi kunyit, dadar, bĕrteh, ayer sa-titek,
    sireh pinang sa-piyak,

Tanda hamba hĕndak minta' sĕrta bĕrmanja.
Jikalau ada salah,
Kĕramat tĕgur, atau sumpah maki, tĕndang tĕrajang !
Hĕndak minta' pulang puleh sĕdia kala,
Chara adat zaman dahulu mula.
Sudah di-unjong kĕramat tujoh,
Hamba mĕngarak ka-bumi lembang,
Minta' mĕnyampai ka-pada nenek Raja Jin,
Bapa sakalian jin,
Pĕnghulu sakalian jin,
Dudok bĕrtapa di-dalam kandang lĕmbu hitam,
Sĕtongkat bumi, sĕrjang bumi, sĕkipas bumi, siapang bumi, sĕgĕpa
    bumi, sĕlenggang bumi.
Kĕtinggalan Ina Jagak Tudong Pĕlangi,
Nenek Jin Dohor balar sa-ribu, bĕrtapong tujoh.
Minta' mu-panggil balik,
Sa-ribu ĕmpat puloh jisi dari bumi,
Jangan dudok tunggu jaga atas sifat anak Adam ini, nama . . .
Baik jisi di-kampong, jisi di-padang, jisi di-rimba, jisi di-laut, jisi
    di-darat, jisi ĕmpat pĕdahak pĕnjuru alam.
Jin sa-kĕti, dewa sa-kĕti,
Jin bĕlum tĕrkesah,
Tabib hĕndak iseh.
Dalam (To' Mindok) hĕndak kesah.
Minta' hĕndak tĕrima ambil khĕdĕmat (kĕndĕri) ini.
Bukan aku punya pĕrasap kĕndĕri,
Akmal Hakim punya pĕrasap kĕndĕri,
Mindok yang asal,
Pĕrduang (Pĕtĕri) yang mula.

The Introductory Song of the To' Mindok. (Page 82.)

Bismillah hamba !
Kalam bĕlum di-ranchong,
Dawat bĕlum hanchor,
Loh mahfud bĕlum tĕrsurat,
Awal bĕlum tĕrlĕtak,
Akhir bĕlum jadi,
Bumi bĕlum tĕrhampar,
Langit bĕlum tĕrungkop,
Laut bĕlum tĕrlaboh,
Di-dalam gĕlap gĕlĕmat,
Di-dalam kĕlam kabut,
Di-dalam asek maksud,
Jin pun bĕlum jadi,
Dewa pun bĕlum jadi,
Shaitan pun bĕlum jadi,
Iblis pun bĕlum jadi.
Dahulu Allah, kĕmdian Rasul,

Dahulu Rasul, kĕmdian Nabi,
Dahulu Nabi, kĕmdian Adam,
Dahulu Adam, kĕmdian Wali,
Dahulu Wali, kĕmdian Auliya,
Dahulu Auliya, kĕmdian Saksi,
Dahulu Saksi, kĕmdian hamba.
Hamba tunduk ka-bumi ala jĕmala,
Hamba lenggok ka-langit arong jĕmarong,
Sĕlat tĕringat ibu di-bumi,
Bapa di-langit.
Jaga! Jaga! Bapa,
Ali Akbar nama bapa,
Tĕrkandong bapa ĕmpat puloh hari,
Anak sa-orang gĕliga Muhammad,
Hĕndak mĕnjadi ulama bomor,
Sudah tĕrkandong bapa di-langit,
Sampai salam ibu di-bumi,
Alialma nama ibu,
Tĕrkandong ibu sĕmbilan bulan sĕmbilan hari,
Anak sa-orang kandek Muhammad.
Sudah tĕrkandong ibu di-bumi,
Sampai salam nenek yang asal, guru yang mula,
Tanggong tanggong rahsia hamba,
Mĕnjadi tabib ulama bomor,
Sĕlat tĕringat Shaikh Abdulsaman,
Dudok bĕrtapa di-sinar naik,
Shaikh Bantalok bahya sĕtĕru sĕri pĕnguchap,
Dudok bĕrtapa di-sinar rundok,
Shaikh Abdulkadir dudok bĕrtapa di-hulu banir,
Shaikh Abdulaja di-hilir bĕsawan,
Shaikh Mĕnaalok di-dalam ĕmpat tapang pĕnjuru alam dunia.
Sĕlat tĕringat kĕramat tujoh alam bumi,
Yang mĕmĕgang sakat, mĕmĕgang daerah, mĕmĕgang rantau,
Suda hamba mĕnyampai kĕramat tujoh.
Hamba hĕndak pintas tanjong, mĕngambil rantau,
Jika jauh, hamba ambil dĕkat,
Jika belok, hamba pintas bĕtul,
Mĕnyampai ka-pada jin sa-kĕti sa-ribu ĕmpat puloh, di-kubang bumi.
Bukan tabib hĕndak puja kampong,
Bukan tabib hĕndak tolak agong,
Bukan tabib hĕndak bayar hasil,
Tabib hĕndak minta' atas sifat nama . . .
Pulang puleh sĕdia kala,
Chara adat zaman dahulu.
Sang Gana raja di-kampong,
Taga Gana hulubalang di-dusan,
Malim Langjuna kĕliling kampong,
Luk-lik-di-kampong,

Daeng di-kampong,
Awang sějangkah panjang, sělimbai lěpas, dahi sulah, rambut
    kěreteng, matá merah, gigi panjut, dada lebar, tangan kědal,
    kaki sopak.
Jěmalang tujoh di-kàmpong,
Mu jangan dudok mari ka-pada orang sakit,
Měnyampai ka-pada Mamuk jin hitam halilintar,
Jin kuning panah Ranjuna,
Kilat barat sulong tahun,
Jangan mu dudok agah těrtawa atas sifat nama . . .
Měnyampai ka-pada Sultan ěmpat, Sultan Ahmad, Sultan Ajimat,
    Sultan Punggok raja di-kampong, Raja Muda di-kampong.
Maya di-kampong, Těruna di-dusun,
Pětěri tujoh di-kampong,
Hitam běrsayap bala,
Ěmpat tapang kampong.
Jangan dudok agah těrtawa atas sifat nama . . .
Měnyampai ka-pada anak dewa tujoh,
Jěmala di-padang, bara api, chagar maut, mělalu api, pukat kikis,
    soyak kapan, liyang měnanti,
Irun Dana tělaga darah.
Anak jin běrkota tinggi,
Awang misai rěpeng,
Awang misai gěmiteh,
Awang sětunjang bělukar,
Awang Sěkěling Bahna,
Budak nenek mahi di-hutan,
Pělana di-padang,
To' Buru tujoh muka ka-langit hantu chěrang,
Jikalau ada těr-salah atas sifat nama . . .
Mu-panggil balěk sakalian juwok-mu :
Hulubalang dada belok Panglima Mansur,
Jin pari, hantu laut,
Anak raja gěronggong Mansur,
Budak nenek Sultan Bahar bala di-laut,
Panglima Ipoh, Panglima Jěpoh, Panglima Bagos, Panglima Bugis.
Budak nenek Ton Teja Kuda Pila,
Sa-gěnap těranas batu,
Di-pachu wilahar tasek měraban.
Jikalau ada salah ta' kěna,
Minta' mu-panggil balěk sakalian jisi-mu,
Di-sinar rundok,
Anak Jin, sikapak api, běliong tanggar, sipahat putar, mělalu api,
Budak nenek Sultan Běrmas, sělindong angin.
Di-sinar naik Mamuk, jin hitam rědup matahari.
Jin kuning sinar matahari,
Budak nenek Shaikh Bara Api,
Jin Hitam Gělumbong Ajar,

Jin Merah Sĕgĕlang Gahna,
Angkatan hulubalang gajah mĕnta,
Gĕmala-nya gila,
Jin Hitam kĕlam kabut,
Jin Kuning kĕlam gantong,
Sa-bĕlah kaki di-pintu langit,
Sa-bĕlah kaki di-pintu bumi,
Budak nenek Sang Nyanya,
Ajal jin amiru'l maut,
Anak Raja Taon, chuchu Raja Pĕraon,
Pĕnghulu bala sakalian alam.
Sa-ribu ĕmpat puloh di-dalam dunia,
Utusan Balong Ajar Pĕtĕri Bala,
To' Pasak, Pak unggal anak jin,
Sĕrakal Api, Kĕpiat Api,
Mĕlalu Api, Pĕlatong Api,
Angkatan mas raja hantu,
Sa-ratus ĕmpat puloh lapan,
Tujoh pĕrjana langit, tujoh pĕrjana bumi.
Sa-isian laut, sa-isian darat, jin dari bumi, dewa di-kayangan,
Nenek Sang Sĕnohong,
Sang Kaki, Bĕtara Kala.

The Bestirring Song of the To' Bomor Mindok. (Page 85.)

Asal raja dudok tidor di-gĕrai kĕchil,
Bikah (bingkas) bangun chapai kĕndi kĕchil mĕmbasoh muka,
Suda basoh muka,
Ambil kĕlubong mĕngadap ka-sinar rundok,
Mĕnguchap shahadat dua kalimah,
Memuji Tuhan sĕlawatkan Nabi,
Sudah sĕlawatkan Nabi,
Dudok bĕrsila lalu chapai tepak sireh kĕchil,
Lalu ambil guda kĕchil pĕti gewang,
Ambil kain chindai bĕrmas, bĕrsayap sandang di-pakaikan.
Ambil baju kuning layangan dewa sarok di-badan,
Baju mĕlĕkit di-kulit manis,
Ambil licha bĕrmas buboh ka-rambut.
Lalu mĕngadap gomba bĕrasap.
Hamba nak gĕrak raja yang asal, dewa yang usul,
Sulong Nurdin, pĕnganjur Raja,
Sulong Sayang, pĕnganjur Dewa,
Sulong Gĕtar Sari, pĕnganjur Balang,
Sulong Taman Sari, pĕnganjur Jin.
Hamba nak gĕrak jaga raja di-gunong, dewa di-kayangan,
Mamuk di-kĕbun, Balang di-anjong,
Jaga sakali dĕngan raja ĕmpat,
Raja Bĕrsawan, Bĕrsawan Raja,
Raja Mĕndara Raib, Mĕndara Lelang,

Sĕri Maharaja, Angin Tanah Mahshar.
Jaga Angin baka, Angin pĕsaka,
Baka ayah, pĕsaka mak bonda,
Jaga sa-kali bimbaran ĕmpat, pahlawan ĕmpat, mĕgat ĕmpat, balang
    ĕmpat,
Balang Abubakar, Balang Umar, Balang Usman, Balang Ali.
Jaga sa-kali Angin Sharĕat, roma dĕngan kulit,
Angin Hatĕkat, daging dĕngan darah,
Angin Tarĕkat, urat dĕngan tulang,
Angin Marifat, nyawa dĕngan bĕneh.
Angin ĕmpat di-dalam, ĕmpat di-luar, ĕmpat di-kanan, ĕmpat
    di-kiri, ĕmpat di-bawah, ĕmpat di-atas,
Jaga kĕluar di-pintu sir, pintu atĕkat, pintu chinta, pintu rasa.
Hati mana tuan tidak bĕlas,
Hati mana tuan tidak rindu,
Hati mana tuan tidak sayu,
Hati mana tuan tidak sayang,
Liyok lintok tĕrkulai-balai,
Sĕperti sulor bĕrmain angin,
Sĕperti punggok mĕrindu bulan,
Sĕperti kuwang mĕngulit anak,
Sĕperti gajah mĕngayak gading.
Lalu tĕrjaga Mamuk gĕmala kuda hijau,
Jĕlumung Dewa,
Siyap dĕngan kuda kĕreta,
Raja dudok nanti hari yang baik, kĕtika yang molek,
Jong payong siyapkan payong,
Jong tombak siyapkan tombak,
Lalu Raja bikah-bangun mĕngadap ka-timor jaga,
Tohok jangkah dĕngan tiga jangkah, tohok limbai dĕngan tiga
    limbai,
Sĕrta nobat mĕmbĕlahkan gunong, kisaran payong,
Umbang bĕrlenuk ka-pada gua singa malim,
Raja pintaskan tanjong,
Mĕnuju ka-alam dua-bĕlas,
Jĕmbatan pintu tujoh, jalan sĕmbilan,
Di-gunong Sĕtong, bandaran nyawa.

The Exorcism of the To' Bomor Pĕtĕri. (Page 89.)

Alam bumi Adam,
Asal tanah sa-kĕpal dari olak shurga,
Asal ayer dalam sungai shurga,
Asal api dalam uwap nĕraka,
Asal angin dalam ĕmpat nasir ('anaṣir),
Asal Di jadi roma kulit,
Asal Wadi jadi daging darah,
Asal Mani jadi tulang urat,
Asal Manikam jadi nyawa bĕneh.

Roma kulit Jibra'il jadi,
Daging darah Mika'il jadi,
Urat tulang Asraf'il jadi,
Nyawa bĕneh Azra'il jadi.
Di-mana tĕmpat jin tumpang bĕrtĕdoh ?
Di-mana tĕmpat jin tumpang bĕrtenggek ?
Jika mu dudok di-kaki,
Kaki itu pĕrjalani Allah, pĕrjalani Muhammad.
Jika mu dudok di-pĕrut,
Pĕrut itu laut Allah, laut Muhammad.
Jika mu dudok di-tangan,
Pĕnyĕmbah Allah, pĕnyĕmbah Muhammad.
Jika mu dudok di-hati,
Rahsia Allah, rahsia Muhammad.
Jika mu dudok di-jantong,
Jantong itu istana Abubakar.
Jika mu dudok dalam paru-paru,
Paru-paru itu istana Umar.
Jika mu dudok di-dalam limpa,
Limpa itu istana Usman.
Jika mu dudok di-dalam ĕmpĕdu,
Ĕmpĕdu itu istana Ali.
Jantong, paru-paru, limpa, ĕmpĕdu, rumah tangga nyawa,
Bukan tĕmpat rumah tangga jin,
Bukan tĕmpat rumah tangga iblis,
Bukan tĕmpat rumah tangga pĕnyakit,
Bukan tĕmpat rumah tangga seksa.
Hai jin, asal mu kĕluar di-dalam uwap lidah nĕraka, yang tiada
    bĕrasap,
Aku tahukan asal bapa-mu nama Harijin,
Nama ibu-mu Marijin,
Nama anak-mu Narijin.

The Farewell Song of the To' Bomor Mindok to Nenek Jin Hitam.
(Page 92.)

Pĕrgi-lah nanti di-hujong bumi,
Sĕrta sakalian jisi kĕlaparan,
Dari-pada ĕmpat pĕnjuru alam,
Tĕrima hasil chukai kĕrajat,
Himpunkan sakalian jin,
Jisi, iblis, shaitan dan hantu,
Dari laut dan darat, hutan dan lĕmbah, bukit, gunong, dan kampong,
Dan makan jamuan ini.

The Passage from Taju's-Salatin, quoted by Dr. Winstedt.
(Page 34.)

Tĕlah di-jadikan kĕadaan manusia itu daripada ĕmpat pĕrkara,
yang bĕrlainan pĕri-nya, dan di-katakan 'anasir arba' nama-nya,

dan suatu daripada ĕmpat pĕrkara itu mĕlawan akan sa-suatu, sapĕrti tanah dan ayer dan angin dan api ; dan kĕĕmpat pĕrkara itu ada-lah kĕadaan sa-sa-orang manusia sa-lama ada-nya itu ada, dan pĕri kĕĕmpat pĕrkara itu, yang ada pada kĕadaan sa-sa-orang manusia, ada-lah bĕrlain-lainan sĕntiasa pada sĕgala manusia jua, tiada dĕngan ikhtiar-nya sa-hingga tiada ada ia dĕngan sĕntosa sa-lama hidup-nya ; harna Tuhan Allah brikan dalam tuboh sa-sa-orang manusia bĕbĕrapa pĕrkara, yang suatu daripada itu mĕlawan akan suatu dĕngan pĕri-nya dan dĕngan khasiat-nya . . . Jikalau pĕri sĕgala pĕrkara itu sĕdang-lah pada tuboh manusia itu ; hanya jikalau bukan sĕdang itu dan ada-lah kurang atau lĕbeh, maka bagai-bagai pĕnyakit datang pada tuboh manusia dari sĕbab ini.

APPENDIX II

CLASSIFICATION IN NATURAL ORDERS OF THE POISONOUS PLANTS.

Natural Order.	Botanical Name.	Section.
Anonaceæ .	Alphonsea ceramensis, Scheff.	Kĕnĕrak.
	A. reticulata, Linn. . .	Do.
	A. ventriculosa, Hook. fil. and Thoms.	Do.
	Anona murticata, Linn. .	Do.
	Cananga odorata, Linn. .	Chĕraka.
	Goniothalamus tapis, Miq. .	Kĕnĕrak.
	Oxymitra macrophylla, Baill.	Do.
	Unona dasmychala, Bl. .	Do.
Menispermaceæ .	Anamirta cocculus, Linn. .	The Kris, p. 4.
Papaveraceæ .	Papaver somniferum, Linn. .	Arsenic, Cyanide of Potassium, Datura, Mercury, Pĕdĕn-dang Gagak Pinang, Tangis Sarang Burong
Dipterocarpaceæ.	Balanocarpus maximus, King	Datura.
Rutaceæ . .	Glycosmis citrifolia, Lindl. .	Do.
Bixaceæ . .	Gynocardia odorata, Roxb. .	Kĕpayang.
	Hydnocarpus inebrians, Valh.	Do.
	H. venenata, Gærtn. . .	Do.
	H. Wightiana, Bl. . .	Do.
	Pangium edule, Reinwt. .	Do.
	Taraktogenos Kurzii, King .	Do.
Meliaceæ . .	Heynea trijuga, Roxb. .	Tangis Sarang Burong.
	H. sumatrana, Miq. . .	Do.
Anacardiaceæ .	Gluta benghas, Linn. . .	Jitong.
	G. coarctata, Hook. fil. .	Do.
	G. virosa, Ridl. . . .	Do.
	Stagmaria verniciflua, Jack .	Rĕngas.
	Melanorrhœa Curtisii, Oliv. .	Do.
	M. Wallichii, Hook. fil. .	Do.
	Rhus vernicifera, D.C. . .	Do.
Moringaceæ .	Moringa pterygosperma, Gærtn.	Datura, Papaya.

Natural Order.	Botanical Name.	Section.
Leguminosæ	Afzelia (intsia) retusa, Kurz..	Měrbau Ayer.
	Derris elliptica, Benth..	Tuba.
	D. uliginosa, Benth.	Do.
	Pithecolobium lobatum, Benth.	Do.
	Mucuna, sp.	Kachang Bulu Rimau.
	Mucuna giganteum, D.C.	Do.
Melanostomaceæ.	Medinila, sp.	Upas Tree.
Lythraceæ.	Lawsonia alba, Lam.	Chěraka.
Papayaceæ.	Carica papaya, Linn.	Papaya.
Cucurbitaceæ	Benicasa cerifera, Savi	Chěraka.
	Momordica charantia, Linn..	Do.
	Hodgsonia capnocarpus, Ridl.	Akar Klapayang.
	Trichosanthes, sp.	Pěděndang Gagak.
Araliaceæ	Aralidum pinnatifidum, Miq..	Upas Tree.
Rubiaceæ	Gardenia Griffithii, Hook. fil..	Chěraka.
Plumbaginaceæ	Plumbago rosea, Linn.	Do.
	P. zeylanica, Linn.	Do.
Apocynaceæ	Cerbera odollam, Gærtn.	Běbuta.
	C. thevetia, Linn. (T. neriifolia, Juss.).	Pokok Batu Pělir Kambing
	Nerium odorum, Soland.	Do.
	Rauwolfia perakensis, King and Gamble.	Do.
	R. serpentina, Benth.	Do.
	R. sinensis, Hamsl.	Do.
	R. verticillata, Baill.	Do.
	R. vomitoria, Afzel	Do.
Ascelepiadaceæ	Sarcolobus globosus, Wall.	Akar Batu Pělir Kambing.
	S. spanoghei, Miq.	Do.
	S. virulentus, Griff.	Do.
Loganiaceæ	Strychnos ovalifolia, Wall.	Upas Climber.
	S. tieuté, Bl.	Do.
Solanaceæ	Datura alba, Nees	Datura.
	D. fastuosa, Linn.	Do.
Verbenaceæ	Vitex pubescens, Vahl..	Do.
Piperaceæ	Piper nigrum, Linn.	Pepper.
Thymelæaceæ	Aquilaria malaccensis, Lam..	Datura.
	Wikstrœmia, Ridleyi and Gamble	Děpu Pělandok.
Euphorbiaceæ	Cnesmone javanica, Miq.	Jělatang.
	Croton caudatus, Griesb.	Chěraka.
	C. tiglium, Linn..	Chěngkian.
	Excœcaria agallocha, Linn.	Běbuta.

Natural Order.	*Botanical Name.*	*Section.*
Euphorbiaceæ .	Jatropha curcas, Linn. . .	Chĕngkian.
Urticaceæ . .	Antiaris toxicaria, Bl. . .	Upas Tree.
	Cannabis indica, Linn. .	Datura.
	Laportea crenulata, Forst. .	Jĕlatang.
	L. stimulans, Miq. . .	Do.
Dioscoreaceæ .	Dioscorea triphylla, Lam. .	Gadong.
	D. hirsuta, Blume . .	Do.
Palmaceæ .	Areca catechu, Linn. . .	Pinang.
	Arenga saccharifera, Labill. .	Langkap.
	A. Westerhouti, Griff. . .	Do.
	Caryota mitis, Lour. . .	Bĕrĕdin.
	Orania macrocladus, Mart. .	Ibul.
Bromeliaceæ .	Ananas sativa, Linn. . .	Pine-apple.
Araceæ . .	Alocasia denudata, Eng. .	Kĕladi.
	Amorphophallus Prainii, Hook. fil.	Do.
	Colocasia antiquorum, Schott.	Do.
	Raphidophera giganteum, Schott.	Rengut.
Gramineæ . .	Bambusa spinosa, Bl. . .	Bamboo.
	B. vulgaris, Schrad. . .	Do.
	Dendrocalamus flagellaris, Munro.	Do.
	D. strictus, Nees and Ham. .	Do.
	Oxytenanthera s i n u a t a, Gamble.	Do.

APPENDIX III

A LIST OF KELANTAN POISONS

OBTAINED FROM THE ANIMAL KINGDOM

Malay Name.	Page.	Scientific Name.	Habitat.	Active Principle.	Pharmacology.
Chalotong	145	Spirostreptus.	Kelantan thick forest.	see jělantor.	Expressed juice used with *rengut*.
Chichak	228	Hemidactylus frenatus (house lizard).	dwellings.	undetermined.	White of the egg used with *papaya*.
Děndang	140	Coleoptera.	on a fern. *daun paku hijau.*	cantharidin.	A single beetle in cakes is a poisonous dose.
Ěmpědu	8	Fel (gall or bile).	—	undertermined.	An excipient used in many poisonous compounds.
,, běruang	185	Helarctos malayanus (honey bear).	Malayan jungle.	,,	Used with *rengut*.
,, burong chěchawi	9	Dissemurus platurus.	,, ,,	,,	Used as an aphrodisiac.
,, burong gagak	186	Corvus macrorhynchus.	,, ,,	,,	Used with *rengut*.
,, ikan buntal	185	Tetrodon fluviatilis	,, rivers.	tetrodonin.	Used with *rengut* and datura.
,, ikan kěli	118	Clarius magur.	,, swamps.	undertermined.	Used with datura.
,, katak pisang	134	Rana erythraea.	ponds.	,,	Given with gambier in a " betel-chew".
,, katak puru	136	Bufo melanostictus.	ditches.	,,	A favourite excipient.
,, landak	177	Hystrix longicauda.	jungle.	,,	Used with opium and *pěděndang gagak*.

Malay Name.	Page.	Scientific Name.	Habitat.	Active Principle.	Pharmacology.
Êmpêdu ular puchok	134	Dryophis prasinus.	trees.	undetermined.	Given alone; also with datura and potassium cyanide.
Gêronggong laut	185	Scyphosa.	China Sea.	,,	Used with rengut.
Ikan buntal	121	Tetrodon fluviatilis.	rivers.	tetrodonin.	Spawn poisonous.
,, kêli	118	Clarius magur	padi fields.	undetermined.	Gall used with datura.
,, pari	125	Trygon.	China Sea.	,,	Used with rengut: spine poisonous.
,, sêmbilang	119	Plotosus	,, ,,	see text.	Fins poisonous.
Jêlantor	145	Spirostreptus.	dense jungle.	hydrocyanic acid, camphor; quinone.	Used with rengut: see Chalutong.
Kêchar lakum	185	Nanina humphreysiana.	villages.	undetermined.	Used with rengut.
,, lotong	145	Atopos maximus.	thick forest.	,,	Used with rengut.
Kêsing	144	Rhynchota.	villages.	,,	Used with millepedes.
Kura katup	133	Cyclemys amboinensis.	rice fields.	,,	Used with the cobra.
Pinang kotai bukit	145	Zephronia.	hills.	see jêlantor.	Used with rengut.
Ular têdong sendok	133	Naia tripudians (black cobra).	jungle.	a neurotoxin.	Used with the tortoise.
Ulat bulu darat	139	Caterpillar of moth. Aloa sanguinolenta.	villages.	see text.	Hairs used with rengut.
,, ,, laut	148	Chloia flava.	China Sea.	undetermined.	Bristles used with rengut.

OBTAINED FROM THE VEGETABLE KINGDOM

Malay Name.	Page.	Scientific Name.	Habitat.	Active Principle.	Pharmacology.
Bamboo	153	Bambusa spp.	jungle.	mechanical irritant.	Hairs used with *rengut* and pounded glass.
Běbula	155	Excœcaria agallocha.	sea coast.	oil of euphorbia.	Used with blood of flying fox; sap causes blindness.
Batu pělir kambing (pokok)	234	Rauwolfia perakensis.	river banks.	undetermined. see text.	Fruit used combined with wild yams.
Batu pělir kambing (akar)	150	Sarcolobus globosus.	sea coast.	undetermined.	Seeds used to poison dogs.
Běrědin	158	Caryota mitis.	jungle.	,,	Berries used in wells.
Běrkat	175	Arenga saccharifera.	hills.	,,	Pulp of fruit used.
Běek	228	Carica papaya.	villages.	carpaine.	Sap used ; also seeds as an abortifacient.
Binjai	137	Mangifera caesia.	,,	undetermined.	Sap used with *rěngas.*
Chandu	220	Papaver somniferum.	India and China.	morphine and other alkaloids.	Used with datura, arsenic, pinang, etc.
Chěngkian	160	Croton Tiglium.	villages.	toxalbumin.	Root as an abortifacient.
Chěraka	202	Plumbago rosea.	,,	plumbagin.	Root as an abortifacient.
Damar lěban	216	Vitex pubescens.	forest.	undetermined.	A sap burnt with datura.
,, *mata kuching*	216	Balanocarpus maximus.	,,	,,	Cat's-eye resin burnt with datura.
Daun gatal	166	Laportea stimulans.	ravines.	,,	see *jělatang.*
Děbu kundur	137	Benicasa cerifera.	villages.	,,	Bloom of ash-pumpkin used with *rěngas.*

Malay Name.	Page.	Scientific Name.	Habitat.	Active Principle.	Pharmacology.
Dĕpu pĕlandok	221	Wikstroemia Ridl.	villages.	undetermined.	Berries: a fish-poison.
Gadong	222	Dioscorea triphylla.	near villages.	dioscorine.	Used with datura.
Gĕharu	215	Aquillaria malaccensis.	forest.	undetermined.	Bark burnt with datura.
Ibul	164	Orania macrocladus.	hills.	see text.	Seeds used as a poison.
Inai	202	Lawsonia alba.	villages.	undetermined.	Root used with chĕraka.
Ipoh (akar)	187	Strychnos ovalifolia.	jungle.	brucine.	Bark used: an arrow poison.
Ipoh (batang)	191	Antiaris toxicaria.	forest.	antiarin.	Sap used: an arrow poison.
Jĕlatang	166	Laportea stimulans.	ravines.	undetermined.	Flowers and leaves given in cakes.
Jĕring	240	Pithecolobium lobatum.	jungle.	,,	Pods poisonous.
Jitong	168	Gluta benghas.	,,	? an acid glucoside.	Sap used with rengut.
Kachang bulu rimau	169	Mucuna sp.	villages.	undetermined.	Hairs from dry pod used.
Kachang rimau	170	Mucuna giganteum.	river banks.	,,	Stinging hairs on leaves.
Kĕchubong	204	Datura alba.	villages.	hyoscine and hyoscyamine.	Whole plant poisonous: seeds specially used.
Kĕladi	171	Alocasia denudata.	,,	undetermined.	Juice of tuber used.
Kĕnanga	203	Cananga odorata.	,,	,,	Root used with chĕraka.
Kĕnĕrak	225	Goniothalamus tapis.	,,	an alkaloid.	Root used with chĕraka.
Kĕpayang	225	Pangium edule.	,,	a cyanogenetic glucoside.	Oil from seeds given in cakes.

Malay Name.	Page.	Scientific Name.	Habitat.	Active Principle.	Pharmacology.
Klapayang (akar) .	152	Hodgsonia heteroclita.	river banks.	? an alkaloid.	Raw seeds reputed poisonous.
Lada hitam .	229	Piper nigrum.	villages.	piperine.	Seeds used as an abortient agent.
Langkap .	175	Arenga obtusifolia.	jungle.	undetermined.	Pulp of fruit used.
Likir .	173	Amorphophallus Pranii.	villages.	,,	Juice of tuber used.
Mérbau Ayer	175	Afzelia (Intsia) retusa.	tidal rivers.	,,	Seeds poisonous.
Mérunggai .	220	Moringa pterygosperma.	villages.	an alkaloid.	Used with papaya.
Miang rěbong	154	Bambusa spp.	jungle.	mechanical irritant.	Used with rengut and pounded glass.
Nanas .	234	Ananassa sativa.	villages.	bromelin.	Juice of unripe fruit used as an abortifacient.
Nérapih .	220	Glycosmis citrifolia.	,,	undetermined.	Inner bark used with datura and chandu.
Papaya .	228	Carica papaya.	,,	carpaine.	Sap used : also seeds.
Pěděndang gagak	177	Tricosanthes spp.	river banks.	undetermined.	Fruit used with opium and bile of the porcupine.
Pinang .	230	Areca catechu.	villages.	arecoline and other alkaloids.	Green fruit used with opium.
Rěngas .	178	Melanorrhœa spp.	forest.	? an acid glucoside.	Sap used with toad-venom.
Rengut. .	183	Epipremnum giganteum.	jungle.	undetermined.	Half-rotted fruit used with other irritants.

19

Malay Name.	Page.	Scientific Name.	Habitat.	Active Principle.	Pharmacology.
Tangis sarang burong ·	186	Heynea trijuga.	jungle.	undetermined.	Berries used with opium and areca nut.
Tuba · · ·	236	Derris elliptica.	villages.	derrid [rotenone].	Sap of root used mostly as a fish-poison.

Obtained from Inorganic Sources

Malay Name.	Page.	Scientific Name.	Habitat.	Active Principle.	Pharmacology.
Bijeh · · ·	269	Grains of alluvial tin.	Malay States.	mechanical irritant.	Used as a blinding powder by Malay thieves.
Kapur tohor ·	269	Quicklime.	,,	,,	Used with pepper as a blinding powder.
Potas · ·	264	Cyanide of Potassium.	imported.	a cardiac poison.	Used alone, and combined with opium and datura.
Raksa · ·	266	Mercury (quicksilver).	,,	an irritant poison.	Used alone, and combined with datura, opium and arsenic.
Sĕrbok kacha ·	268	Pounded glass.	,,	mechanical irritant.	Used with bamboo hairs.
Tuba tikus ·	253	White arsenic.	,,	an irritant poison.	Used with the pips of the sour lime.
Warangan puteh ·	253	,, ,,	,,	,, ,,	Another Malay name for *tuba tikus*.

INDEX